CULTURE AND CORPORATE GOVERNANCE

Research Series:
Issues in Corporate Behaviour and Sustainability

Series Editors:
Güler Aras
David Crowther

Culture and Corporate Governance

Edited by
GÜLER ARAS
Yildiz Technical University, Turkey

&

David Crowther
De Montfort University, UK

Social Responsibility Research Network

Published by
Social Responsibility Research Network
www.socialresponsibility.biz

Published in Leicester, UK, 2008

ISBN: 978-0-9551577-1-4

Printed in Romania

Contents

About the editors

Güler Aras is Professor of Finance and Director of the Graduate School at Yildiz Technical University, Istanbul, Turkey. She is the author or editor of 10 books and has contributed over 150 articles to academic, business and professional journals and magazines and to edited book collections. She has also spoken extensively at conferences and seminars and has acted as a consultant to a wide range of government and commercial organisations. Her research is into financial economy and financial markets with particular emphasis on the relationship between corporate social responsibility and a firm's financial performance.

David Crowther is Professor of Corporate Social Responsibility at De Montfort University, UK. He is the author or editor of 25 books and has also contributed 250 articles to academic, business and professional journals and to edited book collections. He has also spoken widely at conferences and seminars and acted as a consultant to a wide range of government, professional and commercial organisations. His research is into corporate social responsibility with a particular emphasis on the relationship between social, environmental and financial performance.

Their joint research is concerned with sustainability, sustainable development and with governance issues.

About the Contributors

Maria Aluchna PhD is assistant professor at Department of Management Theory, Warsaw School of Economics, Poland. She specializes in corporate governance as well as in strategic management. She was awarded Deutscher Akademischer Austauschdienst (DAAD) scholarship for research stay and Universität Passau and Polish-American Fulbright Commission scholarship for the research stay at Columbia University. She received Polish Science Foundation award for young researchers (2004, 2005). She serves on two boards (as Vice-Chairman and Secretary). Since January she is the editor in chief of Warsaw Stock Exchange portal on corporate governance best practice.

Professor Dr. **Mustafa A. Aysan** has been teaching since 1959 and became a full professor at Istanbul University in 1974. He has published 14 books in finance, accounting, state-owned enterprises and corporate governance. He was also involved in advisory and board membership positions in business from 1970. He served as the Chairman of the Planning and Budgeting Committee of the Parliament (1981) and as the Minister of Transport (1982-83). Currently he is a member of the Board of Finansbank and Chairman of the bank's Audit Committee, while continuing to teach Corporate Governance at the graduate school of a private university.

Dr. **Iti Bose** is a Research Associate at Shailesh J. Mehta School of Management, Indian Institute of Technology, Bombay, India. She began her career as a Lecturer in Political Science. She did her PhD (Political Economy) from Kolkata. Awarded with Postdoctoral Fellowship twice by the University Grants Commission (UGC) of India, she was associated with University of Bombay for her first postdoctoral project on Industrial Growth. Currently, she is working on Corporate Governance and Social Responsibility as part of her second postdoctoral project and associated with IIT Bombay, for the same.

Ana-Maria Davila-Gomez is associate professor in the Department of Administrative Sciences at the University of Quebec, Canada. Her current research includes managers' challenges towards more social responsible organizations, as well as human virtues and responsiveness from management education. She holds a Ph.D. from the *École des hautes etudes commerciales de Montréal*, and an MBA and an Industrial Engineer degrees from the *Universidad del Valle*, Colombia. For seven years, she worked at various private and public organizations in Colombia (e.g. governmental service, telecommunications, and manufacturing) supporting and implementing Information Technology (IT) and Business Process Reengineering projects.

Professor Dr **Hasnah Haron** acts as the Deputy Director (Academic) of Advanced Management Centre at the School of Management; Universiti Sains Malaysia Her research interest is in the area of auditing, financial reporting, ethics, corporate social responsibility and education. She has written several books and modules on management and financial accounting. She sits on the Editorial Board of Malaysian Accounting Review and is currently, the Editor-in-Chief of the Asian Academy of Management Journal. She is also currently the Vice-President of the Asian Academy of Management. Dr. Hasnah is also active in professional activities.

Professor Dr **Daing Nasir Ibrahim** is the Director, Advanced Management Centre of Universiti Sains Malaysia. Professor Daing is a Chartered Accountant, a Fellow of the Certified Practicing Accountants of Australia. (FCPA) and was Vice President of its Malaysia Division. He sits on the Council of the Malaysian Institute of Accountants and on several of its committees. His areas of expertise are Management Accounting and Control, Corporate Governance, and Research Methodology. He is a member of the advisory board of the Kuala Lumpur Malay Chamber of Commerce and a member of the Board of Directors of Usains Holding.

Izabela Koladkiewicz Ph.D. is an Assistant Professor at the Leon Kozminski Academy of Entrepreneurship and Management (LKAEM) in Warsaw, Poland. Her current research interests include corporate governance, knowledge management and family business. She is a lecturer in corporate governance at the LKAEM. She is an author of several books and papers concerning corporate governance.

Lobar G. Mukhamedova has a Masters degrees in Business Computing (University of Westminster) and International Tourism (Tashkent State Economy University) and is currently Course Leader for Business Computing at Westminster International University in Tashkent, Uzbekistan. She also works closely with final year students in developing their research projects, and has been coordinating the production of a multimedia guide to CSR for SMEs in Uzbekistan as well as developing curriculum for the teaching of CSR in the universities of Uzbekistan.

Alovsat Muslumov is Associate Professor of Finance at Dogus University, Istanbul, Turkey. He joined Dogus University faculty in 2001 after receiving his Ph.D. degree from Bogazici University. Alovsat Muslumov teaches finance and accounting in Dogus University. He serves as visiting professor at Bogazici University, Istanbul Bilgi University, and Yeditepe University as well. His research focuses on current financial issues. He is the author of books and numerous research papers published in finance and economics journals. His two books were awarded with best scientific work awards of Association of Turkish Young Businessmen & Entrepreneurs and Association of Institutional Investors Board in Turkey.

Mr Onyeka K Osuji is a Lecturer-in-Law at the University of Exeter, School of Law Cornwall Campus. Mr Osuji obtained law degrees from the University of Nigeria and University of Nigeria. He also attended the Nigerian Law School and qualified as a barrister and solicitor of Nigeria. He also qualified as a solicitor of England and Wales. Mr Osuji's interest is broadly on law and business. In particular, he interested in company law, corporate governance, corporate social responsibilities, contract law, information technology law, multinational enterprises, consumer law and general commercial law.

Dr. Riham Rizk is a Teaching Fellow and Programme Director for the Bachelor of Arts degree in Accounting and Finance at Durham Business School, UK. Dr. Rizk's main areas of research include International Disclosure Practices, CSR, Business Ethics and the Influence of Religion on Accounting and Finance.

Roshima Said is a Senior Lecturer of Universiti Teknologi Mara (UiTM) and currently pursuing her Ph.D in Universiti Sains Malaysia (USM) .She had been Accounting Coordinator for School of Accounting, Universiti Teknologi Mara, Kedah for two years. Her research interest is Corporate Governance, Corporate Social Responsibility and Accounting Education. She has conducted a number of researches that were presented at international and local seminars and conferences, and published in proceedings and journal. . She has written a book on partnership accounting and modules on financial accounting.

Saiful is a senior lecturer of Accounting Department of Bengkulu University, Indonesia. Currently he is also a PhD student of School of Management Universiti Sains Malaysia. He has done some researches in area of financial accounting, capital market, and corporate governance, such as earning management, impact of merger and acquisition on stock performance, investment strategy in emerging market, corporate transparency, and corporate social responsibility. .He has published several articles in local and international journal. He has also presented several articles in so some international conferences.

Daniel Stevens is currently Head of Research and Consultancy at Westminster International University in Tashkent, Uzbekistan and works with both students and staff in developing their research capacity. He is also course leader for the MA in International Business and Management. His own research interests include issues related to the development of civil society in Uzbekistan, particularly the way in which government, international donors and business relate to it. He has been coordinating the project on Corporate Social Responsibility and SMEs at the university.

Loong Wong teaches at the University of Canberra, Australia. He has an active research interest in international business, businesses in China and East Asia, e-commerce, human rights and corporate social responsibility issues. He has published widely, including amongst others Social Responsibility Journal, Asian Business and Management, Prometheus and Journal of Contemporary Asia and is also an activist in the peace, environmental and human rights movement for over 20 years.

Associate Professor Dr **Yuserrie Zainuddin** started his career as a lecturer in management accounting at the School of Management, Universiti Sains Malaysia. His research interest is in management accounting and control systems. He has published in local and international journal. He supervised PhD, DBA and master candidates. Currently his holds a position as the Deputy Dean of Academic and Student's Development at the School of Management, Universiti Sains Malaysia. He teaches management accounting courses for undergraduates and management control systems for MBA and DBA as well as international business management, research methodology and consultation.

Preface

Although the relationship between organisations and society has been subject to much debate, often of a critical nature, evidence continues to mount that the best companies make a positive impact upon their environment. Furthermore te evidence continues to mount that such socially responsible behaviour is good for business, not just in ethical terms but also in financial terms in other words that corporate social responsibility is good for business as well as all its stakeholders. Thus ethical behaviour and a concern for people and for the environment have been shown to have a positive correlation with corporate performance. Indeed evidence continues to mount concerning the benefit to business from socially responsible behaviour and, in the main, this benefit is no longer questioned by business managers. The nature of corporate social responsibility is therefore a topical one for business and academics. This book is designed to act as a forum for the debate and analysis of some of the contemporary issues in this broad area. In doing this it is based upon contributions from people from a wide variety of disciplines and geographic regions leading to diverse views and a stimulating interchange.

This book focuses upon one of the factors that influence business behaviour and thereby contribute towards its social responsibility, namely the question of corporate governance. This we take as a part of the topic of this book. The other part is that of culture because culture is central to both individual behaviour and therefore to corporate behaviour. The purpose of the book therefore is to explore the relationship between culture and the operation of corporate governance around the world. In doing so we will inevitable also consider the relationship between these and corporate performance and corporate social responsibility. This is also something we consider at our conferences.

In September 2008 the 7th International Conference on Corporate Social Responsibility took place in Durham, UK. The conference was jointly organized by Durham University and the Social Responsibility Research Network and hosted by Durham University. This book is a direct outcome of this conference and it is a policy of the organisers to publish a book related to each conference. The focus of this book is culture and its relationship to corporate governance and this book contains contributions from scholars from around the world who have written about their views concerning a variety of important aspects of this issue. The conference itself is the 7th in the series and is part of an ongoing series of conferences on this topic which are taking place in many different parts of the world. Full details of past and future conferences can be found at the conference website: www.davideacrowther.com/csrhome.html.

The beginnings of this conference programme were in 2003 when on three days in September around 140 delegates from nearly 30 countries from around the world gathered in London at London Metropolitan University for the first of an annual series of international conferences on the topic of Corporate Social Responsibility. Over the three days the delegates engaged in discussion on a range of issues concerning this topic and around 100 papers were presented. Topics covered ranged from business ethics to social reporting to implications for biodiversity to sustainable construction, reflecting the interdisciplinary nature of the backgrounds and expertise of the participants. Conversation about many of the important issues raised during the conference continued into the evenings at the dinners organised for delegates at a variety of London hotels and the success of the conference will be continued into a variety of collaborative projects instigated among the international delegates during the conference. In the intervening years conferences have been held in Malaysia, India and Turkey as well as the UK, while future conferences are scheduled to take place in other parts of the world.

Although there are a number of colleagues who have attended all of these conference, each has seen many people attending for the first time. Consequently the network of colleagues engaged in CSR research continues to increase and this will continue into the future conferences which are also planned. A direct outcome of this has been the formation of the Social Responsibility Research Network (www.socialresponsibility.biz) with the aim of fostering the collaborative, cross-cultural interdisciplinary and international research on any aspect of its social responsibility agenda. The Social Responsibility Research Network (SRRNet) is a body of scholars who are concerned with the Social Contract between all stakeholders in global society and consequently with the socially responsible behaviour of organisations. The Network has grown steadily and now comprises around 400 members from countries worldwide and is surely a valuable resource for comparative research.

Apart from organising conferences, the Network has its own journal Social Responsibility Journal www.emeraldinsight.com/info/journals/srj/srj.jsp which is published by Emerald. The journal is concerned with social responsibility, which is of course an essential part of citizenship. This is interpreted by this journal in the widest possible context. The journal is international in its perspective and believes that in the global environment in which we live any author should speak to the greatest possible audience. It seeks to promote an ethos of inclusion and consequently embraces a broad spectrum of issues and a wide range of perspectives. The journal is interdisciplinary in scope and encourages submission from any discipline or any part of the world which addresses any element of the aims of the journal. It encompasses the full range of theoretical, methodological or substantive debates in this area. It particularly welcomes contributions which address the links between different disciplines and / or implications for societal, organisational or individual behaviour.

The Network has also extended its activities into book publishing and this is the second volume that it has published. This, and future volumes will be published as a series of research books, entitled Issues in Corporate Behaviour and Sustainability. We also publish a newsletter periodically and details of all of the Networks activities can be found on its website www.socialresponsibility.biz. These various activities will however remain a minor part of the activities of the Network, with the main focus being upon the conferences and upon facilitating collaboration among like-minded people around the world.

The rationale for the conferences has been based on the fact that over the last decade the question of the relationship between organisations and society has been subject to much debate. The conferences are designed to act as a forum for the debate and analysis of contemporary issues in this broad area. In doing so they attract people from a wide variety of disciplines and geographic regions for an exchange of views. The broad range of topics which are of concern in the area of Corporate Social Responsibility are reflected not just in the conferences which we hold but also in the contents of the journal. The worldwide interest in, and concern for, the subject matter is also reflected by the range of backgrounds from which participants at the conference hail from not just in terms of areas of expertise but also in terms of geographical locations. This also is reflected in the contributions to this book. We hope that readings them creates an interest which will encourage you to join the discourse and to participate in a future conference.

Güler Aras & David Crowther
January 2008

INTRODUCTION

Chapter 1

Exploring Frameworks of Corporate Governance

Güler Aras & David Crowther

Introduction

Corporate governance can be considered as an environment of trust, ethics, moral values and confidence as a synergic effort of all the constituents of society that is the stakeholders, including government; the general public etc; professional / service providers and the corporate sector. One of the consequences of a concern with the actions of an organisation, and the consequences of those actions, has been an increasing concern with corporate governance (Hermalin 2005). Corporate governance is therefore a current buzzword the world over. It has gained tremendous importance in recent years. There is a considerable body of literature which considers the components of a good system of governance and a variety of frameworks exist or have been proposed. This chapter examines and evaluates these frameworks while also outlining the cultural context of systems of governance. Our argument in this chapter is that corporate governance is a complex issue which cannot be related to merely the Anglo Saxon approach to business; indeed it cannot be understood without taking geographical, cultural and historical factors into account in order to understand the similarities, differences and concerns relating to people of different parts of the world. In part therefore this chapter also serves as an introduction which sets the scene for the other chapters in the book as well as outlining the purpose of the book and the contributions within this theoretical and practical context.

Good governance is essential for good corporate performance and one view of good corporate performance is that of stewardship and thus just as the management of an organisation is concerned with the stewardship of the financial resources of the organisation so too would management of the organisation be concerned with the stewardship of environmental resources. The difference however is that environmental resources are mostly located externally to the organisation. Stewardship in this context therefore is concerned with the resources of society as well as the resources of the organisation. As far as stewardship of external environmental resources is concerned then the central tenet of such stewardship is that of ensuring sustainability. Sustainability is focused on the future and is concerned with ensuring that the choices of resource utilisation in the future are not constrained by decisions taken in the present (Aras & Crowther 2007a).

This necessarily implies such concepts as generating and utilising renewable resources, minimising pollution and using new techniques of manufacture and distribution. It also implies the acceptance of any costs involved in the present as an investment for the future.

A great deal of concern has been expressed all over the world about shortcomings in the systems of corporate governance in operation and its organisation has been exercising the minds of business managers, academics and government officials all over the world. Often companies' main target is to become global while at the same time remaining sustainable as a means to get competitive power. But the most important question is concerned with what will be a firms' route to becoming global and what will be necessary in order to get global competitive power. There is more then one answer to this question and there are a variety of routes for a company to achieve this. Corporate governance can be considered as an environment of trust, ethics, moral values and confidence as a synergic effort of all the constituents of society that is the stakeholders, including government; the general public etc; professional / service providers and the corporate sector.

Of equal concern is the question of corporate social responsibility what this means and how it can be operationalised (Aras & Crowther 2007b). Although there is an accepted link between good corporate governance and corporate social responsibility the relationship between the two is not clearly defined and understood. Thus many firms consider that their governance is adequate because they comply with The Combined Code on Corporate Governance, which came into effect in 2003[1]. Of course all firms reporting on the London Stock Exchange are required to comply with this code, and so these firms are doing no more than meeting their regulatory obligations. Many companies regard corporate governance as simply a part of investor relationships and do nothing more regarding such governance except to identify that it is important investors / potential investors and to flag up that they have such governance policies. The more enlightened recognise that there is a clear link between governance and corporate social responsibility and make efforts to link the two. Often this is no more than making a claim that good governance is a part of their CSR policy as well as a part of their relationship with shareholders.

It is recognised that these are issues which are significant in all parts of the world and a lot of attention is devoted to this global understanding. Most analysis however is too simplistic to be helpful as it normally resolves itself into simple dualities: rules based v principles based or Anglo-Saxon v Continental. Our argument is that this is not helpful as the reality is far more complex. It cannot be understood without taking geographical, cultural and historical factors into account in order to understand the similarities, differences and concerns relating to people of different parts of the world. The aim of this book is to redress this by asking subject experts from different parts of the world to explain the issues from their particular perspective.

---

[1] It was revised in 2006.

Corporate Governance

One of the main issues, therefore, which has been exercising the minds of business managers, accountants and auditors, investment manages and government officials again all over the world is that of corporate governance (Aras 2008). Often companies main target is to became global while at the same time remaining sustainable as a means to get competitive power. But the most important question is concerned with what will be a firms' route to becoming global and what will be necessary in order to get global competitive power. There is more then one answer to this question and there are a variety of routes for a company to achieve this.

Probably since the mid-1980s, corporate governance has attracted a great deal of attention. Early impetus was provided by Anglo-American codes of good corporate governance[2]. Stimulated by institutional investors, other countries in the developed as well as in the emerging markets established an adapted version of these codes for their own companies. Supra-national authorities like the OECD and the World Bank did not remain passive and developed their own set of standard principles and recommendations. This type of self-regulation was chosen above a set of legal standards (Van den Barghe, 2001). After big corporate scandals corporate governance has become central to most companies. It is understandable that investors' protection has become a much more important issue for all financial markets after the tremendous firm failures and scandals. Investors are demanding that companies implement rigorous corporate governance principles in order to achieve better returns on their investment and to reduce agency costs. Most of the times investors are ready to pay more for companies to have good governance standards. Similarly a company's corporate governance report is one of the main tools for investor' decisions. Because of these reason companies can not ignore the pressure for good governance from shareholders, potential investors and other markets actors.

On the other hand banking credit risk measurement regulations are requiring new rules for a company's credit evaluations. New international bank capital adequacy assessment methods (Basel II) necessitate that credit evaluation rules are elaborately concerned with operational risk which covers corporate governance principles. In this respect corporate governance will be one of the most important indicators for measuring risk. Another issue is related to firm credibility and riskiness. If the firm needs a high rating score then it will have to be pay attention for corporate governance rules also. Credit rating agencies analyse corporate governance practices along with other corporate indicators. Even though corporate governance principles have always been important for getting good rating scores for large and publicly-held companies, they are also becoming much more important for investors, potential investors, creditors and governments. Because of all of these factors, corporate governance receives high priority on the agenda of policymakers, financial institutions, investors, companies and academics.

---

[2] An example is the Cadbury Report

This is one of the main indicators that the link between corporate governance and actual performance is still open for discussion. In the literature a number of studies have sought investigated the relation between corporate governance mechanisms and performance (eg Agrawal and Knoeber, 1996; Millstein and MacAvoy, 2003) Most of the studies have showed mixed result without a clear cut relationship. Based on these results, we can say that corporate governance matters to a company's performance, market value and credibility, and therefore that company has to apply corporate governance principles. But most important point is that corporate governance is the only means for companies to achieve corporate goals and strategies. Therefore companies have to improve their strategy and effective route to implementation of governance principles. So companies have to investigate what their corporate governance policy and practice needs to be.

Corporate Governance Principles

Since corporate governance can be highly influential for firm performance, firms must know what are the corporate governance principles and how it will improve strategy to apply these principles. In practice there are four principles of good corporate governance, which are:

> Transparency,
> Accountability,
> Responsibility,
> Fairness

All these principles are related with the firm's corporate social responsibility. Corporate governance principles therefore are important for a firm but the real issue is concerned with what corporate governance actually is.

Management can be interpreted as managing a firm for the purpose of creating and maintaining value for shareholders. Corporate governance procedures determine every aspect of the role for management of the firm and try to keep in balance and to develop control mechanisms in order to increase both shareholder value and the satisfaction of other stakeholders. In other words corporate governance is concerned with creating a balance between the economic and social goals of a company including such aspects as the efficient use of resources, accountability in the use of its power, and the behaviour of the corporation in its social environment.

The definition and measurement of good corporate governance is still subject to debate. However, good corporate governance will address all these main points:

- Creating sustainable value
- Ways of achieving the firm's goals
- Increasing shareholders' satisfaction
- Efficient and effective management
- Increasing credibility
- Ensuring efficient risk management

- Providing an early warning system against all risk
- Ensuring a responsive and accountable corporation
- Describing the role of a firm's units
- Developing control and internal auditing
- Keeping a balance between economic and social benefit
- Ensuring efficient use of resources
- Controlling performance
- Distributing responsibility fairly
- Producing all necessary information for stakeholders
- Keeping the board independent from management
- Facilitating sustainable performance

As can be seen, all of these issues have many ramifications and ensuring their compliance must be thought of as a long term procedure. However firms naturally expect some tangible benefit from good governance. So good governance offers some long term benefit for firms, such as:

- Increasing the firm's market value
- Increasing the firm's rating
- Increasing competitive power
- Attracting new investors, shareholders and more equity
- More or higher credibility
- Enhancing flexible borrowing condition/facilities from financial institutions
- Decreasing credit interest rate and cost of capital
- New investment opportunities
- Attracting Better personnel / employees
- Reaching new markets

Systems of governance

It is probably true to say that there is a considerable degree of convergence[3] on a global scale as far as systems of governance are concerned, and this convergence is predicated in the dominance of the Anglo Saxon model of the state, the market and of civil society. As a consequence there tends to be an unquestioning assumption (see for example Mallin 2004) that discussions concerning governance can assume the Anglo Saxon model as the norm and then consider, if necessary, variations from that norm (see Guillen 2001). In this chapter we take a very different position which explains the significant contribution of this book that there were historically 4 significant approaches to governance.

Each has left its legacy in governance systems around the world and any consideration of global convergence cannot be undertaken seriously certainly as far as any prognosis is concerned without a recognition of this. Thus for us the Anglo Saxon

---

[3] See chapter 12 for a fuller discussion of this convergence.

model is important but just one of the 4 models we wish to examine. The others which we have considered here we have described as the Latin model, the Ottoman model and the African model. We start by outlining the salient features of each.

The Anglo Saxon model of governance

The Anglo Saxon model of governance is of course familiar to all readers of this book. It is founded on rules which must be codified and can therefore be subject to a standard interpretation by the appropriate adjudicating body. It has a tendency to be hierarchical and therefore imposed from above; and along with this imposition is an assumption of its efficacy and a lack therefore of considerations of alternatives. In this model therefore the issues of governance, politics and power become inseparably intertwined.

The abuses which have been revealed within this system of governance[4] have exposed problems with the lack of separation of politics from governance. This has led to the suggestion that there should be a clear distinction between the two. The argument is that politics is concerned with the processes by which a group of people, with possibly divergent and contradictory opinions can reach a collective decision which is generally regarded as binding on the group, and therefore enforced as common policy. Governance, on the other hand, is concerned with the processes and administrative elements of governing rather than its antagonistic ones (Solomon 2007). This argument of course makes the assumption that it is actually possible to make the separation between politics and administration. For example both the UK and the USA have governance procedures to make this separation effective for their national governments and different procedures in each country but in both countries the division is continually blurred in practice. Many would argue, and we concur, that the division is not possible in practice because the third factor of power is ignored whereas this is more important. Indeed it is our argument that it is the operation of this power in practice that brings about many of the governance problems that exist in practice. We discuss this in greater detail later in the chapter but part of our argument is that theories and systems of governance assume that power relationships, while not necessarily equal, are not too asymmetric. If the relationship is too asymmetric then the safeguards in a governance system do not operate satisfactorily whereas one of the features of globalisation is an increase in such power asymmetries. We will return to this later.

As we have already identified, the Anglo Saxon model is hierarchical but other forms of governance are allowed and even encouraged to operate within this framework.

Thus the market form features prominently in the Anglo Saxon model while the network and consensual forms can also be found. It is therefore apparent that it is not the form of governance which epitomises the Anglo Saxon model; rather it is the

---

[4] For example in the UK there is at present (2007) an ongoing criminal investigation into the activities of the ex-Prime Minister, Tony Blair, his colleagues and senior members of the Labour Party with regard to the way in which the (national) Honours system has been used to reward people for donations made for political purposes. Similarly many people would, as far as the USA is concerned, blame failures in the governance system generally for the debacle of the Enron affair. These two countries are of course the principle exponents of the Anglo Saxon model of governance.

dependence on rules and adjudication which distinguishes this system of governance.

The Latin model of governance

The Latin model of governance tends to be less codified than the Anglo Saxon model and finds less need for procedures for adjudication. This is because it is founded in the context of the family and the local community. In some respects therefore it is the opposite of the Anglo Saxon model, being based on a bottom up philosophy rather than a hierarchical top down approach. Thus this model is based on the fact that extended families are associated with all other family members and therefore feel obligated. And older members of the family are deemed to have more wisdom and therefore assume a leadership role because of the respect accorded them by other family members. As a consequence there is no real need for formal codification of governance procedures and the system of adjudication does not need to be formalised it works very satisfactorily on an informal basis. Moreover this model is extended from the family to the local community and works on the same basis.

In many ways the network form of governance is based on this Latin model, insofar as it is predicated in informal relationships of mutual interest, and without the need for codification: this need is not required because of the interest of all parties in maintaining the working relationships which exist. Thus tradition can be said to play a part in this model of governance trust based on tradition because it has worked in the past and can be expected to continue working into the future. The network form however is based on a lack of significant power inequalities whereas the Latin model definitely does have a hierarchy and power is distributed unequally. The power if distributed according to age however and therefore it is acceptable to everyone because they know that they will automatically rise up the hierarchy thereby acquiring power as they age. The process is therefore inevitable and deemed to be acceptably fair.

The Ottoman model of governance

The Ottoman Empire existed for 600 years until the early part of the twentieth century. Although the empire itself is well known, few people know too much about it. Throughout Europe, at least, the reality is obscured by the various myths which abound and were mostly created during the latter part of the nineteenth century primarily by rival states and for political propaganda purposes. The reality was of course different from the myths and the empire had a distinct model of governance which was sufficiently robust to survive for 600 years, although much modern analysis suggests that the lack of flexibility and willingness to change in the model was one of the principle causes of the failure of the empire. We do not wish to enter into this debate and will restrict ourselves to an analysis of this distinct model of governance.

According to the fifteenth century statesman, Tursun Beg, it is only statecraft which enables the harmonious living together of people in society and in the Ottoman empire there were two aspects to this statecraft the power and authority of the rule (the Sultan) and the divine reason of Sharia (via the Caliph) (Inalcik 1968). In the Ottoman Empire these two were combined in one person. The Ottoman Empire was of course Islamic, but notable for its tolerance of other religions. It has been argued

(Cone, 2003), that the Islamic understanding of governance and corporate responsibility shares some fundamental similarities with the Rawlsian concept of social justice as mutual agreement among equals (motivated by self interest). All parties must be fully aware of the risks attendant on a particular course of action and be accepting of equal liability for the outcomes, good or bad. Muslims see Islam as the religion of trade and business, making no distinction between men and women and seeing no contradiction between profit and moral acts (Rizk 2005). The governance system was effectively a form of patronage which operated in a hierarchical manner but with the systems and procedures being delegated in return for the benefits being shared in an equitable manner. This enabled a very devolved form of governance to operate effectively for so long over such a large area of Asia, Europe and Africa. It is alien to the Anglo Saxon view because the systems involved payment for favours in a way that the Anglo Saxon model would interpret as corrupt but which the Ottoman model interprets simply as a way of devolving governance. It is interesting to observe therefore that the problems with failure of governance in the current era could not have occurred within the Ottoman model because there was no space left for the necessary secrecy and abuse of power.

The African model of governance

Africa is a continent which is normally ignored when any analysis of governance systems is considered, or it is merely assumed that the Anglo Saxon model has been adopted with the colonial regimes and that nothing preceded this. This is of course a false assumption as there were some complex civilisations and methods of commerce in existence prior to the European interventions. These operated largely upon the basis of kinship, tribal membership and shared belonging to various networks. Thus governance as networks is the dominant feature of the African model. These different networks of communication are classified as internal to the community or an inter-group (or intra-organisational) network and external to the community, or an inter-organisational network in the terminology of Fulk and Boyd (1991), with these classifications being specific to each network. This is distinct from the local neighbourhood communities in which a network of ties is inherent (Tilley 1974, Wellman & Leighton 1979).

      In the main these can be considered as a network of weak ties (Granovetter 1973) which are based upon social interaction around a commonality of interests and upon shared memberships rather than based upon friendship. In this respect it is pertinent to note that the dominant model here supports the findings of Ericksen & Yansey (1980) that strong ties are made more use of by less well educated people. Equally Pool (1980) demonstrates that networks operate more effectively when an effective communication system exists. The nature of this network can be argued to increase the effectiveness of its achievement of the strategic goals expressed earlier. However, it can also be seen to actually increase the effectiveness of the network as a communication, and hence governance, mechanism.

The concept of global governance

All systems of governance are concerned primarily with managing the governing of associations and therefore with political authority, institutions, and, ultimately, control. Governance in this particular sense denotes formal political institutions that aim to coordinate and control interdependent social relations and that have the ability to enforce decisions. Increasingly however, in a globalised world, the concept of governance is being used to describe the regulation of interdependent relations in the absence of overarching political authority, such as in the international system. Thus global governance can be considered as the management of global processes in the absence of form of global government. There are some international bodies which seek to address these issues and prominent among these are the United Nations and the World Trade Organisation. Each of these has met with mixed success in instituting some form of governance in international relations but are part of a recognition of the problem and an attempt to address worldwide problems that go beyond the capacity of individual states to solve (Rosenau 1999).

To use the term global governance is not of course to imply that such a system actually exists, let alone to consider the effectiveness of its operations. It is merely to recognise that in this increasingly globalised world there is a need for some form of governance to deal with multinational and global issues. The term global governance therefore is a descriptive term, recognising the issue and referring to concrete cooperative problem-solving arrangements. These may be formal, taking the shape of laws or formally constituted institutions to manage collective affairs by a variety of actors   including states, intergovernmental organisations, non-governmental organisations (NGOs), other civil society actors, private sector organisations, pressure groups and individuals). The system also includes of course informal (as in the case of practices or guidelines) or temporary units (as in the case of coalitions). Thus global governance can be considered to be the complex of formal and informal institutions, mechanisms, relationships, and processes between and among states, markets, citizens and organizations, both inter- and non-governmental, through which collective interests on the global plane are articulated, rights and obligations are established, and differences are mediated.

Global governance is not of course the same thing as world government: indeed it can be argued that such a system would not actually be necessary if there was such a thing as a world government. Currently however the various state governments have a legitimate monopoly on the use of force on the power of enforcement. Global governance therefore refers to the political interaction that is required to solve problems that affect more than one state or region when there is no power of enforcing compliance. Improved global problem-solving need not of course require the establishing of more powerful formal global institutions, but it would involve the creation of a consensus on norms and practices to be applied. Steps are of course underway to establish these norms and one example that is currently being established is the creation and improvement of global accountability mechanisms. In this respect, for example, the United Nations Global Compact[5] described as the world's largest voluntary corporate responsibility initiative brings together companies, national and international agencies, trades unions and other labour organisations and various organs of civil society in order to support universal environmental protection, human rights and social principles. Participation is entirely voluntary, and there is no enforcement of the principles by an outside regulatory body. Companies adhere to these practices both because they make economic sense, and because their stakeholders, including their shareholders (most individuals and institutional investors) are concerned with these issues and this provides a mechanism whereby they can monitor the compliance of companies easily. Mechanisms such as the Global Compact can improve the ability of individuals and local communities to hold companies accountable.

Cultural and geographical factors

The tenor of the debate about governance can be considered to be an argument between two competing positions: the free market economic model and the concomitant greater corporate autonomy versus greater societal intervention and government control of corporate action. The latter would imply the regulation of reporting through the governmental adoption of standards while the former would imply the continuance of the current voluntary approach. There is clear evidence that the free market proponents are winning the argument. They point to the global spread of capitalism, arguing that this reflects a recognition that social well-being is dependent on economic growth. Conversely, in the UK, the Combined Code on Corporate Governance, came into effect in 2003. This has the effect that all firms reporting on the London Stock Exchange are required to comply with this code, and so these firms are required to do so in order to meet their regulatory obligations. Thus the discussion regarding the extent of regulation continues.

Resolving this argument would seem to be impossible because the various proponents assume divergent philosophical positions in the ethics v regulation debate as well as in more fundamental understandings of human nature. There is of course no definitive answer to this conflict and we want to use this book to suggest that this debate is to a large extent pointless. It is our argument that the most important factor affecting the operation of governance systems is normally ignored from the analysis as we seek to introduce governance systems with universal application. This factor is that of culture. Culture is of course a set of shared attitudes, values and beliefs which are based to a large extent upon common backgrounds and experiences. They determine such things as our understanding of appropriate behaviour and reacting to circumstances. It is our argument that similarities in culture lead towards similar

---

[5] See www.unglobalcompact.org

behavioural patterns whereas differences in culture lead to differences. This cultural component of corporate behaviour sets the tone of governance systems in a way which is very complex and is based in part upon the different systems described earlier.

Our argument and the purpose for this book is that cultural differences are normally excluded from any analysis of governance but these differences mean that any universal code is applied so differently in different cultures as to render the code almost meaningless. In other words we maintain that culture is the most important determinant of the operation of any system of governance. In order to illustrate this point we have assembled a set of contributions from people of different cultures and from different geographical locations. So let us look at these contributions, which we have organised into three sections, dealing with governance issues, regional issues and cultural issues. These issues are interrelated in the various chapters but we have organised it like this in order to highlight the main factors involved.

The first section deals with governance issues and in chapter 2 therefore we start by considering the perennial question of regulation versus self-regulation. In this chapter Osuji pick up the growth in the on-financial aspects of governance reporting and disclosure and questions whether self-regulation can be trusted to protect the public interest norms inherent in such reporting. After examining the various options and both sides of the argument he concludes that external regulation is necessary to give veracity to such governance reporting, as well as being able to supply sanctions for non-compliance. In chapter 3 Bose takes up another perennial issue that of globalisation. She argues that the trend toward globalisation has intensified the debate about the proper role of business and government in addressing the social and environmental concerns associated with business operations. She identifies that enterprises are recognising that sustainable business success and shareholder value cannot be achieved solely through maximising short-term profits, but instead through market-oriented yet responsible behaviour, and that companies are aware that they can contribute to sustainable development by managing their operations in such a way as to enhance economic growth and increase competitiveness whilst ensuring environmental protection and promoting social responsibility, including consumer interests. Thus for her this has become an imperative. In chapter 4 Muslumov tackles another significant issue, namely that of insider trading. He uses an empirical study of such activity in the Istanbul Stock Exchange to demonstrate that insider trading significantly affects stock price volatility during and after the trade and therefore argues that such activity destabilizes the market.

Section two is concerned with regional issues and in the first chapter in this section Aluchna and Koladkiewicz are concerned with Poland as an example of a transitional economy. They present the process of building code of best practice from the perspective of emergence of corporate governance system, aiming at the analysis of the code characteristics relating to suggested guidelines and challenges identified in Polish public companies listed on the stock exchange and problematic practice adopted by corporate bodies or dominant shareholders. In doing so they demonstrate that ideas of best practice and corporate governance recommendations change to reflect the current stage of development of the economy of a country. In chapter 6 Said and colleagues are concerned with Corporate Governance and Corporate Social Responsibility in Malaysia. They state that in response to problems of corruption in the private sector the government, in 2004, launched the National Integrity Plan which aimed at promoting an accountable and corrupt-free society. Their chapter is based on a study which examines whether good corporate governance has a positive influence on the level of Corporate Social Responsibility in Malaysian Public Listed Companies. They conclude that better corporate governance will lead to a higher corporate social responsibility. In chapter 7 Aysan is also concerned with governance issues in a developing economy   in his case that of Turkey. He shows that, as the Turkish companies were mostly family firms dominated by founders and/or their immediate relatives, the owners and the managers are not yet used to the principles of Corporate Governance. In this chapter therefore he investigates the relationship of the Turkish Business Culture and the state of implementation of principles of Corporate Governance in quoted and non-quoted companies of Turkey. In addition, relationship of cultural characteristics of the Turkish Society are investigated and analyzed for determining whether these characteristics were supporting or against the development of Corporate Governance implementations in quoted and non- quoted companies in Turkey. The three chapters in the section all deal with different issues in different developing countries but all highlight key features of corporate governance that show them to be dependant upon the state of development of the economy and upon cultural issues which represent the norms in their respective country.

The final section therefore is concerned with a variety of cultural issues. In the first chapter Wong examines what he describes as the cultural imperative. He states that there appears to be an emerging convergence towards best-practice standards on corporate governance, but also a recognition that no single model of governance can exist. He seeks to examine the influence of culture on disclosure, transparency and enforcement practices, drawing on East Asian examples, arguing that prevailing legal and institutional forms in Asia mitigate against effective governance systems and practices and that relationship-based business practices further exacerbate the issue. Thus he suggests that cultural, historical and institutional factors and contexts are critical influential factors to consider in developing better and more effective governance practices but concludes that an uncritical acceptance of this cultural imperative is flawed and that a critical interrogation of culture and its exegesis is essential to unpack the different and contending claims of culture. In the next chapter Stevens and Mukhamedova examine the way in which a particular feature of culture in Uzbekistan, the *mahalla* community organization plays a central role in the way in which corporate social responsibility is understood and practiced amongst small and medium enterprises in that country. After examining this distinct feature of Uzbek culture they conclude with some observations about how the particular case of SMEs in Uzbekistan suggests broader lessons about how corporate social responsibility evolves as it encounters new cultures and institutional frameworks.

In Chapter 10 Davila Gomez takes a very different perspective, looking inside the corporation rather then to its external environment. As she states, with globalisation, organizations become a space where multiculturalism is a source of conflicts or agreements that needs to be addressed. In this chapter therefore she discusses the previous reality in an aim to understand some of the causes and implications for human well-being derived as an imposition from the concept of corporate culture. Equally, she examine how organizational theory has addressed these issues, trying to unveil some limits and possibilities, in an aim to reflect at the end about some alternatives, that considering transculturality, may help managers in the imperative to be open and active towards wholeness. To conclude she argues that we need to pass from a corporate culture of competition to a transcultural experience of collaboration. In chapter 11 Rizk investigates the relationship between corporate governance and Islam. She considers this relationship to be extensive and significant, arguing that Islam is much more than a religion and that the Qur'an is not merely about religions but has much more to do with rules of conduct, both social and economic. Her argument is that Moslems are governed by moral rules and mechanisms designed to achieve progress through the ideal use of resources and the protection of human values.

Finally we conclude by highlighting some important issues and arguing that the importance of culture has not been sufficiently taken into account in the debates about governance and codes of governance. We finish by arguing that any code of governance must be designed to be sufficiently flexible to allow for the full extent of cultural variation throughout the world.

References

Agrawal A & Knoeber C R (1996); Firm Performance and Mechanisms to Control Agency Problems between Managers and Shareholders; *Journal of Financial and Quantitative Analysis,* 31 (3), 377-398

Aras G (2008); Corporate Governance and the Agency Problem in Financial Markets; in D Crowther & N Capaldi (eds), *Ashgate Research Companion to Corporate Social Responsibility*; Aldershot; Ashgate (forthcoming)

Aras G & Crowther D (2007a); Is the global economy sustainable?; in S Barber (ed), *The Geopolitics of the City*; London; Forum Press, 165-194

Aras G & Crowther D (2007b); The Development of Corporate Social Responsibility; *Effective Executive*; Vol X No 9, September, 18-21

Cone, M (2003); Corporate Citizenship: The Role of Commercial Organizations in an Islamic Society; *Journal of Corporate Citizenship*; Vol. 9; pp 49-66.

Erricksen E & Yansey W (1980); Sex ties and status attainment; unpublished paper, Temple University Department of Sociology

Fulk, J. & Boyd, B. (1991); Emerging Theories of Communication in Organisations; *Journal of Management*; 17 (2), 407-446

Granoveter M S (1973); The strength of weak ties; *American Journal of Sociology* 78, 1360-1380

Guillen M F (2001); Is globalisation civilising, destructive or feeble? A critique of six key debates in the social science literature; *Annual Review of Sociology*, 27, 235-260

Hermalin B E (2005); Trends in corporate governance; *Journal of Finance*, LX (5), 2351-2384

Inalcik H (1968); The nature of traditional society: Turkey; in R E Ward & D A Rustow (eds), *Political Modernization in Japan and Turkey*; Princeton, NJ; Princeton University press; pp 49-56

Mallin C (2004); *Corporate Governance*; Oxford; Oxford University Press

Millstein. I.M. and MacAvoy. P.W.(2003); The Active Board of Directors and Performance of the Large Publicly Traded Corporation; *Columbia Law Review,* 8 (5), 1283-1322

Pool I (1980); Comment on Mark Granovetter's the strength of weak ties: a network theory revisited; paper presented at International Communications Association Conference, Acapulco

Rizk R R (2005); The Islamic Perspective to Corporate Social Responsibility; in D Crowther & R Jatan (eds), *International Dimensions of Corporate Social Responsibility* Volume 1; Hyderabad; ICFAI University Press

Rosenau J (1999); Toward an Ontology for Global Governance; in M Hewson & T J Sinclair (eds), *Approaches to Global Governance Theory*; Albany, NY; State University of New York Press

Soloman J (2007); *Corporate Governance and Accountability*; Chichester; Wiley

Tilley C (ed) (1979); *An Urban World*; Boston, Ma; Little Brown; Introduction pp 1-35

Van den Berghe, L.(2001), "Beyond Corporate Governance", *European Business Forum,* Issue 5, Spring

Wellman B & Leighton B (1979); Networks, neighbourhoods and communities; Urban Affairs Quarterly Vol 15 pp 363-390

Part 1
GOVERNANCE ISSUES

Chapter 2

Reporting of Corporate Governance Issues, Policies and Practices: Self-Regulation or Regulation

Onyeka K. Osuji

Introduction

Market regulation and self-regulation of business activities have been expanding in scope. There is also a marked increase in the delegation of regulatory power to private organisations, and business associations or agencies. The method of regulation has often been an issue where some sort of intervention is sought in the activities or operations of business organisations. The extent, form, pattern or degree of regulation has, rightly, been labelled "a sophisticated issue"[1]. Businesses often, if not always, prefer absence of governmental regulation in any aspects of corporate life. This attitude could be seen from the report of the Greenbury Committee. The report was not in favour of "statutory controls, which would be at best unnecessary and at worst harmful" on executive remuneration[2] .Incidentally, the Confederation of British Industry (CBI), "an organisation which speaks on behalf of the business community"[3], established the committee. The chairman of the committee, Sir Richard Greenbury, was "chairman and chief executive officer" of a big UK company[4].

---

[1] D. Milman, (1999) "Regulation of Business Organisations into the Millennium" in D. Milman (ed.) *Regulating Enterprise: Law and Business Organisations in the UK* (Oxford, and Portland, Oregon: Hart Publishing) 1 at 3.
[2] *Directors' Remuneration: Report of a Study Group chaired by Sir Richard Greenbury*, (1995) (London: Gee), ("Greenbury Report") 11, para.1.13.
[3] B. R. Cheffins, (1997) *Company Law: Theory, Structure and Operation*, (Oxford: Clarendon Press) 656.
[4] *Ibid.*

Although the committee favoured self-regulation, it did not rule out external regulation altogether. The committee sought the backing of The Stock Exchange to its code of best practice on executive remuneration[5] .The code of best practice is now part of the listing rules of The Stock Exchange[6].

The practice of publishing non-financial corporate governance reports in one form or the other is now widespread. The critical question is how to determine the effective method for regulating the reporting of non-financial corporate governance issues, policies and practices. What regulatory method can ensure the existence and maintenance of minimum standards in corporate governance reporting? Can self-regulation be trusted to protect the public interest norms inherent in such reporting? Are there issues of legitimacy and credibility? Is there an issue in the fusion of representative and regulatory functions under a self-regulatory system? Are there likely to be issues of conflict of interest? What should be the aims of an effective regulatory regime for corporate governance reporting? What are the flexibility, costs and technical advantages of a relevant regulatory regime? Is the fact that self-regulation is not limited to exhausting the language of the legally prescribed standards of conduct an advantage of self-regulation over prescriptive regulation? What is the role of culture? Are there any culture questions critical to the effectiveness of any regulatory regime for reporting corporate governance issues? Can the apparent success of selfregulation in the professions be extended to the business world in general and corporate governance reporting in particular? This chapter attempts to examine and provide answers to these questions.

Scope of Corporate Governance

According to some scholars, corporate governance may be defined as "the system of checks and balances, both internal and external to companies, which ensures that companies discharge their accountability to all their stakeholders and act in a socially responsive way in all areas of their business activity"[7]. This definition is based on the "perception that companies can maximize value creation over the long term, by discharging their accountability to all of their stakeholders and by optimising their system of corporate governance"[8]. The definition acknowledges that the concept of corporate governance has both internal and external components. The wider

---

[5] Greenbury Report, note 2 above, at 12, 19.
[6] Cheffins, note 3 above, at 656.
[7] J. Solomon and A. Solomon, (2004) *Corporate Governance and Accountability*, (Chichester: John Wiley & Sons Ltd) 14.
[8] *Ibid.* .

conception of corporate governance extends the concept to the interests of different stakeholders, and even interests such as the community, the environment and the relevant national interest[9]. The general view is that corporate governance is important for the welfare of a company and its diverse stakeholders. Stakeholders such as shareholders, creditors, employees, and even suppliers and consumers are exposed to risks by bad or incompetent corporate management[10]. Part of the reasons given for the collapse of large enterprises recently is the failure of, or weakness in, corporate governance[11]

Corporate governance may be examined from two approaches. First, it may be viewed from the 'external' perspective as "the various ways in which society attempts to control company behaviour in the public interest"[12]. Secondly, corporate governance may refer to "structures and processes that ensure that those responsible for managing companies do so in accordance with the legitimate objectives of the business"[13]. This approach focuses on the internal operations of the company. Although corporate governance may be broadly described as including both internal and external operations of a company, the focus of the subject is usually the direction and control of the internal company operations[14]. Some of the key issues in corporate governance include involvement of shareholders, effectiveness of the board of directors, and auditing and internal controls[15].Some of the mechanisms of corporate governance are definition of director duties, membership and role of the board of directors, and disclosure of financial and other information[16].

---

[9] B. S. Butcher, (2000) *Directors' Duties: A New Millennium, A New Approach?* (The Hague: Kluwer) 7. See also E.M. Dodd Jr., (1931-1932) "For Whom Are Corporate Managers Trustees?" 45 *Harv. LR* 1145 at 1160; L.S. Sealy, (1989) "Directors' 'Wider' Responsibilities-Problems Conceptual, Practical and Procedural" 13 *MULR* 164 at 170; G.P. Stapledon, (1996) *Institutional Shareholders and Corporate Governance*, (Oxford: Clarendon Press) 8.

[10] Butcher, note 9 above, at 7. See also B.A.K. Rider, (1978) "Amiable Lunatics and the Rule in Foss v Harbottle" *CLJ* 270 at 286-287.

[11] Cheffins, note 3 above, at 612. For an analysis of the U.S. Sarbanes-Oxley Act 2002 as a response to failure of corporate governance, see R. C. Smith and I. Walter, (2006) *Governing the Modern Corporation. Capital Markets, Corporate Control and Economic Performance*, (New York: Oxford University Press) 242-246.

[12] J. Parkinson, (2006) "Corporate Governance and the Regulation of Business Behaviour" in S. MacLeod (ed.), *Global Governance and the Quest for Justice. Volume II: Corporate Governance*, (Oxford and Portland, Oregon, Hart Publishing) 1 at 1.

[13] *Ibid*. The definition is lifted from D. Higgs, (2003) *Review of the Role and Effectiveness of the Non-Executive Directors*, (London: DTI) 11.

[14] D. Singh, (2006) "Corporate Governance and Banking Supervision" in J. J. Norton and J. Rickford (eds.) *Corporate Governance Post-Enron: Comparative and International Perspectives* (London: BICL) 465 at 467.

[15] *Ibid*.

[16] Parkinson, note 12 above, at 1.

Corporate governance has financial aspects[17]. This is uncontroversial. For instance, the earning of top executives has often attracted "keen interest"[18]. However, there are equally non-financial issues in corporate governance. The modern concept of public relations has moved from traditional marketing process to the identification and satisfaction of the needs and interests of customers, and other stakeholders including the local community[19]. Consequently, modern public relations and corporate governance share the same concerns, including non-financial and social responsibility issues[20]. This connection indicates the existence of non-financial components of corporate governance. Certainly, there are some corporate governance[21] issues that may be classified as non-financial. These include rolling contracts for executive directors, internal control mechanisms[22], voting rights of shareholders and directors, proxy voting, training programmes for directors[23], effectiveness of the board of directors and non-executive directors[24]. The assessment of the performance of the board of directors[25], committees of directors, individual directors and senior executives or employees is a key aspect of corporate governance[26].

---

[17] See Hampel Committee, (1998) *Final Report* ("Hampel Report"), available at: http://www.ecgi.org/codes/documents/hampel_index.htm (last visited on 21-11-2007); Solomon and Solomon, note 7 above, at 50.

[18] Cheffins, note 3 above, at 655. For an analysis of executive remuneration, see 653-708.

[19] M. Cingula, (2006) "Corporate Governance as a Process-Oriented Approach to Socially Responsible Organizations" in P. U. Ali and G. N. Gregoriou, *International Corporate Governance After Sarbanes-Oxley*, (Hoboken, NJ: John Wiley & Sons Inc) 65 at 88-89.

[20] *Ibid* at 89-90.

[21] See generally Solomon and Solomon, note 7 above, at 60.

[22] See Financial Reporting Council, (1999, revised 2005) *Internal Control. Revised Guidance for Directors on the Combined Code* (Turnbull Report), available at: http://www.frc.org.uk/images/uploaded/documents/Revised%20Turnbull%20Guidance%20October%202005.pdf (last visited on 21-11-2007); Solomon and Solomon, note 7 above, at 52.

[23] See Committee on the Financial Aspects of Corporate Governance, (1992) *Report*, (London: Gee), ("Cadbury Report") 24, para.4.19; Solomon and Solomon, note 7 above, at 47.

[24] See D. Higgs, (2003) *Review of the Role and Effectiveness of Board of Non-Executive Directors*, ("Higgs Report"), available at: http://www.berr.gov.uk/files/file23012.pdf (last visited on 21-11-2007); Solomon and Solomon, note 7 above, at 47.

[25] For an examination of the effect of the UK corporate governance codes on board relationship and structure, see T. J. Nichol, (2006) "Board Power Relations and the Impact of the UK's Combined Code on Corporate Governance" in P. U. Ali and G. N. Gregoriou, *International Corporate Governance After Sarbanes-Oxley*, (Hoboken, NJ: John Wiley & Sons Inc) 299.

[26] See Financial Reporting Council, (2003) *The Combined Code on Corporate Governance*, (London) Main Principle A.6; Final NYSE Corporate Governance Rules, section 303A of NYSE's Listed Company Manual Commentary to Rule 9; Australian Stock Exchange Corporate Governance Council, (2003) *Principles of Good Corporate Governance and Best Practice Recommendations*, (Sydney: Australian Stock Exchange) para.8.1; New Zealand Securities Commission, (2004) *Corporate Governance in New Zealand: Principles and Guidelines*, (Wellington) para.2.10; R. Leblanc, (2006) "Assessing the Effectiveness of Boards of Directors and Individual Directors" in P. U. Ali and G. N. Gregoriou, *International Corporate Governance After Sarbanes-Oxley*, (Hoboken, NJ: John Wiley & Sons Inc) 485 at 486.

There have been proposals for annual "reporting measures of board diversity along several dimensions, including the gender, nationality, ethnicity, age and prior experience"of non-executive directors[27].

Financial issues such as executive remuneration[28] and audit may arguably have non-financial aspects especially in the formulation and monitoring of policies. The existence or establishment of remuneration committees[29] may also be classified as non-financial if the question is on the existence, quality or effectiveness of internal checks. Where non-financial reports are subject to audit, the role and effectiveness of the audit committee and internal and external auditors[30] can also have non-financial implications. Similarly, people are concerned about both the extent of executive remuneration and the procedure for approval of such remuneration[31].

Regulation and Expanding Regulation of Corporate Governance Reporting

Regulation may be interpreted in three ways. First, in a narrow sense, regulation is "the promulgation of an authoritative set of rules, accompanied by some mechanism typically a public agency, for monitoring and promoting compliance with these rules"[32]. Secondly, regulation may refer to "all the efforts of state agencies to steer the economy"[33]. In this broader sense, regulation includes both rule-making and measures such as taxes, subsidies, public ownership and redistribution of property[34].

---

[27] L. Tyson, (2003) *The Tyson Report on the Recruitment and Development of Non-Executive Directors*, (London: London Business School) 6-7. See also Parkinson, note 12 above, at 11.

[28] See *Audit Committees Combined Code Guidance*, (2003) ("Smith Report"), available at: http://www.football-research.org/docs/smithreport-30-01-03.pdf (last visited on 21-11-2007); Cadbury Report note 23 above; Solomon and Solomon, note 7 above, at 56.

[29] See Greenbury Report, note 2 above; Solomon and Solomon, note 7 above, at 48.

[30] On financial aspect of this issue, see Cadbury Report, note 23 above; Solomon and Solomon, note 7 above, at 47.

[31] For *e.g.* see M. B. Clinard, (1990) *Corporate Corruption. The Abuse of Power*, (New York: Praeger) 9-10.

[32] J. Jordana and D. Levi-Faur, (2004) "The Politics of Regulation in the Age of Governance" in Jacint Jordana and David Levi-Faur (eds.), *The Politics of Regulation. Institutions and Regulatory Reforms for the Age of Governance* (Cheltenham, UK: Edward Elgar) 1 at 3-4; R. Baldwin, C. Scott and C. Hood, (1998) "Introduction" in R. Baldwin, C. Scott and C. Hood (eds.), *A Reader on Regulation*, (Oxford: Oxford University Press) 1 at 3.

[33] Jordana and Levi-Faur, note 32 above, at 4; Baldwin, Scott and Hood, note 32 above, at 3.

[34] Jordana and Levi-Faur, note 32 above, at 4.

In the broadest sense, regulation may refer to "all mechanisms of social control, including unintentional and non-state processes"[35]. Such definition of regulation extends to "anything producing effects on behaviour...[even] without mechanisms for monitoring and enforcement"[36].

The word "regulation" seems to, naturally, point to some form of governmental intervention, but private regulators "are increasingly engaged in authoritative decision making"[37] in diverse areas. Regulation is not an exclusive preserve of the state. A definition of regulation "in the context of a public agency"[38] as "sustained and focused control exercised by a public agency over activities that are valued by a community"[39] is quite narrow. Although the obvious view of regulation is in the context of legislative mandate, administrative agency and judicial interpretation of rules, "fluidization of regulatory space"[40] is now common while diverse private forms of regulatory authority exist and are still emerging[41]. It is wrong, at least in this age, to believe that the state is the sole source of regulation; in fact, the state may not be the principal regulator in some cases[42]. Authority for regulation is not necessarily associated with state or government institutions[43]. Regulation certainly includes public laws enforced by a state or government agency; but it may also include private arrangements, and even social norms, principles and customs[44].

---

[35] *Ibid.*

[36] Baldwin, Scott and Hood, note 32 above, at 4.

[37] A. C. Cutler, V. Haufler and T. Porter, (1999) "Private Authority and International Affairs" in A. Claire Cutler, V. Haufler and T. Porter (eds.) *Private Authority and International Affairs* (Albany, New York: SUNY Press) 16.

[38] A. McGee, (1999) "The Regulation of Insurance" in D. Milman (ed.) *Regulating Enterprise: Law and Business Organisations in the UK* (Oxford, and Portland, Oregon: Hart Publishing) 145 at 145.

[39] P. Selznick, (1985) "Focussing Organizational Research on Regulation" in R. Noll (ed.) *Regulatory Policy and the Social Sciences* (Berkeley: University of California Press) p.363; cited in *ibid.*

[40] R. D. Lipschutz and C. Fogel, (2002) "Regulation for the Rest of Us?" Global Civil Society and the Privatization of Transnational Regulation" in R. B. Hall and T. J. Biersteker (eds.) *The Emergence of Private Authority in Global Governance* (Cambridge: Cambridge University Press) 115 at 122.

[41] *Ibid* at 125. See also A. C. Cutler, V. Haufler and T. Porter (eds.) (1999) *Private Authority and International Affairs* (Albany, New York: SUNY Press).

[42] R. B. Hall and T. J. Biersteker, (2002) "The Emergence of Private Authority in the International System" in R. B. Hall and T. J. Biersteker (eds.) *The Emergence of Private Authority in Global Governance* (Cambridge: Cambridge University Press) 3 at 5; A. I. Ogus, *Regulation: Legal Form and Economic Theory* (Oxford: Clarendon Press) 1-3.

[43] R. B. Friedman, (1990) "On the Concept of Authority in Political Philosophy" in J. Raz (ed.) *Authority* (Washington Square, New York: New York University Press; Oxford: Basil Blackwell) 64.

[44] Lipschutz and Fogel, note 40 above, at 118.

A regulator supervises, coordinates or ensures compliance with rules. A regulator may be a public agency, a private body or a combination of public and private organisations. The distinction between "government" and "governance" is critical to understanding the role of private regulatory authorities. While government is exclusively state, governance encompasses governmental institutions and non-governmental mechanisms, persons, and organisations.[45] The idea of governance accepts the existence of "multiple authorities that are not necessarily public"[46]. A broad conception of private regulation includes corporate regulation[47] and other "non state actors" and "social actors" or "social groups"[48] participating in public affairs. Some of these private actors take "functional responsibility for seeing that regulations- both national and international- are adhered to by both public and private actors"[49].

---

[45] J. N. Rosenau, (1992) "Governance, Order and Change in World Politics", in J. N. Rosenau and E. Czempiel (eds.) *Governance Without Government: Order and Change in World Politics* (Cambridge: Cambridge University Press) 4-5.

[46] U. Mőrth, (2006) "Soft Regulation and Global Democracy" in M. Djelic and K. Sahlin-Andersson, *Transnational Governance-Institutional Dynamics of Regulation*, (Cambridge: Cambridge University Press) 119 at 123.

[47] R.D. Lipschutz, (2002) "Doing well by Doing Good? Transnational Regulatory Campaigns, Social Activism, and Impacts on State Sovereignty" in J. Montgomery and N. Glazer (eds.) *Challenges to Sovereignty: How Governments Respond* (New Brunswick, N.J.: Transaction) 291-320; V. Haufler, (2001) *Public Role for the Private Sector: Industry Self-Regulation in a Global Economy* (Washington D.C.: Carnegie Endowment for International Peace).

[48] Lipschutz and Fogel, note 40 above, at 116-117.

[49] *Ibid*. See also: A. C. Cutler, (1997) "Artifice, Ideology and Paradox: The Public /Private Distinction in International Law" 4(2) *Review of International Political Economy*, 261-285; E. Ostrom, (1990) *Governing the Commons: The Evolution of Institutions for Collective Action* (Cambridge: Cambridge University Press); D. W. Bromley (ed.) (1992) *Making the Commons Work* (San Francisco: ICS Press); J. Scott, (1998) *Seeing Like a State* (New Haven: Yale University Press) chapter 1; D. Korten, (1998) *Globalizing Civil Society: Reclaiming Our Right to Power* (New York: Seven Stories Press); J.C. Smith, C. Chatfield and R. Pagnucco (eds.) (1997) *Transnational Social Movements and Global Politics: Solidarity Beyond the State* (Syracuse, N.Y.: Syracuse Universe Press); T. Pricen and M. Finger (eds.) (1994) *Environmental NGOs in World Politics* (London: Routledge); M. Keck and K. Sikkink, (1998) *Activists Across Borders: Advocacy Networks in International Politics* (Ithaca, N.Y: Cornell University Press); R. D. Lipschutz and J. Mayer, (1996) *Civil Society and Global Environmental Governance* (Albany, N.Y.: SUNY Press); P. Wapner, (1996) *Environmental Activism and World Civic Politics* (Albany, N.Y.: SUNY Press); R. D. Lipschutz, (1996) "Reconstructing World Politics: The Emergence of Global Civil Society" in J. Larkins and R. Fawn (eds.) *International Society After the Cold War* (London: Macmillan) 101-131; R. B. Hall and T. J. Biersteker (eds.) (2002) *The Emergence of Private Authority in Global Governance* (Cambridge: Cambridge University Press); E. E. Meindinger, (2000) "Private' Environmental Regulation, Human Rights, and Community" in *Buffalo Environmental Law Journal*, available at: http://www.ublaw.buffalo.edu/fas/meindinger/hrec.pdf.

There are historical and existing examples of activities "governed by customs, laws, and contracts among and between individuals and groups, often but not always with the approval or support of the state"[50].

A form of private regulation is corporate self-regulation. Self-regulation may be defined as "...the possibility for economic operators, the social partners, non-governmental organisations or associations to adopt amongst themselves and for themselves common guidelines ... (particularly codes of practice or sectoral agreements)"[51]. A critical element of self-regulation is that corporations regard "the rules and practices to be obligatory"[52]. The obligatory element should be distinguished from mere cooperation among corporations[53]. It is clear that self-regulation cannot be equated with voluntariness. There are cases of self-regulatory schemes that are backed by law and legally enforceable[54]. However, pure self-regulatory schemes are usually voluntary. Under a self-regulatory system, the businesses "regulate their own activities without the requirements or agreements being underpinned by legislation"[55]. Self-regulation[56] has different forms or degrees at the corporation level, industry or sector regulation, or involvement of independent parties.

---

[50] Lipschutz and Fogel, note 40 above, at 121. See also: J. Braithwaite and P. Drahos, (2000) *Global Business Regulation* (Cambridge: Cambridge University Press); C. N. Murphy, (1994) *International Organization and Industrial Change: Global Governance Since 1850* (New York: Oxford University Press).

[51] Definition by the Inter-Institutional Agreement on Better Lawmaking, cited in Better Regulation Commission (formerly Better Regulation Task Force), *The Challenge of Culture Change: Raising the Stakes*, 27 available at: http://www.brc.gov.uk/downloads/pdf/brtftext04.pdf.

[52] A. C. Cutler, (2002) "Private International Regimes and Interfirm Cooperation" in R. B. Hall and T. J. Biersteker (eds.) *The Emergence of Private Authority in Global Governance* (Cambridge: Cambridge University Press) 1 at 27-28.

[53] *Ibid* at 27. For a discussion on cooperation and obligation, see R. O. Keohane, (1989) "International Institutions: Two Approaches" in R. O. Keohane (ed.) *International Institutions and State Power: Essays in International Relations Theory* (Boulder, Colo.: Westview Press) 158-179.

[54] C. Glinski, (2006) "Self-Regulation of Transnational Corporations: Neither Meaning in Law Nor Voluntary" in S. MacLeod (ed.), *Global Governance and the Quest for Justice. Volume II: Corporate Governance*, (Oxford and Portland, Oregon, Hart Publishing) 197 at 198ff.

[55] Better Regulation Commission (formerly Better Regulation Task Force), *The Challenge of Culture Change: Raising the Stakes*, 27 available at: http://www.brc.gov.uk/upload/assets/www.brc.gov.uk/brtftext04.pdf (last visited on 21-11-2007).

[56] For a distinction between 'co-regulation' and 'enforced self-regulation', see I. Ayres and J. Braithwaite, (1992) *Responsive Regulation. Transcending the Deregulation Debate*, (New York: Oxford University Press) 102.

Company law usually imposes demanding disclosure requirements on financial aspects of corporate governance. In most cases, disclosure requirements may "exceed the requirements governing the financial actions themselves"[57]. In contrast, a "gap"[58] usually exists in the disclosure of non-financial components of corporate governance. The regulated non-financial aspects of corporate governance reporting can be found in the corporate annual report requirements, with assumption that regulatory activity is primarily directed at disclosure to shareholders[59].

Prior to the Companies Act (CA) 2006[60], mandatory social-related issues covered in United Kingdom annual reports included charitable donations, employment data, pension fund adequacy, consultation with employees, employee share ownership schemes, employment of the disabled, contingent liabilities and provisions for health and safety or environmental remediation[61]. In addition, some United Kingdom companies' annual reports voluntarily make disclosures on issues such as environmental protection, energy saving, consumer protection, product safety, community involvement, value-added statement, health and safety, racial and sexual equality, redundancies, employee training, mission statement/statement of social responsibility[62]. However, with no attempt to quantify performance or reporting, the contents of annual reports focus only on "creation of images"[63] of active corporate involvement in relevant activity.

CA 2006 now goes further to require directors' report of companies, with the exception of small companies, to contain a business review[64]. For a quoted company, the business review must contain information on environmental, employee[65] and social and community issues[66]. Consideration of these issues is also part of the newly codified directors' duties[67]. The codification of directors' duties was, possibly, in response to calls for the codification of both the legal and equitable duties of directors[68]. Would one now conclude that CA 2006 contains a philosophy in favour of regulation of non-financial aspects of corporate governance? A close look at the relevant statutory provisions indicates that this is not likely to be the case.

---

[57] R. Gray, D. Owen and C. Adams, (1996) *Accountability. Changes and Challenges in Corporate Social and Environmental Reporting*, (Hemel Hempstead: Prentice Hall) 65.

[58] *Ibid* at 64-65.

[59] *Ibid* at 82.

[60] For the background to the CA 2006, see P. Loose and M. Griffiths, (2007) *The Company Director: Powers, Duties and Liabilities 9th Edn*, (Bristol: Jordan) 60-66.

[61] Gray, Owen and Adams, note 57 above, at 89 figure 4.3.

[62] *Ibid*.

[63] D. Crowther, (2004) "Corporate Social Reporting: Genuine Action or Window Dressing" in D. Crowther and L. Rayman-Bacchus, *Perspectives on Corporate Social Responsibility*, (Aldershot: Ashgate) 140 at 158.

[64] CA 2006, s.417(1).

[65] See also CA 2006, s.411, which requires annual accounts of companies, except small companies, to contain information on employee issues.

[66] CA 2006, s.417(5).

[67] CA 2006, s.172.

[68] For instance, see Butcher, note 9 above, at 22-28.

The statutory provisions imply interest in only the financial aspects of the disclosed issues[69]. Moreover, the statutory reports- annual accounts and directors' report- are meant for shareholders only. But acknowledgment of a wider range of interests in corporate governance necessarily involves recognition of the existence and importance of non-financial components of corporate governance.

Regulatory Method

The method of regulation has often been an issue where some sort of intervention is sought in business activities. Recent history of corporate law and practice reveals that even where there is agreement on the need for regulatory intervention in an area, the form of regulation or the status of the regulator is often a controversial issue. The extent, form, pattern or degree of regulation has, rightly, been labelled "a sophisticated issue"[70]. It is likely that the regulation of corporate governance reporting would not be an exception especially when the need for intervention appears not to have received universal support from enterprises. The possible forms of regulation for both financial and non-financial components of corporate governance reporting are public (external), private (self-regulation), and mixed regulation.

Can self-regulation be trusted to protect the public interest norms inherent in corporate governance reporting? The implementation of existing voluntary codes of conduct shows that the potential for abuse of self-regulation of non-financial corporate governance reporting is a distinct and real possibility. Legislative regulation of such reporting can rightly be justified since the existing corporate codes of conduct, most of which are drawn up by businesses individually or collectively or prepared with their active participation and consent, are more or less a system which confers on corporations "a degree of immunity from the consequences of their mistakes"[71] or deliberate misconduct. Although some may, initially or subsequently, receive some form of legal recognition[72], a major problem with self-regulatory systems is that "they can be viewed as essentially derived from contract"[73].

---

[69] See CA 2006, s.417(6).
[70] Milman, note 1 above, at 3.
[71] *Ibid* at 5.
[72] For example, in *R v Takeover Panel ex parte Datafin Plc* [1987] 2 W.L.R 699, the City Code on Takeovers and Mergers issued by the Takeover Panel received formal judicial recognition.
[73] Milman, note 1 above, at 6.

A corporation is not merely a medium for, or an expression of, private contracting; some form of protection and regulation of corporate operations provided by the external instrumentality of law may be required in some cases[74].

The availability of sanctions or redress[75] should be an important factor in the choice of the regulatory method for corporate governance reporting. The availability of redress is critical for the effectiveness of such regulation. For example, a system of regulation for corporate governance reporting should provide options to the regulator on receipt of complaints from consumers or prospective investors who have relied on a corporate governance report. Without doubt, a system of self-regulation may have room for sanctions. Although the UK City Panel on Takeovers and Mergers had no statutory basis[76], but non-compliance with its findings might be regarded as a "regulatory offence" and attract some "sanctions". For instance, non-compliance might be a ground for the Stock Exchange to consider de-listing the concerned company[77]. However, sanctions available to a self-regulatory body must be limited in comparison with the "full weight of the law" open to legislative regulation. Despite the existence of self-regulatory schemes in the advertising business in the United States and Europe, the Federal Trade Commission Act[78] and the Misleading Advertising Directive[79] respectively provide legal means for redress for the consumer[80].

Sanctions available or applied under a self-regulatory system are more likely to be exposed to the risk of legal and other challenges because of the absence of "legal backing". Simply put, most self-regulatory measures lack legitimacy[81]. Some cases brought against the Takeover Panel by businesses aggrieved by some of its decisions illustrate this point[82]. For delegation of authority to be legitimate, the mechanisms for accountability should be trusted[83]. Legislation has the advantage of conferring legitimacy on both the regulatory method and the regulator. Legitimacy is necessary for market stability and credibility[84].

---

[74] A. R. Pinto, (1998) "United States" in A. R. Pinto and G. Visenti (eds.) *The Legal Basis of Corporate Governance in Publicly Held Corporations- A Comparative Approach* (The Hague: Kluwer Law International) 253 at 263.

[75] Better Regulation Commission, note 55 above, at 17.

[76] But now see CA 2006, Pt. 28, chapter 1, s.942ff.

[77] S. Leader and J. Dine, (1998) "United Kingdom" in A. R. Pinto and G. Visenti (eds.) *The Legal Basis of Corporate Governance in Publicly Held Corporations- A Comparative Approach* (The Hague: Kluwer Law International) 219 at 221, 225.

[78] The legislation is available at: http://www.fda.gov/opacom/laws/ftca.htm (last visited on 21-11-2007).

[79] Directive 97/55/EC.

[80] See further Better Regulation Commission, note 55 above, at 10, 12, 43.

[81] A. Ogus, (1995) "Rethinking Self-Regulation" 15 *Oxford Journal of Legal Studies* 97 at 98.

[82] For instance, see *R v Takeover Panel ex parte Datafin Plc* [1987] 2 W.L.R 699.

[83] C. Scott, (2000) "Accountability in the Regulatory State" 27(1) *Journal of Law and Society* 38 at 39.

[84] Lipschutz and Fogel, note 40 above, at 136.

A phenomenon associated with self-regulatory arrangements is that they limit relevant debates to company executives with the result that they are generally "opaque and non-democratic as well as limited in scope"[85]. This may be more disturbing in corporate governance reporting since some of the relevant issues transcend the "corporate world". External legal regulation widens the debating arena and provides more effective protection of those issues.

One inherent difficulty with self-regulation exists where consumers and other "outsiders" are involved. In such cases, the self-regulatory body has dual roles of regulating and at the same time representing or encouraging the members. This is a curious[86] situation that reminds one of the biblical saying that no one can serve two masters with equal love and devotion[87]. In corporate governance reporting, business managers and other interest groups may in most cases be regarded as two separate 'masters' with conflicting expectations. Corporate representatives essentially "represent a money-making, profit-making enterprise"[88] who have an incentive to provide misleading information or suppress unfavourable information about the "quality"[89] or reputation of the corporation. There is evidence to cast doubt on the effectiveness of self-regulatory bodies in protecting the public interest[90]. Independence of the regulator ensures the maintenance of trust and transparency of a regulatory system[91].

This problem with the fusion of both regulatory and representative functions in one body informed some recommendations on the regulation of solicitors by the *Report of the Review of the Regulatory Framework for Legal Services in England and Wales* undertaken by Sir David Clementi ("Clementi Report")[92]. The Clementi Report recommended two separate bodies to be created from The Law Society of England and Wales one, a purely representative organisation, and the other, an independent body to handle consumer and related issues. The recommendation led to the establishment of the Solicitors Regulatory Authority[93] as the regulatory authority for solicitors in England and Wales. The Law Society remains a representative

---

[85] *Ibid* at p.121. See also I. M. Young, (1990) *Justice and the Politics of Difference* (Princeton,N.J.: Princeton University Press) chap 3.

[86] Leader and Dine, note 77 above, at 225.

[87] Luke chapter 16 verse 13, *The Holy Bible, New International Version* (1984) (International Bible Society).

[88] A. A. Berle, (1954) *The 20th Century Capitalist Revolution* (New York: Harcourt and Brace and Company).

[89] Ogus, note 42 above, at 140.

[90] R. Baldwin and M. Cave, (1999) *Understanding Regulation: Theory, Strategy, and Practice* (New York: Oxford University Press) 127. See also Office of Fair Trading, (1998) *Raising Standards of Consumer Care- Progressing Beyond Codes of Practice* (London) 16-17, quoted in R. Baldwin and M. Cave, (1999) *Understanding Regulation: Theory, Strategy, and Practice* (New York: Oxford University Press) 127.

[91] Better Regulation Commission, note 55 above, at 7, 36.

[92] The Clementi Report is available at: www.legal-services-review.org.uk/content/**report**/.

[93] http://www.sra.org.uk/home.page.

organisation.

Japan provides another example of the issue of dual and conflicting roles in the regulation of corporate governance reporting. In 2004, Japan's Certified Public Accountants and Auditing Oversight Board (COPAAB) was placed under the supervision of the public regulator, the Financial Services Agency. The COPAAB was previously a purely self-regulatory body. However doubts on the effectiveness of the COPAAB persist despite the 2004 changes because the body "acts both as a watchdog and as a representative of the accountants"[94].

Regulation of corporate governance reporting shares one objective with consumer protection laws. The objective is the protection of "the public at large including those who do not deal with a business"[95]. In the area of consumer protection, private initiatives or self-regulatory measures exist. The efficacy of exclusive self-regulation in consumer protection must be doubtful. The law has intervened to a significant extent in this area. For example, the European Commission once directed airlines to fashion out, by self-regulation, a compensation scheme for air passengers for delays or cancellations of flights. After a prolonged wait, the European Parliament and Council issued a binding Regulation[96] providing for the compensation scheme. The reaction of the airlines was to challenge the validity of the Regulation before the European Court of Justice (ECJ) on the ground of inconsistency with the Montreal Convention[97]. The ECJ decided in favour of the European institutions[98]. The airlines are now taking steps to implement the Regulation[99]. The result might not have been achieved in the absence of external legal intervention.

The choice of the form or degree of regulation should to, a reasonable extent, depend upon the aims of a particular regulatory regime. For instance, a regulatory regime may try to achieve "equity between the participators in the business", or it may concentrate "on the external conduct of the particular business medium"[100]. Self-regulation or external regulation may work in either situation depending on the circumstances of the particular case. The question in corporate governance reporting is the definition or description of its regulatory aim. The basic aim of an effective regulatory regime for such reporting should be the protection of other interests or

---

[94] "Auditors in Japan- Under Attack" *The Economist* May 13th 2006, 90.
[95] A. McGee, C. Williams and G. Scanlan, (2005) *The Law of Business Organisations* (Exeter: Law Matters Publishing) 300.
[96] Regulation (EC) 261/2004.
[97] Convention for the Unification of Certain Rules for International Carriage by Air.
[98] *Case C334/04- R. (on the application of International Air Transport Association) v Department of Transport*, [2006] ECR 0, decided on 10 January 2006.
[99] For instance see: http://www.easyjet.com/EN/News/20050216_01.html (last visited on 21-11-2007).
[100] Milman, note 1 above, at 4.

interest groups who might rely, or would be interested in relying, on corporate reports. "Relative ignorance"[101] of these other interest groups may be sufficient justification for recourse to external legislative regulation. External legal intervention is justified where rules affect or are likely to affect third parties especially where the potential for abuse exists.[102]

The same reasoning and conclusion apply to cases where there exist real or apparent "opportunities for dishonesty"[103] by the information provider as is the case with non-financial reports. In 1945, the United Kingdom Cohen Committee expressed their satisfaction that "the great majority of limited companies...are honestly and competently managed".[104] This statement might have been true in 1945, but its accuracy may be open to question today in view of the increase in the number of corporate scandals. It is certainly not the correct approach to vouch for the honesty of businesses in reporting of corporate governance issues and activities. Even some commentators who oppose external legal intervention in the business world accept the need for an external regulator to "assess the quality"[105] of rules devised by businesses.

Nike's troubled experience with campaigners, which culminated in the *Nike v Kasky*,[106] showed that the credibility of corporate reports is doubtful when they are solely 'regulated' by the concerned corporation, individually or in association with other or similar businesses. *Kasky v Nike* concerned Nike's response to allegations of operation of 'sweatshop' factories in South East Asia. Among other claims, Nike stated that its wages were "on average double the minimum wage" in those countries where its factories were located, and that its employees "are protected from physical and sexual abuse".[107] Kasky sued Nike claiming that Nike's communications were false and misleading. The case did not go beyond the interlocutory stage, while the parties subsequently reached a settlement on the case.[108] In furtherance of the terms of settlement, Nike's publication in the aftermath of the *Kasky* litigation documented the employment conditions in its factories. The April 2005 report prepared in conjunction

---

[101] McGee, note 38 above, at 145 at 146.

[102] Ogus, note 81 above, at 98-99.

[103] *Ibid.*

[104] Cmnd. 6659 (1945) para. 5.

[105] J. Dine, (1999) "Companies and Regulations: Theories, Justifications and Policing" in D. Milman (ed.) *Regulating Enterprise: Law and Business Organisations in the UK* (Oxford, and Portland, Oregon: Hart Publishing) 291 at 311.

[106] 27 Cal. 4th 939, 946, 45 P.3d 243, 247, 119 Cal. Rptr.2d 296 (Cal. 2002) California Supreme Court.

[107] A. K. Kazer and C. A. Williams, "The Future of Social Reporting is on the Line- Nike v Kasky could undermine the Ability to Require Accurate Reporting" available at http://www.dominiadvisor.com/advisor/About-Domini/News/Press-Release-Archive/Nike_Kasky_Oped_6-03.doc_cvt.htm (last visited on 21-11-2007).

[108] http://www.nike.com/nikebiz/news/pressrelease.jhtml?year=2003&month=09&letter=f (last visited on 21-11-2007).

with some 'independent' parties admitted of poor labour standards in a significant number of Nike's factories especially those located in Asia.[109] Nike's report has been described as an "unusual step"[110]. It is certainly unusual for business organisations to publish such unfavourable corporate information.

External legal regulation would confer some degree of credibility to corporate governance reports and would go a long way in preventing the dissemination (or, at least, effecting the reduction) of the amount of false or misleading corporate governance reports. Credibility is a serious issue for any regulatory scheme for, or on, information provision. Corporate governance reporting is all about the provision of relevant information, which may, in some cases be, or turn out to be, unfavourable to the corporate image or reputation. External legal regulation of corporate governance reporting would also be to the advantage of business enterprises. A corporation should ordinarily have a good defence if it followed the legally prescribed code of practice.[111]

Generally, no person, including corporations, would be willing to provide information adverse to their reputation, or likely to be used against them for any reason. The question is whether an association of businesses would be able to ensure the credibility and transparency of corporate governance information and reports. Although this may be possible, but the tendency to protect reputation or interest also applies where "an association" of "similar persons" is involved. Such "negative" information is usually withheld or understated. Information that would impact positively on the image or interest could be falsified or exaggerated. It is arguable that the huge popularity enjoyed by movies such as *The Insider* (1999),[112] *A Civil Action* (1998) and *Erin Brockovich* (2000)[113] was a reflection of the fact that its story was based on the belief that corporate managers, individually and/or collectively, would prefer providing false or misleading statements when the "truth" conflicts with the perceived corporate interest. *The Insider* was a story of an organisation and industry wide deliberate making of false statements and cover-ups on the effects of a particular product on human health.

Flexibility[114] is often touted as an advantage of self-regulation over external legal

---

[109] Nike's 2004 Corporate Social Responsibility Report is available at: http://www.nike.com/nikebiz/nikebiz.jhtml?page=29 (last visited on 21-11-2007).

[110] N. Baker, (2005) "All Done With Mirrors? Transparency and Business Ethics" 59(4) International Bar News 4 at 6.

[111] Better Regulation Commission, note 55 above, at 13.

[112] The movie was produced by Touchstone Pictures and Spyglass Entertainment.

[113] D. B. Sicilia, (2004) "The Corporation Under Siege: Social Movements, Regulation, Public Relations, and Tort Law since the Second World War" in K. Lipartito and D. B. Sicilia (eds.), Constructing Corporate America. History, Politics, and Culture, (Oxford: Oxford University Press) 188 at 209.

[114] Better Regulation Commission, note 55 above, at 5, 14.

regulation. The argument goes that business organisations need "to be allowed some flexibility and some freedom from mandatory rules and formalities".[115] Other commentators have further argued that "private, ad-hoc and discretionary standards" in the business world are preferable to "explicit, predictable and fixed legal rules".[116] Without doubt the process of legislation or amending statute may make it more difficult to modify rules of a regulatory scheme to adapt with changing situations. But the question is how useful is the flexibility argument to corporate governance reporting?

First, inflexibility is not always a disadvantage. It can provide and promote certainty[117] and predictability in a regulatory environment. Second, external legal regulation is not always or necessarily inflexible. A legislative framework may anticipate the need for a sufficiently dynamic regulatory scheme by providing the necessary procedures or processes. The use of subordinate legislation is a good illustration. Third, there are situations where the legal intention is and should be to provide less flexible rules. For instance, the concept of fiduciary duty in company law is usually inflexible, even to the extent of hindering its exclusion by private contracting.[118]

It is also said that self-regulation is appropriate for areas of complex or technical issues which may require high level of expertise.[119] This does not constitute an insurmountable obstacle for external legal regulation of corporate governance reporting. The issue is just one of reporting corporate practice in selected areas; it would not normally involve technical questions. But where expertise may be needed such as in the verification of information supplied, no rule prevents the law from relying on the practice of the experts in the field. There is precedence in business taxation where recourse is usually had to "generally accepted principles of accounting" in the determination of corporate profit.[120] In any event, law's role is to set

---

[115] L. S. Sealy, (1984) Company Law and Commercial Reality (London: Sweet & Maxwell) 13. See also L. S. Sealy, (1984) Company Law and Commercial Reality (London: Sweet & Maxwell) 5.

[116] Cutler, note 52 above, at 35, relying on W. Scheuerman, (1999) "Economic Globalization and the Rule of Law" 6(1) Constellations: An International Journal of Critical and Democratic Theory 3-25.

[117] Better Regulation Commission, note 55 above, at 16.

[118] R. C. Clark, (1985) "Agency Costs Verses Fiduciary Duties" in J. W. Pratt and R. J. Zeckhauser (eds.) Principles and Agents: The Structure of Business.

[119] Better Regulation Commission, note 55 above, at 7, 32.

[120] Gallagher v Jones; Threfall v Jones [1993] STC 537 (Court of Appeal) noted in J. Freedman (1993) "Ordinary Principles of Commercial Accounting-Clear Guidance or a Mystery Tour?" BTR 468; Johnston v Britannia Airways Ltd [1994] STC 763; Herbert Smith v Honour [1999] STC 173; Odeon Associated Theatres Ltd v Jones [1973] Ch 288, 48 TC 257. The relationship between tax law and accounting has generated wide literature, for e.g.: G. Macdonald, (2002) The Taxation of Business Income- Aligning Taxable Income with Accounting Income- a discussion paper (London: The Tax Law Review Committee, The Institute of Fiscal Studies); A. Wilson, (2001) "Financial Reporting and Taxation: Marriage is out of the Question" BTR 86; S. Green, (1995) "Accounting Standards and Tax Law: Complexity, Dynamism and Divergence" BTR 445; G. Whittington, (1995) "Tax Policy and Accounting Standards" BTR 452; A. Broke, (1995) "Accounting Standards and Taxable Profit: An Accountant's View" BTR 457; G. Macdonald, (1995) "Matching Accounting and Taxable Profits: Reflections on Gallagher v Jones" BTR 484.

the guidelines and law should not regard itself as bound[121] by expert practice.

It appears that there is widespread support, even among critics of self-regulatory schemes for business organisations, for the point that self-regulation enjoys cost-compliance, administration and enforcement advantages over external legal regulation.[122] However, this cost analysis suffers from some weaknesses, especially with reference to the regulation of non-financial corporate governance reporting. Cost is a logical consequence of any regulatory system, whether it is external or internal. Although proponents of the cost argument would point out that a self-regulatory scheme is cheaper than external regulation, the extension of the argument to corporate governance reporting raises some difficulty. The preparation, drafting, monitoring, and enforcement of rules for such reporting must have some cost implications for the regulator. Why and how it would be cheaper for a self-regulatory body than an external regulator to perform these roles are important questions. For the regulated, cost would be involved in the preparation and submission of the corporate governance report. Would it make any difference that an external regulator instead of a trade association directs the preparation or submission, for instance? Would the status of the regulator affect issues such as the internal corporate procedure for gathering and processing information? Would it have been cheaper for corporations to submit their annual reports and financial statements to their self-regulatory bodies instead of external regulatory authorities?

The critical issue for any regulatory scheme is achieving a cost efficient system of regulation. High cost of implementation or application may sometimes defeat the aims of any regulatory scheme irrespective of the status of the regulator. Regulators, whether external or internal, state-imposed or voluntary, need be aware of this issue. Sometimes, the attitude of individuals involved in a regulatory scheme may affect its cost. For instance, individuals might take unusually long time to approve reports. This might not have anything to do with the fact the individual works for an external regulator or a self-regulatory body.

Insistence on unnecessary or expensive requirements or formalities is not an inherent or exclusive part of external legal regulation; neither is a self-regulatory scheme synonymous with reduction of formalities and enforcement costs.

---

[121] Lord Denning had a similar view in respect of accounting and tax law: *Heather v PE Consulting Group* [1973] 1 All ER 843.

[122] For instance see: Ogus, note 81 above, at 97-98; Sealy, note 37 above, at 26-29; Cutler, note 52 above, at 31; P. Milgrom, D. North and B. Weingast, (1990) "The Role of institutions in the Revival of Trade: The Law Merchant, Private Judges, and the Champagne Fairs" 2(1) *Economics and Politics*; Better Regulation Commission, note 55 above, at 15.

The key issue is simply one of regulatory design and implementation.[123] Even poorly designed deregulatory measures, including self-regulatory systems, can result in complexity and increased compliance costs.[124] Regulatory cost usually depends on the enabling legislation. The relevant legislation may well design a cost-effective system of regulation. For instance, United Kingdom company law policy at some point sought a comparatively cheap and straightforward incorporation procedure. The measures adopted included the relaxation of incorporation formalities and the removal of minimum capital requirement. Following the decision in *Centros*[125] that companies are free to use the United Kingdom as place of incorporation, the United Kingdom appears to enjoy comparative advantage in incorporation.[126]

It is true that "…behavioural signals provided by legislation, regulations and common-law rules are not exhausted by the language of their legal standards of conduct".[127] But this does not mean that self-regulation could or should be regarded as a viable alternative or replacement for external legal guidance in corporate governance reporting. What is required is a mechanism for setting and monitoring minimum standards. Only external legal intervention in such reporting can set effective minimum standards. Law's duty is to set minimum standards. This will not prevent businesses from supplementing the legal standards with their own voluntary codes. Third parties including consumers[128] are likely to benefit in that situation.

Self-regulation has achieved only modest success[129] in addressing corporate abuses. Self-regulatory organisations have not fared better. Such organisations have "repeatedly lacked forcefulness and perseverance in addressing conflict issues".[130]

---

[123] Better Regulation Commission, note 55 above, at 16.

[124] J. Freedman, (2003) "Small Business Taxation: Policy Issues and the UK" in Warren, *Taxing Small Business*, Australian Tax Research Foundation Conference Series 23, 13 at 14. See also J. Freeman, (2003) "One Size Fits All- Small Business and Competitive Legal Forms" 3 *JCLS* 123.

[125] [1999] ECR 1-1459 (ECJ).

[126] J. Freedman, (2003) "Small Business Taxation: Policy Issues and the UK" in Warren, *Taxing Small Business*, Australian Tax Research Foundation Conference Series 23, 13 at 34.

[127] J. Mashaw, (1985) "The Economic Context of Corporate Social Responsibility" in K. J. Hopt and G. Teubner (eds.) *Corporate Governance and Directors' Liabilities- Legal, Economic and Sociological Analyses on Corporate Social Responsibility* (Berlin; New York: Walter de Gruyter) 55 at 58. See also D. Engel, (1979) "An Approach to Corporate Social Responsibility" 32 *Stanford Law Review* 1.

[128] R. Lowe and G. Woodroffe, (2004) *Consumer Law and Practice 6th Edn* (London: Sweet & Maxwell) 313.

[129] Clinard, note 31 above, at 159.

[130] R. C. Smith and I. Walter, (2006) *Governing the Modern Corporation. Capital Markets, Corporate Control and Economic Performance*, (New York: Oxford University Press) 272.

One other disadvantage of self-regulation is that it promotes 'free-rider' situation. In the absence of penalties or sanctions, the perceived benefits of self-regulatory systems also apply to organisations that do not participate fully or at all in the system.[131] Private enforcement without "credible oversight is of questionable value"[132]

Another possible argument in favour of self-regulation concerns the relationship between legal regulation and the culture of an industry. In most legal systems, there is a connection between culture and law. Law can express culture and vice versa.[133] Both legal regulation and culture are important determinants of corporate or sector practice. But legal regulation can result in changes in culture.[134] Culture can, on the other hand, also lead to changes in legal regulation. The efficacy of external legal regulation is enhanced where such regulation enjoys support from the culture of the particular industry or sector. Where this appearance of mutuality is absent, legal rules may be observed more in the letter than in its spirit, while advantage is taken of the slightest loophole in the legal regulation. The fact is that changing expectations of the people to be affected by legislation aids the effectiveness of legislation and observance of its tenets.[135] A commentator once observed that "[c]hanging the mindsets of those who lead opinion within the industry is also essential and must accompany (or even precede) attempts to change behaviour patterns by legislation."[136]

The effectiveness of a regulatory scheme for corporate governance reporting would be greatly ensured if it receives the support of the industry.[137] However the need for regulation and culture alignment may not provide a strong justification for recourse to self-regulation of corporate governance reporting. First, businesses are generally against or even hostile to any form of regulation, except facilitative regulation[138] and they share the belief that law "facilitates the conduct of trade".[139]

---

[131] R. Sullivan, (2006) "Legislating for Responsible Corporate Behaviour: Domestic Law Approaches to an International Issue" in S. MacLeod (ed.), *Global Governance and the Quest for Justice. Volume II: Corporate Governance*, (Oxford and Portland, Oregon, Hart Publishing) 183 at 186. See also N. Gunningham and J. Rees, (1997) "Industry Self-Regulation: An Institutional Perspective" 19(4) *Law & Policy* 363 at 393.

[132] J. O'Brien, (2006) "The Politics of Symbolism: Sarbanes-Oxley in Context" in P. U. Ali and G. N. Gregoriou, *International Corporate Governance After Sarbanes-Oxley*, (Hoboken, NJ: John Wiley & Sons Inc) 9 at 23.

[133] See generally, L. Rosen, (2006) *Law as Culture. An Invitation*, (Princeton and Oxford: Princeton University Press).

[134] McGee, note 38 above, at 158.

[135] *Ibid* at 160.

[136] *Ibid* at 158.

[137] Better Regulation Commission, note 55 above, at 36.

[138] Sealy, note 115 above, at 3-4.

[139] *Schroeder v Music Publishing Co. Ltd v Macaulay* [1974] 1 W.L.R 1308 at 1316 (Lord Diplock).

Businesses are hostile to any "code of prescriptive rules or bureaucratic supervision by some central government agency".[140] But this "business attitude" has not stopped law's intervention, from time to time, in different areas of corporate practice.

Second, situations may arise where the law deliberately does not insist on securing the support of the subjects of the new regulation; in such instances, compliance is enforced despite the reluctance of the operators in that particular field.[141] Issues such as labour standards in corporate governance reporting are of such seriousness and importance to justify a regulatory scheme imposed on businesses irrespective of their attitude. Legal intervention has occurred in several areas of business practice, sometimes even in the face of active business opposition to such legal intervention. The compensation scheme for airline passengers imposed by the European Commission on the airline industry is an example. Third, the coincidence of culture with regulation cannot necessarily stop or prevent persons or organisations that, for one reason or the other, would chose to flout the rules.

There is one difficulty common to legally mandated corporate reporting obligations. This is the problem of laxity. For example, company law generally requires information on issues such as financial statements and accounts, and details of directorship or shareholdings to be supplied or made available to interested persons, "but few people dealing with a company take advantage of [such provisions]"[142]. It may well be that corporate governance reporting (being a combination of financial and non-financial issues) would not be different. It is also possible to argue that reports would be in a state worse than pure financial statements, since 'fewer people' generally appear interested in non-financial information.

However, the possibility of limited interest in non-financial corporate governance reports is not sufficient reason to exclude their external legal regulation. Clearly, it does not matter that few members of a class of persons are willing to take advantage of provisions of legal provisions directed at their protection. How many people do exercise their voting rights? Is the abolition of voting rights the correct approach to the problem of few numbers of voters? Should the fundamental rights or minority rights clauses be scrapped since not all, or just few people are interested in taking advantage of those provisions? Law's role is to create the regulatory framework, while only "interested persons" apply the regulatory measures. Although regulations are apparently established for all, regulations are, in reality, only for 'interested persons'.

Success or otherwise of self-regulation in professions is largely irrelevant in

---

[140] Sealy, note 115 above, at 22.
[141] Better Regulation Commission, note 55 above, at 13.
[142] McGee, Williams and Scanlan, note 95 above, at 9.

corporate governance reporting. A distinction should be drawn between self-regulatory schemes in or for professions and business. Most professional self-regulatory regimes have five core functions of providing entry standards and training; rule making; monitoring and enforcement; complaints and discipline.[143] The entry standards and barriers to professions plus "ongoing disciplinary arrangements" are "designed to ensure a high level of competence and probity".[144] In most cases, the relationship between the professional service provider and the other party is regarded as a fiduciary one.[145] These qualities, which might suggest the relative success of self-regulation in professions, are largely absent in a purely business setting such as corporate governance reporting.

Conclusion

External mechanisms are the "most effective strategy" in ensuring and preserving "corporate adherence to the rules of the game" and for the resolution of the "public interest issues"[146] in corporate governance reporting. Self-regulation may be effective in private issues, but external legal mechanism is more effective and efficient where the question concerns a public "issue of responsibility within society".[147] Corporate governance reporting is definitely one of such issues.

The growing trend "toward greater privatization of [social] regulation and less...accountability" is already of "considerable concern"[148] and should not be extended to corporate governance reporting. Privatised regulatory mechanisms cannot work effectively and in a convincing manner in such reporting. Corporate governance reporting is an area where there is a marked need for distinction between the regulator and the regulated. Corporate governance reporting is certainly not a situation that the business world should be given "freedom to find its own way, to assert its own values and priorities".[149] A positive answer to the important question for regulation[150] posed by the Roman philosopher, Juvenal, thus: *Quis custodiet ipsos custodies* (Who will guard the guardians themselves) cannot be found in self-regulation for corporate governance reporting.

---

[143] D. Clementi, (2004) *Report of the Review of the Regulatory Framework for Legal Services in England and Wales,* ("Clementi Report"), available at: http://www.legal-services-review.org.uk/content/report/ (last visited on 21-11-2007).

[144] McGee, note 38 above, at 154.

[145] *Ibid.* at 154-155 discusses the nature of the relationship in the legal profession.

[146] D. Krause, (1985) "Corporate Social Responsibility: Interests and Goals" in K. J. Hopt and G. Teubner (eds.) *Corporate Governance and Directors' Liabilities- Legal, Economic and Sociological Analyses on Corporate Social Responsibility* (Berlin; New York: Walter de Gruyter) 95 at 117.

[147] Lord Wedderburn of Charlton, (1985) "The Legal Development of Corporate Responsibility-For Whom Will the Mangers be Trustees?" in K. J. Hopt and G. Teubner (eds.) *Corporate Governance and Directors' Liabilities- Legal, Economic and Sociological Analyses on Corporate Social Responsibility* (Berlin; New York: Walter de Gruyter) 1 at 44.

[148] Lipschutz and Fogel, note 40 above, at 121.

[149] Sealy, note 115 above, at 68.

[150] O'Brien, note 132 above, at 20.

Chapter 3

Government Policies For Business Behaviour Under Globalisation: A Micro Analytical Perspective

Iti Bose

Summary

Economic globalisation   sometimes called corporate globalisation or just neoliberalism has made great strides over the past 20 years, driven by international trade agreements (free trade) and the removal of regulatory and other controls on corporate activity. The trend toward globalisation has intensified the debate about the proper role of business and government in global "corporate social responsibility" (CSR), which involves business efforts to address the social and environmental concerns associated with business operations. The growth in global trade and the dramatic increase in foreign direct investment in developing countries raise questions regarding CSR-related issues such as labor, environment, and human rights.

Globalisation is the process by which all peoples and communities come to experience an increasingly common economic, social and cultural environment. By definition, the process affects everybody throughout the world. It is a system designed and created for one overall purpose: to give primacy always and everywhere to corporate values above all other values. In the process, it has engineered a power shift of awesome proportions- away from national, regional and local governments and communities to transnational corporations, bankers, and the global bureaucracies they have created to administer and enforce their worldwide corporate agenda.

CSR is a concept whereby companies integrate social and environmental concerns in their business operations and in their interaction with their stakeholders on a voluntary basis. There is today a growing perception among enterprises that sustainable business success and shareholder value cannot be achieved solely through maximising short-term profits, but instead through market-oriented yet responsible behaviour. Companies are aware that they can contribute to sustainable development by managing their operations in such a way as to enhance economic growth and increase competitiveness whilst ensuring environmental protection and promoting social responsibility, including consumer interests. In this context, an increasing number of firms have embraced a culture of CSR.

The OECD Guidelines for Multinational Enterprises are one of the world's foremost corporate responsibility instruments and are becoming an important international benchmark for corporate responsibility. They contain voluntary principles and standards for responsible business conduct in such areas as human rights, disclosure of information, anti-corruption, taxation, labour relations, environment, and consumer protection. They aim to promote the positive contributions multinational enterprises can make to economic, environmental and social progress.

The adhering countries are the source of most of the world's foreign direct investment and are home to most major multinational enterprises. Although many business codes of conduct are now publicly available, the Guidelines are the only multilaterally endorsed and comprehensive code that governments are committed to promoting.

Introduction

Business is facing challenging times world-wide. Increased competition and commercial pressure are combining with rising regulatory standards and consumer demand to create a whole new playing field for business. Traditional expectations of business are also changing. It is no longer enough to simply employ people, make a profit and pay taxes. Companies are now expected to act responsibly, be accountable and benefit society as a whole. This is the new agenda of corporate social and environmental responsibility (CSER) or corporate citizenship. From a trickle, it has become a wave sweeping boardrooms across the world. Astute business leaders have been quick to embrace this new ethos spotting its potential for .triple bottom line. benefits: profit for the economic bottom line, the social bottom line and the environmental bottom line.

There is presently an increasing interaction of national economic systems all over the world through the growth in international trade, investment and capital flows. This interaction is seen by many as a worldwide drive toward globalisation and a globalised economic system. Furthermore with the tremendous development in modern communications and information technologies, knowledge and culture can be shared around the world simultaneously. Globalisation is a new reality, an economic, political and socio-cultural phenomenon which has an increasing impact on the way enterprises function whether at the local or global level.

People around the globe are more connected to each other than ever before. Information and money flow more quickly than ever. Goods and services produced in one part of the world are increasingly available in all parts of the world. International travel is more frequent. International communication is commonplace. This phenomenon has been titled "globalisation." Globalisation is a process of interaction and integration among the people, companies, and governments of different nations, a process driven by international trade and investment and aided by information technology. This process has effects on the environment, on culture, on political systems, on economic development and prosperity, and on human physical well-being in societies around the world.

This current wave of globalisation has been driven by policies that have opened economies domestically and internationally. In the years since the Second World War, and especially during the past two decades, many governments have adopted free-market economic systems, vastly increasing their own productive potential and creating myriad new opportunities for international trade and investment. Governments also have negotiated dramatic reductions in barriers to commerce and have established international agreements to promote trade in goods, services, and investment. Taking advantage of new opportunities in foreign markets, corporations have built foreign factories and established production and marketing arrangements with foreign partners. A defining feature of globalisation, therefore, is an international industrial and financial business structure.

Business ethics and corporate social responsibility

Corporate social responsibility or CSR is a business term means different things to different people both inside and outside of corporations. Firstly. corporate social responsibility is the humane duty of companies to improve or regulate labor practices shutting down sweatshops in developing countries and the industrial centers of Group 8 nations, feeding the hungry, volunteering in schools, building homes for the homeless, fending for migrant farmers, creating goodwill in the community. Secondly, corporate social responsibility is closely linked to sustainable development and business decisions based on ethical considerations and environmental consequences.

The World Business Council for Sustainable Development[1] says, "Corporate Social responsibility is the continuing commitment by business to behave ethically and contribute to economic development while improving the quality of life of the workforce and their families as well as of the local community and society at large." CSR is all about mastering a communications challenge -- to define what the company is doing, why it is doing it, and to maximize the goodwill that results. Corporate social responsibility will remain an important differentiator in business today.

---

[1] The World Business Council for Sustainable Development (WBCSD) is a CEO-led, global association of some 200 companies dealing exclusively with business and sustainable development.

The term is often used interchangeably for other terms such as Corporate Citizenship and is also linked to the concept of Triple Bottom Line Reporting (TBL), which is used as a framework for measuring an organisation's performance against economic, social and environmental parameters. The rationale for CSR has been articulated in a number of ways. In essence it is about building sustainable businesses, which need healthy economies, markets and communities. The key drivers for CSR are:[2]

- Enlightened self-interest - creating a synergy of ethics, a cohesive society and a sustainable global economy where markets, labour and communities are able to function well together.
- Social investment - contributing to physical infrastructure and social capital is increasingly seen as a necessary part of doing business.
- Transparency and trust - business has low ratings of trust in public perception.
- There is increasing expectation that companies will be more open, more accountable and be prepared to report publicly on their performance in social and environmental arenas.
- Increased public expectations of business globally companies are expected to do more than merely provide jobs and contribute to the economy through taxes and employment.

As recently as a decade ago, many companies viewed business ethics only in terms of administrative compliance with legal standards and adherence to internal rules and regulations. Today the situation is different. Attention to business ethics is on the rise across the world and many companies realize that in order to succeed, they must earn the respect and confidence of their customers. Like never before, corporations are being asked, encouraged and prodded to improve their business practices to emphasize legal and ethical behavior. Companies, professional firms and individuals alike are being held increasingly accountable for their actions, as demand grows for higher standards of corporate social responsibility.

Social responsibility and business ethics are often regarding as the same concepts. However, the social responsibility movement is but one aspect of the overall discipline of business ethics. The social responsibility movement arose particularly during the 1960s with increased public consciousness about the role of business in helping to cultivate and maintain highly ethical practices in society and particularly in the natural environment.

---

[2] Source: Positive Outcomes website http://www.positiveoutcomes.com.au

Fig 1. Business Ethics and Corporate Social Responsibility

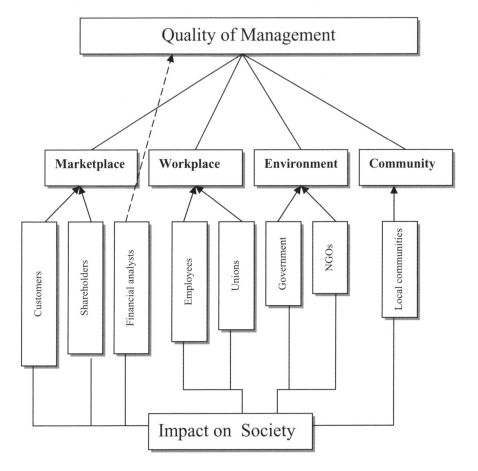

Role of Government for Business Policy

Governments create the rules and frameworks in which businesses are able to compete against each other. From time to time the government will change these rules and frameworks forcing businesses to change the way they operate. Business is thus keenly affected by government policy. Key areas of government policy that affect business are:

Economic policy

A key area of government economic policy is the role that the government gives to the state in the economy. Between 1945 and 1979 the government increasingly interfered in the economy by creating state run industries which usually took the form of public corporations. However, from 1979 onwards we saw an era of privatisation in which industries were sold off to private shareholders to create a more competitive business environment.

Taxation policy affects business costs. For example, a rise in corporation tax (on business profits) has the same effect as an increase in costs. Businesses can pass some of this tax on to consumers in higher prices, but it will also affect the bottom line. Other business taxes are environmental taxes (e.g. landfill tax), and VAT (value added tax). VAT is actually passed down the line to the final consumer but the administration of the VAT system is a cost for business.

Another area of economic policy relates to interest rates. In this country the level of interest rates is determined by a government appointed group - the Monetary Policy Committee which meets every month. A rise in interest rates raises the costs to business of borrowing money, and also causes consumers to reduce expenditure (leading to a fall in business sales).

Government spending policy also affects business. For example, if the government spends more on schools, this will increase the income of businesses that supply schools with books, equipment etc. Government also provides subsidies for some business activity - e.g. an employment subsidy to take on the long-term unemployed.

Legal changes

The government of the day regularly changes laws in line with its political policies. As a result businesses are continually having to respond to changes in the legal framework.

Examples of legal changes include:

- The creation of a National Minimum Wage which has recently been extended to under-18's.
- The requirement for businesses to cater for disabled people, by building ramps into offices, shops etc.
- Providing increasingly tighter protection for consumers to protect them against unscrupulous business practice.

Today British business is increasingly affected by European Union (EU) regulations and directives as well as national laws and requirements.

The OECD Guidelines for Multinational Enterprises

Over the past two years, OECD has conducted a major review of its *Guidelines for Multinational Enterprises* to ensure their continued relevance and effectiveness in the rapidly changing global economy.

The theme of the OECD Ministerial level meeting that approved the revised Guidelines was "Shaping Globalisation". The integration of national economies into one global economy is accelerating and intensifying, driven by new technologies and new opportunities. These new opportunities are not only to reap profit, but also to stimulate development and improved social conditions around the world. The revised Guidelines will be an important instrument for shaping globalisation. They provide a government-backed standard of good corporate conduct that will help to level the playing field between competitors in the international market place. They will also be a standard that corporations themselves can use to demonstrate that they are indeed important agents of positive change throughout the developing as well as the developed world.

The *Guidelines* are recommendations on responsible business conduct addressed by governments to multinational enterprises operating in or from the 33 adhering countries. While many businesses have developed their own codes of conduct in recent years, the OECD *Guidelines* are the only multilaterally endorsed and comprehensive code that governments are committed to promoting. The *Guidelines* express the shared values of the governments of countries that are the source of most of the world's direct investment flows and home to most multinational enterprises. They apply to business operations world-wide.

This initiative is very timely. It is widely recognised that foreign investment is important for economic growth and that multinational enterprises contribute to economic, social and environmental progress. At the same time, public concerns remain about the impact of their activities on home and host countries. The new *Guidelines* represent an important step in responding to some of these concerns while improving the climate for international investment. The basic premise of the *Guidelines* is that principles agreed internationally can help prevent conflict and to build an atmosphere of confidence between multinational enterprises and the societies in which they operate. The *Guidelines* are not a substitute for, nor do they override, applicable law. They represent standards of behaviour supplemental to applicable law and, as such, do not create conflicting requirements.

The new text of the *Guidelines* contains far-reaching changes that reinforce the economic, social and environmental elements of the sustainable development agenda. Recommendations have been added on the elimination of child labour and forced labour, so they now cover all internationally recognised core labour standards. A recommendation on human rights has been introduced, and new chapters on combating corruption and consumer protection have been added. The environment section now encourages multinational enterprises to raise their environmental performance through improved internal environmental management and better contingency planning for environmental impacts. The chapter on disclosure and transparency has been updated to reflect the *OECD Principles on Corporate Governance* and to encourage social and environmental accountability.

The OECD Committee on International Investment and Multinational Enterprises (CIME) remains the responsible body for clarifying the meaning of the Guidelines and overseeing their effectiveness.

Fig 2. Implementation of guidelines

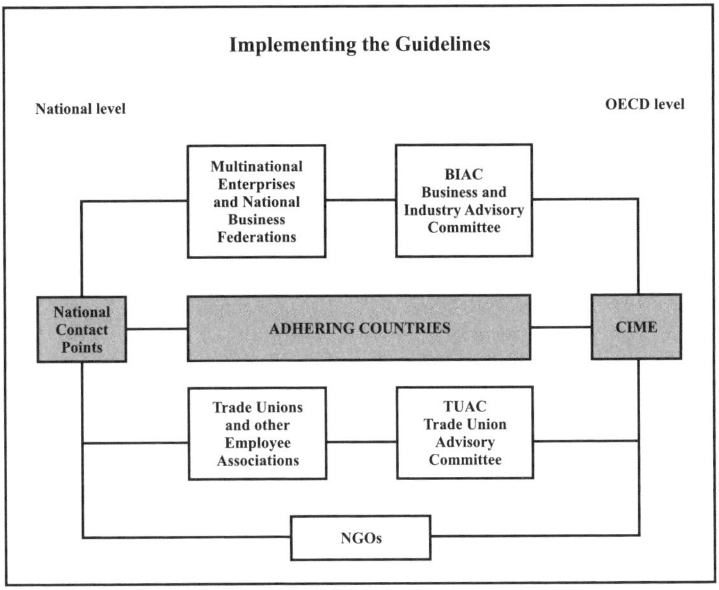

Implementing the Guidelines

National level   OECD level

Multinational Enterprises and National Business Federations — BIAC Business and Industry Advisory Committee

National Contact Points — ADHERING COUNTRIES — CIME

Trade Unions and other Employee Associations — TUAC Trade Union Advisory Committee

NGOs

Source: The OECD Guidelines for Multinational Enterprises

Corporate Citizenship and the Role of Government

Corporate citizenship or corporate social responsibility (CSR) means understanding and managing a company's influence on society and all its stakeholders. Good corporate citizenship integrates social, ethical, environmental, economic and philanthropic values in the core decision-making processes of a business. Corporate citizenship has supporters and detractors from across the political and ideological spectrum, business, non-government organisations (NGOs) and the general public.

The focus of the corporate citizenship debate over the last few years has been on the business case on why being good is good for business. More recently, the focus has shifted to the relationship between public policy and corporate citizenship and the role, if any, for government. Recent trends and evidence provides good grounds for believing that there is a role for government (public policy) in the area of corporate citizenship, but that role is not necessarily a regulatory one. While corporate citizenship has traditionally been regarded as an activity that companies engage in voluntarily, the growth and influence of the 'corporate citizenship movement' has led to increasing calls for governments in several countries to regulate the social behaviour of companies. Similar to the need for companies to understand the business case for corporate citizenship, governments should understand the public policy case for corporate citizenship.

> "The important thing for business and society at large to understand is the limit to voluntary action, which is the point where government needs to intervene. If we are to live within the earth's capacity and share its resources equitably, economies must be transformed. That cannot be done by business alone"[3]

When global justice activists took to the streets in the late 1990s to demand reforms such as higher wages and better working conditions for laborers around the world, corporate strategists saw the writing on the wall: Adopt voluntary codes of conduct or face increased government regulation. They opted for self-regulation.

Asia Pacific Perspective

Corporate social responsibility is represented by the contributions undertaken by companies to society through its core business activities, its social investment and philanthropy programmes and its engagement in public policy. In recent years CSR has become a fundamental business practice and has gained much attention from chief executives, chairmen, boards of directors and executive management teams of larger international companies. They understand that a strong CSR program is an essential element in achieving good business practices and effective leadership. Companies have determined that their impact on the economic, social and environmental landscape directly affects their relationships with stakeholders, in particular investors, employees, customers, business partners, governments and communities.

---

[3] Cowe R and Porritt J (2002), Government's Business   Enabling Corporate Sustainability, Forum for the Future, p3.

The Asia Pacific context is distinct. On the one hand, there are long-standing traditions of respect for family and social networks, and high value placed on relationships, social stability and education. Diverse religions and cultures also bring distinct attitudes towards community social behaviour and engagement as well as support and philanthropic contributions. Governments in the region also play distinct roles often stronger in terms of influence on economic and social priorities, yet not as advanced in terms of social safety nets. This has resulted in the drivers for corporate citizenship being very different from those in other regions.

Many of the large corporations in Asia Pacific are private, and many do not have the same public pressures on corporate behaviour that public companies in Europe and North America have for progress on corporate social responsibility, although this is changing. Yet many of the larger companies in Asia Pacific have strong localized philanthropic programmes. Also, regional companies that are engaged in supply chains of major global corporations and local affiliates of global corporations from Europe and America have significant pressures and a strong business case to develop corporate citizenship policies and practices within the region, not least on the environment, human rights and labour standards.

India- a case study

CSR is not a new concept in India. It has been well established in India by the organizations having strong values for families. Historically also it CSR has been a strong influence on business, government and society (Sundar 2000, Srivastava and Venkateshwaran 2000). The corporate sector in India very often blames the government for poor governance and lack of farsightedness. The question that comes every time into mind is, do the corporate sector performs its duty to contribute to the overall growth of the country? Does it have right to blame the government for poor governance? Does it contribute to nation building?

In India, most of the corporate do not have a clear policy on social responsibility. While developed countries like England have separate ministries to look after the issue of corporate social responsibility, in India, the government does not have a clear policy on the issue. Out of very few companies who contribute to the social development, the basic intention was not to ensure the good of the nation, rather a business policy to stay away from the tax net. The corporate and the government should try to build up a relationship between the business and the society. The concept of corporate social responsibility (CSR) has so far failed to take deep root in India because the nomenclature is not properly defined. The CSR is in a nascent stage. Much needs to be done to bring changes in attitude towards CSR and bring awareness among the corporate about their social responsibilities. The corporate should be made aware about the changing nature of business due to globalisation, transformation of market environment and deepening of competition. The market economy has paved the way for enterprise-led development and a new cultural perspective is taking place in Indian business environment that has a strong bearing on social responsibilities.

Social responsibility encompasses the sectors like health, education, employment, income and quality of life. It should be binding on the corporate sector to work on the above aspects, which are thought to be primary social indicators. They have enough money to serve the nation on the above segments of the society. They should not forget that if general health of the mass were good, they would have better buying capacity.

In 1970, Milton Friedman of New York Times rightly wrote: "the social responsibility of business is to increase profits." This view is often held and propounded by those who do not see much merit in companies being engaged in issues of Social Responsibility other than the making of profit. However, increasingly, the profit case, evident indicators that are tangible and the altruistic/ philanthropic/ ethical case, evident in the intangibles are getting blurred. In this context the purpose is to highlight the need for a paradigm shift in the importance of greater investment in intangibles to enhance corporate value.

Significance of CSR for India

The ideal corporate citizenship has ethical and philosophical dimension, particularly in India here wide gap exists between people in terms of income and living standards as well as social status. A latest survey by the Tata Energy Research Institute (TERI) called 'Altered Images: the 2001 State of Corporate Responsibility in India Poll' Traces Back The History Of CSR In India and suggests that there are four models of CSR.

Ethical model: The origin of the first ethical model of corporate responsibility lie in the pioneering efforts of 19 th century corporate philanthropists such as the Cadbury brothers in England and the Tata family in India. The pressure on Indian industrialists to demonstrate their commitment to social development increased during the independence movement, when Mahatma Gandhi developed the notion of 'trusteeship', whereby the owners of property would voluntarily manage their wealth on behalf of the people.

Gandhi's influence prompted various Indian companies to play active roles in nation building and promoting socio-economic development during the 20th century. The history of Indian corporate philanthropy has encompassed cash or kind donations, community investment in trusts and provision of essential services such as schools, libraries, hospitals, etc. Many firms, particularly family-run businesses', continue to support such philanthropic initiatives.

Statist model: A second model of CSR emerged in India after independence in 1947, when India adopted the socialist and mixed economy framework, with a large public sector and state-owned companies. The boundaries between the state and society were clearly defined for the state enterprises. Elements of corporate responsibility, especially those relating to community and worker relationships, were enshrined in labour laws and management principles. This state sponsored corporate philosophy still operates in the numerous public sector companies that have survived the wave of privatization of the early 1990s.

Liberal Model: Indeed, the worldwide trend towards privatization and deregulation can be said to be underpinned by a third model of corporate responsibility that companies are solely responsible to their owners. This approach was encapsulated by the American economist Milton Friedman, who in 1958 challenged the very notion of corporate responsibility for anything other than the economic bottom line.
Many in the corporate world and elsewhere would agree with this concept, arguing that it is sufficient for business to obey the law and generate wealth, which through taxation and private charitable choices can be directed to social ends.

Stakeholder Model: The rise of globalisation has brought with it a growing consensus that with increasing economic rights, business also has a growing range of social obligations. Citizen campaigns against irresponsible corporate behaviour along with consumer action and increasing shareholder pressure have given rise to the stakeholder model of corporate responsibility. This view is often associated with R. Edward Freeman, whose seminal analysis of the stakeholder approach to strategic management in 1984 brought stake holding into the mainstream of management literature (Freeman, 1984). According to Freeman, 'a stakeholder in an organisation is any group or individual who can affect or is affected by the achievement of the organisation's objectives.'

Perception and practices of CSR in India

A survey was conducted by ORG-MARG for TERI-Europe in several cities of India in 2001. The basic purpose of the survey was to capture perceptions and expectations (related to corporate responsibility) of the following three sets of stakeholders such as general public, workers (skilled, semiskilled and un-skilled) and corporate executives (head of corporate relation, labour relations, welfare dept. and manufacturing dept. in MNCs, large and medium sized Indian companies). The poll gathered that people believe that companies should be actively engaged in social matters. A majority of the general public feels that companies should be held fully responsible for roles over which they have direct control. These include providing good products
and cheaper prices, ensuring that operations are environment friendly, treating employees fairly without any discrimination based on gender, race or religion and applying labour standards globally. More than 60% of the general public felt that the companies should also be held responsible for bridging the gap between the rich and the poor, reducing human rights abuses, solving social problems and increasing economic stability.

CSR as business success: CSR is considered to be an important aspect of business success through efficient resource management, environment protection, employment, eco-friendly atmosphere, etc.

Recognising CSR

All that the government can do is, first, to set a good example in their own public sector units, and secondly, to create a mechanism for awarding some sort of formal recognition to good work done in this area like the export awards or environmental management awards being given at present.

The government or the apex organisations of industry could create a CSR Accreditation Council which would assess the work done by the applicant companies and award a star rating to each as is being done by the National Academic Accreditation Council to Universities.

Income-tax rebate used to be offered to a company undertaking rural development schemes but its working proved unsatisfactory. Moreover, any tax rebate scheme would involve a distinct possibility of abuse and too much verification and might well make CSR itself too cumbersome.

CSR at level C should first become visible enough for many companies to be attracted to and inspired by it.

To facilitate this, the apex organisations of business may set up CSR Exchanges in the various regions.

In these exchanges, the corporates would register their preferred areas of operation and their core capabilities and the citizen groups would register their priority felt needs so that the two could be matched and concrete, successful CSR projects could materialise quickly.

CSR for consumers

Is there any way customers and investors can be made to encourage CSR? In some Western countries, there are agencies that guide investors towards 'ethical investment,' i.e., in companies practising good CSR. There are also consumer groups organising campaigns against companies whose practices violate CSR. Eco-labeling of products could be widened in scope to include total CSR.

Such developments are still to take roots in India where price and product brand image still count more than the company's social image. Innovative, intense consumer and investor education needs to be taken up seriously if CSR is to become second nature to companies instead of being considered an external ingredient added reluctantly to normal business management

While financial incentives for practicing motivational reinforcement from the government, the customers and the investors is necessary to reinforce companies' CSR behaviour.

Tata Group

Innovating while protecting the environment is one of the commitments the Tata Group, one of India's biggest business conglomerates of which Tata Steel is a subsidiary, has made towards what it calls "nation-building", which it sees as part of its responsibility towards wider society. The group, which has 93 companies in seven sectors including chemicals, energy, consumer products and technology, is one of India's oldest businesses and has a well-established tradition of giving back to society.

The Tata Group does this through trusts, such as the Tata Institute for Fundamental Research, the Tata Institute for Social Sciences and the Tata Memorial Hospital. These philanthropic trusts, endowed by the Tata family, are 65.9% shareholders in Tata Sons, the holding company for the group.

With a philanthropic culture that dates back to the mid-19th century, the Tata Group has long been involved in community initiatives across India, and has tried to adhere to consistent principles and values across all its operations.

In 1998, the group decided to formalise these value systems and the Tata Code of Conduct was formed. The code is composed of 25 clauses of expected corporate and employee behaviour. These include "corporate citizenship", which demands an active involvement in communities with an aim to making them self-reliant; "political non-alignment", which prohibits companies either directly or indirectly supporting or funding any political party, candidate or campaign; "ethical conduct", which imposes a broad duty on directors, management and employees; and "conflicts of interest", which prevents management from engaging in any transaction that can personally benefit themselves or their families.

Implementation of the Tata code of conduct at company level is ensured by the Ethics Office, headed by an ethics counsellor.

Going local: Among the many annual events and activities the Ethics Office organises is "ethics month" at Tata Steel, designed to generate "awareness, sensitisation and reinforcement" of the behaviour expected of employees and suppliers. Training and induction programmes are held for new employees and they are expected to sign an allegiance to the Tata code of conduct when accepting a job. Suppliers, too, are expected to sign a memorandum of understanding, violation of which could result in blacklisting.

The ethics counsellor, who is independent of any department within the company, is the first port of call for employees who wish to blow the whistle on violations of the code.

But if they wish to report to a higher authority, they can seek the attention of the company's managing director or chief executive, who also carries the title of chief ethics officer at Tata companies. The company is currently deliberating on how it can factor in ethical behaviour in the performance management system of executives and develop a toolkit to assess prospective employees on their value-orientation at the time of recruitment.

Corporate governance: Corporate responsibility experts in India believe the governance structure at Tata group to be extremely good, owing much to the philanthropic nature of the companies' ownership and high-level disclosure about group activities.

The stake the trusts own in the holding company demonstrates the group's commitment to uplift society not through what it calls "patchwork philanthropy" but by supporting individuals, causes and institutions that have the potential to improve the overall quality of life in India.

The trusts symbolise one of the Tata group's core beliefs: "What comes from the people goes back to the people many times over."[4] Last year, the Tata trusts won the corporate citizen of the year award at the Economic Times Awards for Corporate Excellence.

Conclusion

The business of the 21-st century will have no choice but to implement CSR. The sooner corporate houses realize this and aggressively pursue this process, the better off they will be. The laws need to be formulated to help in reinforcing CSR practices.

Indian CSR has traditionally been a matter of classical paternalistic philanthropy, financially supporting schools, hospitals and culture institutions. However, far from being an add-on motivated by altruism and personal glory, the philanthropic drive has been driven by business necessity. With minimal state welfare and infrastructure provision in many areas, companies had to ensure that their workforce had adequate housing, healthcare and education and simultaneously the country grows at a fast pace.

The CSR should not be merely a statement of intent. It should be made compulsory for the corporate operating in India. This will definitely help in upholding human rights. In this context, the following measures may be made mandatory to ensure participation of the corporate in social development:

- Incorporation of a section on social actions in annual reports of companies
- Appointment of an independent social accounting committee to measure, monitor, evaluate and report impact of CSR in annual reports
- Separate department to look after the CSR
- Periodic training programmes and awareness camps to train personnel on CSR
- Linkage between CSR and financial success should be established
- A certain percentage of profit should be earmarked for social development that should reflect in the annual balance sheets of companies.

---

[4] Philosophy of J.N.Tata , Founder of Tata House

According to Milton Friedman, the only social responsibility of business is to comply with the law of the land and stay profitable.

Any other non-economic or social activities are the responsibility of the State using the taxes collected from profitable businesses. Peter F. Drucker considers profitability the first and the basic social responsibility of business as no other responsibility, social or otherwise, can be fulfilled by any losing business.

References

Amitabh Kundu (2005); Infrastructure financing and emerging pattern of urbanization: a perspective; Planning Commission report.

Ashok Leyland Report on Corporate Social responsibility 2005-06.

Balasubramaniam N K , Kimber D & Siemensma F (2005); Emerging Opportunities of Tradition Reinforced?; Journal of Corporate Citizenship, CC 17

Bhattacharya C B & Sen S (2004); When, Why and How Consumers respond to Corporate Social Initiatives; California Management Review, vol. 47

Davis, K. (1983). 'An expanded view of the social responsibility of business'. In Beauchamp, T. L. and Bowie, N. E. (Eds), Ethical Theory and Business, Englewood Cliffs, NJ: Prentice-Hall, 947

Dawar, N. & Chattopadhyay, A. (2000); Rethinking Marketing Programs for Emerging Markets; Davidson Institute Working Paper Series

Deardorff A V (2003); What Might Globalisation's Critics Believe?; The World Economy, 26(5), 639-658

Economic Outlook for 2006-07, Economic Advisory Council to Prime Minister August 2006.

EU Green Paper (2001), Promoting a European Framework for Corporate Social Responsibility, Brussels, Commission of the European Communities, Retrieved on August 27, 2004 from_www.btplc.com/Societyandenvironment /Reports/GreenpaperonCSR.pdf , http://www.csmworld.org

Helpman, E, (1984); A Simple Theory of International Trade with Multinational Corporations; Journal of Political Economy, 92(3), 451-71, June

Husted B W & de Jesus Salazar J (2006); Taking Friedman Seriously: Maximizing Profits and Social Performance, Journal of Management Studies, January

K.G. Nair (2004), "Economic Reforms and Regional Disparities".

Kumar and V. Balsari (2002), "Corporate Responsibility in India: A changing Agenda?" Business Social Partnership: Beyond philanthropy Conference, IIM Calcutta, India, December 2002.

Markusen, James R. & Venables, Anthony J., 1998. "Multinational firms and the new trade theory," Journal of International Economics, Elsevier, vol. 46(2), pages 183-203, December.

Ninth Five year Plan report of Planning Commission.

Pravin Krishna, (1998); Regionalism And Multilateralism: A Political Economy Approach; The Quarterly Journal of Economics, MIT Press, vol. 113(1), 227-250, February.

Inderson P V (2005); Vision 2020; Planning Commission Report.

Robbins, N. (2000); Position Paper on Emerging Markets and Human Rights; Henderson Global Investors

Rodrik, D. (1995); Political economy of trade policy; in G. M. Grossman & K. Rogoff (ed.), Handbook of International Economics, edition 1, volume 3, chapter 28, 1457-1494

Elsevier Sunder, P. (2000); Beyond Business: From Merchant Charity to Corporate Citizenship New Delhi; Tata Mcgraw Hill; United nations report on Human development

Index 2005-06.

Warhust, A. (2001); Corporate Citizenship and Corporate Social Investment: Drivers of Tri-Sector Partnerships; *Journal of Corporate Citizenship*, spring, pp 57-73.

Wood, D. J. (1991); Corporate social performance revisited; *Academy of Management Review*, 16, 691 718. www.earthtrends.com

Chapter 4

The Impact of Insider Trading on the Stock Price Volatility in an Emerging Market Setting: Evidence from Istanbul Stock Exchange[*]

Alovsat Muslumov

Abstract

This study examines stock price volatility effects of the insiders trading in Istanbul Stock Exchange. Our results indicate that insider trading significantly affects stock price volatility during and after the trade. Sub-sample analyses show that sell positions, the trades of the traders more related with the company, larger trades, trades in the smaller stocks, and trades that follow contrarian pattern causes in the more volatility after the trade period. These results indicate that insider trading destabilizes the market.

Introduction

Insider trading is defined as trades of the individuals using publicly unavailable privileged information set. The debate about the merits of insider trading centers around the economic efficiency and morality dimensions. Insider trading is strictly conceived morally wrong and often persecuted as legally forbidden, since the usage of privileged information to gain profits causes in the loss of investors' confidence to markets and leads to the serious asymmetric information problem[1]. But in the other hand, it is argued that economic environment functions as a moderating variable in the insider trading and economic efficiency relationship, and under certain economic conditions insider trading may promote welfare as well (Leland 1992). The debate

---

[*] I thank Murat Dogu for providing me insiders trading data and helpful comments.
[1] See Cinar (1999) for the discussion of insider trading from the ethical viewpoint.

have been solved against insider trading and though, insider trading was not illegal even in most developed until the beginning of the 1990s, today all of developed countries and almost 80 percent of emerging countries have their own insider trading laws (Bhattacharya and Daouk 2002) which is the proof of the shared consensus against insider trading among policy-makers and market regulators. The extensive cross-sectional analysis of the effects of insider trading enforcements on the cost of equity report that better insider trading regulations reduce cost of equity (Bhattacharya and Daouk 2002).

Most empirical work on the insider trading are concentrated on the abnormal profitability of the insider trading and report that insider traders outperform the market in developed markets such as USA (Jaffe 1974, Finnerty 1976, Seyhun 1986, Lin and Howe 1990), UK (Friedrich *et al.* 2002, Fidrmuc *et al.* 2006), Germany (Betzer and Theissen 2007), Italy (Barucchi *et al.* 2006), Spain (Del Brio *et al.* 2002), Hong-Kong (Cheuka *et al.* 2006). These results indicate that even in the markets with strong regulatory environments insider trading signals information content to the market. For the emerging markets, there is hardly any evidence.

Our study examines the effects of insider trading on the stock price volatility in an emerging market setting focusing on the insider trading activities in Istanbul Stock Exchange, the main securities stock exchange of Turkey. The intensity of the insider trading in the emerging markets makes these markets interesting laboratories for the insider trading studies. It was argued that the intensity of the insider trading mitigates the effects of corporate news announcements on stock prices. For example, Bhattacharya *et al.* (2000) reports that Mexican main stock market (Bolsa Mexicana de Valores) appears to be insensitive to the corporate news announcements. This insensitiveness was caused by insider trading, which results in the price adjustment in the market before the announcement is announced.

The effects of the insider trading on the stock price volatility is a relatively less studied area of the insider trading field. The relationship between insider trading and stock price volatility is not well established in the economic theory. On the one hand, it is claimed that insider trading brings precious information to the market and market rapidly adjusts the prices (Leland 1992). Therefore, insider trading would be associated with few jumps which may increase stock price volatility for a short term, while stabilizing stock prices in the long term. On the other hand, the majority of the theoretical studies argue that insider trading increase stock price volatility for a long term as well through several channels. For example, insiders gain may undermine other investors confidence to the market, therefore, other investors expecting insiders move may sell their shares (Ausubel 1998) which would impair market liquidity (Leland 1992) and increase the volatility of stock prices. Moreover, insider trading may lead to the market manipulation. Strong market power of corporate insiders and large traders allows them to manipulate prices and corner the market which leads to the higher market volatility and adverse effects on the other asset prices (Allen *et al.* 2006). The ability of insiders to manipulate the timing and content of the information release to the market may also increase the volatility of stock prices (Benabou and Laroque 1992). Odean (1998) theoretically links volatility to the overconfidence of the insider traders and argues that if the insiders are overconfident, then volatility in the market increases. Cross-sectional empirical evidence suggests that more frequent insider trading prevalent in stock markets are associated with more volatile stock markets (Du and Wei 2004).

The structure of the paper is as follows. Section 2 considers the data, regulatory background and research design. The empirical results are presented in Section 3 and concluding remarks are contained in Section 4.

The Regulatory Background, Data and Research Design

Istanbul Stock Exchange (ISE) started its operations in 1986 and reached to the total market capitalization of 250 billions USD by the end of January 2008 with 319 listed companies. The capital market in Turkey is regulated by the Capital Market Board. Insider trading enforcements set by Capital Market Board prohibits profiting from privileged information not announced to the public and foresees strong punishments for those who violate these rules. According to the insider trading decree of Capital Market Board dated 20.07.2003, influential owners (those with shareholding of more than 5 percent either directly or indirectly), members of board, top level corporate managers have to report their trades. These reporting have to be submitted to Istanbul Stock Exchange till the end of the day (i.e. 12:00 pm midnight). The public declaration of the announcements are made through Daily Bulletins of ISE at the same day if the declaration is submitted till 18:00 evening, or next day if the declaration is submitted late. Though, the majority of the announcements are made till 18:00, there are some cases where announcements are made later. Since our study is focused on the volatility of impact of insider trading announcement, we have defined announcement date as ($t=0$) and collected information about the trades of the insiders from Daily Bulletins of ISE.

The insider trading dataset used in this study is hand-collected from the corporate news announcements published in the Daily Bulletins of ISE and covers February 02, 2005 June 29, 2007 period. Our dataset include the information about the date of the insider transaction, the identity of the insider, the degree of relationship with the company, number of shares traded and average price of the trading. The total number of the insiders' trades is 7224, whose descriptive statistics are reported in Table 1.

We should emphasize on the source of the data and possible associated problems in the interpretation of the empirical results. In our study, we are using self-reported legal trading of insiders and mutual funds since it is only publicly available data about insider trades. Using the self-reported insider trades dataset leads to the self-selection bias, since corporate managers are not expected to report their illegal trades. Even if corporate managers are too honest, they are not in the condition to report all trades of the other insiders. This self-selection bias contaminates the information content of the available insider trading data which is widely cited problem in the empirical literature (Du and Wei 2004).

Table 1: Descriptive Statistics

Number of Securities	211
Total number of insiders' trades	7,224
Total trading volume (million $)	10,927
$ Purchase / $ total (dollar value)	67.27 %
Average Dollar volume per trading ($)	1,513,073
Median Dollar volume per trading ($)	58,831
Average-daily return volatility (basis points)	9.65
(calculated over research window: Feb-02-2005 to June-29-2007)	

In our study, we construct the pre-announcement, announcement and post-announcement windows of insiders' trades with various length. We use benchmark pre-announcement (-50, -3) window which refers to the period that starts 50 days before the trade and ends 3 days before the trade. Shorter pre-announcement windows such as (-25, -3), (-15, -3) and (-5, -3) windows are also constructed and examined. Our trade announcement window covers the period starting 2 days before the trade and ending 2 days after the trade. Post-announcement windows are constructed symmetrically to those of pre-announcement window and covers (+3, +5), (+3, +15), (+3, +25) and (+3, +50) post-announcement windows defined with respect to the trade date.

The unconditional volatilities in the announcement windows are calculated following Chiyachantana *et al.* (2006). Individual stock volatilities are calculated by averaging the logarithmic differences of successive daily prices (p). For the announcement window with t days length, average daily volatility of the individual stock (σ_2) is calculated as:

$$\sigma_j^2 = \sum_{t=1}^{n} \left[\log\left(p_{j,t}\right) - \log\left(p_{j,t-1}\right) \right]^2 \bigg/ n \qquad (1)$$

Since changing stock volatilities around announcement date can be caused by the volatility in the market, we also calculate market-adjusted volatility using the following formula (m denotes market price):

$$\sigma_{mj}^2 = \sum_{t=1}^{n} \left\{ \left[\log\left(p_{j,t}\right) - \log\left(p_{j,t-1}\right) \right] - \left[\log\left(m_{j,t}\right) - \log\left(m_{j,t-1}\right) \right] \right\}^2 \bigg/ n \qquad (2)$$

Empirical Results

The results of the daily average unconditional volatilities are given in Table 2. We have employed several pre-announcement windows which started 50-day, 25-day, 15-day and 5-day before the insiders' trade and ended 3-day before the insiders' trade. Post-announcement windows are constructed symmetrically. They all start from 3-day after the insiders' trade and end 5-day, 15-day, 25-day and 50-day after the announcement. Announcement window covers the period of 2-day before and 2 days after the insiders' trade. The regular reported figures are individual daily volatilities, whereas market-adjusted volatilities are reported in parentheses.

According to the findings for all insider transactions, average daily volatilities of pre-announcement window is 9.15 basis points which is 0.5 basis points lower than the average daily volatilities of all ISE stock during the research period which is reported in Table 1. Volatility increases as announcement date approaches and rise to 9.97 basis points in (-15, -3), 10.93 basis points in (-5, -3) pre-announcement windows. These volatilities are significantly higher than the volatility of benchmark (-50, -3) pre-announcement window. Compared to pre- and post-announcement windows, average daily volatilities culminate at the announcement window with 11.75 basis points which suggest that insider trading is associated with high volatility in the trading window. Though, average stock volatilities decline sharply by 2.20 basis points immediately after announcement window, average stock market volatility remains at 10.13 basis points level after insiders' transactions in (+3, +50) post-announcement window which is significantly higher than (-50, -3) pre-announcement window average. This means that the effect of the insiders' transaction do not appear to be temporary since we observe the lasting high volatility in the longest post-announcement window we have employed.

There could be simultaneous sales and purchases of the stocks by insiders at the same day. If total number of purchased shares is higher than total number of the sold shares, this transaction is defined as buy decision. Sale decision is registered if the opposite holds. If good news is expected, to make the money insiders buy the asset. However, if bad news is expected insiders sell short at high price and wait for the price to fall. The effects of insiders' sales and buys affect volatilities of assets asymmetrically due to the leverage effect which is defined as the negative correlation between asset returns and changes in volatility (French *et al.* 1987; Glosten, Jagannathan, and Runkle 1993; Avramov *et al.* 2006). Previous researches (for example, Bekaert and Wu 2000; Wu 2001) argue that bad news foster stock sales which reduces stock value and increases financial leverage, making the stock riskier and, hence, its volatility higher. However, good news which results in the stock purchases doesn't increase asset volatility significantly.

TABLE 2: VOLATILITY AROUND INSIDER TRADING

This table reports volatility average daily around for several preannouncement (-50, -3; -25, -3; -15, -3; -5, -3), announcement (-2, +2), and postannouncement (+3, +5; +3, +15; +3, +25; +3, +50) windows defined with reference to the date of insider trading announcement. The reported statistics in the parentheses refers to the average daily stock volatilities adjusted for the market volatility, whereas the regular statistics re   fers to the average volatilities on individual stocks. Estimates of average daily volatilities are reported in terms of basis points. In addition to the all trades study, we conduct subsample analyses defined in terms of trading position, trader type, rela   tionship of the trader with the company, relationship of trader with company, percentage of share ownership of trader after trade, trade volume / total equity ratio, index coverage of stocks (ISE -30 and ISE-100), industry of the stock traded, and momentum versus contrarian trading. We compare volatilities for each time -windows with that of preannouncement (-50, -3) window and report the statistical significance levels of the difference in volatilities with asterisks next to the numbers. ***, **, and * indicate statistical significance at 1 percent, 5 percent and 10 percent levels, respectively. The last row in each partition reports the difference in volatility across groups for a given time interval.   †††, ††, and † indicate statistical significance at 1 percent, 5 percent and 10 percent levels, respectively.

	N	Preannouncement window				Announcement Window	Postannouncement window			
		(-50, -3)	(-25, -3)	(-15, -3)	(-5,-3)	(-2, +2)	(+3, +5)	(+3, +15)	(+3, +25)	(+3, +50)
Average volatility										
All Trades	7189	9.15	9.38	9.97*	10.93**	11.75***	9.55	9.27	9.45	10.13**
		(8.19)	(8.38)	(8.92)	(9.81*)	(10.94***)	(8.65)	(8.22)	(8.38)	(8.97**)
Trading Position										
Buy	4437	8.43	8.52	8.71	8.63	8.64	7.71	8.05	8.54	8.93
		(7.46)	(7.50)	(7.62)	(7.58)	(7.65)	(6.80*)	(7.10)	(7.57)	(7.94)
Sell	2752	10.30	10.77	11.99**	14.63**	16.79***	12.53	11.24	10.94	12.08***
		(9.36)	(9.81)	(11.03**)	(13.42**)	(16.26***)	(11.62)	(10.03)	(9.68)	(10.64*)
Difference (buy − sell)		-1.88†††	-2.25†††	-3.28†††	-6.00†††	-8.15†††	-4.82†††	-3.19†††	-2.40†††	-3.16†††
		(-1.90†††)	(-2.31†††)	(-3.41†††)	(-5.85†††)	(-8.61†††)	(-4.82†††)	(-2.93†††)	(-2.11†††)	(-2.71†††)

TABLE 2: VOLATILITY AROUND INSIDER TRADING (CONTINUED)

	N	Preannouncement window				Announcement Window	Postannouncement window			
		(-50, -3)	(-25, -3)	(-15, -3)	(-5, -3)	(-2, +2)	(+3, +5)	(+3, +15)	(+3, +25)	(+3, +50)
Trader Type										
Member of Board	979	14.40 (12.88)	14.18 (12.68)	14.91 (13.26)	16.73 (14.96)	15.04 (13.96)	15.80 (14.21)	15.51 (13.64)	15.74 (14.28)	20.25** (18.84***)
Top-level Manager	85	17.74 (16.57)	8.08 (7.12*)	8.90 (7.82)	9.20 (8.24**)	13.73 (12.83)	6.00* (5.80*)	6.56* (6.13*)	10.78 (10.08)	8.87 (8.06)
Shareholder	3954	8.74 (7.94)	9.37** (8.51**)	10.17*** (9.27***)	10.88*** (9.88***)	12.88*** (12.09***)	9.43* (8.62*)	9.07 (8.10)	9.19* (8.13)	9.35** (8.16)
Institutional Investor	2171	7.19 (6.21)	7.36 (6.33)	7.51 (6.48)	8.53*** (7.50*)	8.35*** (7.64***)	7.15 (6.38)	6.99 (6.13)	7.10 (6.14)	7.08 (6.06)
Difference (Member of Board – Institutional Investor)		7.21††† (6.67†††)	6.82†† (6.35†††)	7.40†† (6.78†††)	8.20†† (7.46†)	6.68††† (6.32†††)	8.65†† (7.83†)	8.52†† (7.52†††)	8.65††† (8.14†††)	13.17††† (12.79†††)
Relationship with Company										
Related	4536	10.23 (9.25)	10.41 (9.40)	11.20 (10.13)	11.92 (10.75)	12.83** (11.92**)	10.39 (9.39)	10.29 (9.14)	10.54 (9.39)	11.76** (10.49**)
Not Related	2653	7.39 (6.46)	7.72 (6.73)	7.96* (6.97*)	9.33*** (8.29***)	10.01*** (9.36**)	8.19* (7.43**)	7.63 (6.73)	7.70 (6.74)	7.51 (6.53)
Difference (related – not rel.)		2.84††† (2.79†††)	2.69††† (2.67†††)	3.24††† (3.16†††)	2.59 (2.46)	2.82†† (2.56†)	2.20 (1.96)	2.66††† (2.40†††)	2.84††† (2.64†††)	4.25††† (3.96†††)

TABLE 2: VOLATILITY AROUND INSIDER TRADING (CONTINUED)

	N	Preannouncement window				Announcement Window	Postannouncement window			
		(-50, -3)	(-25, -3)	(-15, -3)	(-5, -3)	(-2, +2)	(+3, +5)	(+3, +15)	(+3, +25)	(+3, +50)
Percentage of Share Ownership after Trade										
Share ≥ 50 %	598	9.30	9.74	10.64	11.87*	12.47**	10.07	9.03	9.33	9.25
		(8.88)	(9.32)	(10.27)	(11.60*)	(12.24**)	(10.37)	(9.05)	(9.01)	(8.50)
50 % > Share ≥ 25%	910	15.25	14.75	15.42	17.39	13.97	14.98	14.04	13.04	18.98
		(14.07)	(13.51)	(14.12)	(16.12)	(12.62)	(13.22)	(12.34)	(11.58)	(17.63)
25 % > Share ≥ 10%	1700	7.46	7.67	7.98	8.61**	9.85***	8.53**	8.23**	8.27**	8.56***
		(6.76)	(6.90)	(7.19)	(7.84**)	(9.37***)	(7.65*)	(7.17)	(7.23)	(7.44***)
10 % > Share ≥ 5%	2058	7.82	8.24	8.69**	9.40***	9.66***	8.79*	8.32*	8.82***	8.64***
		(6.82)	(7.30*)	(7.73**)	(8.37***)	(8.86***)	(7.85**)	(7.44**)	(7.82***)	(7.56***)
5 % > Share ≥ 1%	1107	9.14	9.30	9.71	11.44**	10.53**	7.96*	7.82***	7.67***	7.66***
		(7.98)	(8.06)	(8.26)	(9.61*)	(9.78***)	(7.15*)	(6.91***)	(6.77*)	(6.64*)
1 % > Share	816	8.95	9.58	10.96*	10.89*	19.71***	9.01	10.47	11.83*	10.93*
		(7.62)	(8.05)	(9.44)	(9.25*)	(18.29***)	(8.09)	(8.71)	(10.12)	(9.17)
Difference (Group 1 – Group 6)		0.34†††	0.16†††	-0.32†††	0.97†	-7.24†††	1.06	-1.43†††	-2.50†††	-1.68†††
		(1.25†††)	(1.27†††)	(0.83†††)	(2.35†)	(-6.04†††)	(2.28)	(0.35†††)	(-1.11†††)	(-0.67†††)
Trade Volume / Equity										
Large Trades (> 1%)	3849	9.11	9.63**	10.31***	11.54***	14.07***	11.32	10.77**	10.47***	10.42***
		(8.07)	(8.53*)	(9.15**)	(10.42***)	(13.03***)	(10.01)	(9.44*)	(9.10**)	(8.98**)
Small Trades (≤ 1%)	3340	9.18	9.12	9.60	10.27	9.26	7.65***	7.66***	8.36	9.82
		(8.31)	(8.22)	(8.67)	(9.16)	(8.70)	(7.18**)	(6.91***)	(7.60)	(8.97)
Difference (Large – Small)		-0.07	0.51	0.71	1.27	4.81†††	3.68††	3.11†††	2.11††	0.60
		(-0.24)	(0.32)	(0.48)	(1.26)	(4.32†††)	(2.83†)	(2.53†††)	(1.50†)	(0.01)

TABLE 2: VOLATILITY AROUND INSIDER TRADING (Continued)

	N	Preannouncement window				Announcement Window	Postannouncement window			
		(-50, -3)	(-25, -3)	(-15, -3)	(-5, -3)	(-2, +2)	(+3, +5)	(+3, +15)	(+3, +25)	(+3, +50)
Index Coverage of Stock (ISE-30)										
Covered in ISE-30	397	7.96 (5.12)	8.70 (5.79)	9.85 (6.82)	8.52 (5.23)	22.11* (19.37)	6.98 (4.39)	8.89 (6.09)	8.15 (5.24)	8.41 (5.41)
Not covered in ISE-30	6792	9.22 (8.37)	9.42 (8.53)	9.97 (9.05)	11.07* (10.08**)	11.15** (10.45***)	9.70 (8.90)	9.29 (8.34)	9.53 (8.56)	10.23** (9.18**)
Difference (Covered − Not Covered)		-1.26 (-3.24†††)	-0.72 (-2.74††)	-0.12 (-2.22)	-2.55 (-4.85)	10.97††† (8.92†††)	-2.72 (-4.51)	-0.41 (-2.25)	-1.38 (-3.32††)	-1.82 (-3.77†††)
Index Coverage of Stock (ISE-100)										
Covered in ISE-100	1470	8.61 (6.32)	8.79 (6.55)	9.53 (7.21)	10.02 (7.76)	12.78* (10.65*)	8.16 (6.25)	8.87 (6.70)	10.15 (7.86)	10.09** (7.57**)
Not covered in ISE-100	5719	9.28 (8.66)	9.53 (8.85)	10.08 (9.36)	11.16* (10.33)	11.49** (11.02***)	9.90 (9.26)	9.37 (8.60)	9.27 (8.51)	10.14* (9.33)
Difference (Covered − Not Covered)		-0.68 (-2.34†††)	-0.75 (-2.30†††)	-0.55 (-2.14†)	-1.14 (-2.58)	1.29 (-0.37)	-1.75 (-3.01)	-0.50 (-1.90†)	0.88 (-0.65)	-0.06 (-1.76††)
Industry										
Manufacturing	2430	10.22 (9.52)	10.02 (9.36)	10.40 (9.78)	11.03 (10.41)	10.75 (10.30)	9.66 (9.38)	9.83 (9.19)	10.55 (9.90)	12.76** (12.03**)
Service	685	6.92 (6.58)	6.90 (6.48)	7.12 (6.74)	9.11 (9.14)	7.36 (7.22)	6.92 (6.29)	6.23* (5.86*)	6.01** (5.60***)	6.83 (6.28)
Technology	85	9.08 (7.02)	9.46 (6.96)	8.21 (5.50)	8.35 (5.00)	9.07 (8.65)	7.63 (5.32)	7.32* (5.39**)	8.16 (6.29)	7.70 (5.65)
Financial	1220	9.86 (8.09)	10.54 (8.77)	11.65** (9.70*)	11.86*** (9.69**)	16.03*** (14.45*)	10.62 (9.09)	10.71 (9.10)	10.47 (8.70)	10.35 (8.28)
Mutual Funds	2769	8.43 (7.46)	8.94* (7.86)	9.64*** (8.49††)	11.00** (9.64†)	12.04*** (11.04***)	9.74** (8.52**)	8.99* (7.66)	8.95* (7.64)	8.57 (7.28)
Difference (buy − sell)		1.78††† (2.06†††)	1.08†† (1.51††)	0.76† (1.29)	0.03 (0.77)	-1.28†† (-0.74†)	-0.08 (0.87)	0.84† (1.53†)	1.60††† (2.26†††)	4.19††† (4.74†††)

TABLE 2: VOLATILITY AROUND INSIDER TRADING (Continued)

	N	Preannouncement window				Announcement Window	Postannouncement window			
		(-50, -3)	(-25, -3)	(-15, -3)	(-5, -3)	(-2, +2)	(+3, +5)	(+3, +15)	(+3, +25)	(+3, +50)
Momentum versus contrarian trading										
Momentum	3546	9.10	9.46	10.39*	9.70	10.68*	8.51	9.20	9.56	9.73
		(8.15)	(8.51)	(9.40*)	8.89)	(10.12**)	(7.72)	(8.17)	(8.50)	(8.56)
Contrarians	3753	9.19	9.31	9.56	12.09*	12.77***	10.53	9.34	9.35	10.52**
		(8.22)	(8.26)	(8.47)	(10.68)	(11.72***)	(9.52)	(8.27)	(8.26)	(9.37*)
Difference (momentum – contrarian)		-0.09	0.16	0.84	-2.38	-2.10	-2.02	-0.14	0.22	-0.79
		(-0.06	(0.25	(0.93	(-1.78	(-1.60	(-1.79	(-0.10	(0.24	(-0.81

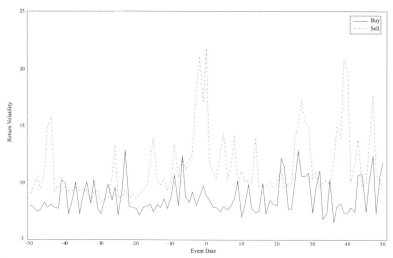

Figure 1: Average Raw Daily Volatility from 50 days before to 15 days after insider trading announcement

Our results clearly show that leverage effects exist in the case of insider trading. There are significantly higher average daily volatilities in the stock sales position in all of the employed pre-announcement, announcement, and post-announcement windows ranging from 1.88 basis points to 8.15 basis points. Differences in the volatilities between stock sales and stock purchases subsets start with 1.88 basis points in longest pre-announcement window (-50,-3) and gradually increases as announcement window approaches. The difference reaches to 6.00 basis points in (-5, -3) pre-announcement window which is the closest announcement window to the announcement date. The volatility difference between sell and buy categories reaches to its maximum level of 8.15 basis points in the (-2, +2) announcement window. Though, differences between sell and buy categories starts to fade after the occurrence of announcement, it remains still higher than pre-announcement levels which is 3.16 basis points in (+3, +50) post-announcement window compared to 1.88 basis points in (-50, -3) pre-announcement window.

Interestingly, buy position of insiders doesn't affect the volatility of stocks significantly during the announcement and post-announcement windows. Raw volatilities and market-adjusted volatilities are not statistically significant at conventional levels. However, as it is suggested in Figure 1, sell positions are strictly associated with the higher volatilities immediately before, during and after announcement dates. Average raw daily volatilities peaks to the 16.79 basis points in the (-2, +2) announcement window which is almost two times more than the those of in the buy position. The average raw daily volatility even increases to 21.82 basis points at the announcement date.

The sample is further classified into four categories according to the trader type including member of board, top-level manager, shareholder, and institutional investors. Our results indicate that the differences among average daily volatilities of the four categories are statistically significant. Over the (-50, -3) pre-announcement window, average daily volatility are highest in the top-level managers category followed by members of board, shareholders, and institutional investors categories. The average daily volatilities in shareholders and members of board categories significantly increase in the (+3, +50) post-announcement window, which suggests lasting effects of the trades on the stock price volatility. However, the decreases in the average stock price volatilities of the remaining two categories (top-level managers and institutional investors) are not statistically significant.

The members of board are active participants to the corporate activities in emerging markets which are usually characterized by weaker regulatory environments, lower property rights protection, ineffective enforcement of regulations, and lower levels of political and economic stability (Makino *et al*, 2004). Family holding companies constitute dominant form of large business organization in Turkey (Demirağ and Serter 2003). Boards of Turkish firms are usually smaller in size[2] and often include family member directors. Since the separation of the ownership and management are not fully realized, board members may also undertake managerial roles as well. Therefore, the trading activities of members of board are expected to affect heavily market volatilities. Our results indicate that the trades of members of board affect daily average volatilities for a longer period after the announcement. Post-announcement (+3, +50) window average volatility of the trades of members of the board is 20.25 basis points, which is 5.85 basis points higher than the average volatility of pre-announcement (-50, -3) window. Therefore, the trades of members of board have a lasting impact on the volatility.

Interestingly, stock price volatility decreases after the transaction of the top-level managers. Average daily volatilities of the (-50, -3) pre-announcement window decreases from 17.74 basis points to the 13.73 basis points in the (-2, +2) announcement window, though this decrease is not statistically significant. However, immediately after the announcement it decreases further to 6.00 basis points at (+3, +5) post-announcement window and 6.56 basis points at (+3, +15) post-announcement window. These values are significantly different than that of (-50, -3) pre-announcement window.

Shareholder transactions are associated with high volatilities during the announcement and post-announcement windows. While average daily volatility equals to 8.74 basis points in the (-50, -3) pre-announcement window, it increases gradually to 9.37 basis points in the (-25, -3) pre-announcement window, 10.17 basis points in the (-15, -3) pre-announcement window, and 10.88 basis points in the (-5, -3) pre-announcement window. Average daily volatilities reach to the maximum level of 12.88 basis points at the (+2, +2) announcement window, and later starts to decline gradually.

---

[2] According to the author's calculation, average board size in Turkish companies whose shares are actively traded in ISE is around 6. Unbalanced panel data of 720 observations covering 197 firms and 1999-2002 years are used in this calculation.

Though, the average daily volatility in (+3, +50) post-announcement window equals to 9.35 basis points, which is significantly higher than the average level in (-50, -3) pre-announcement window.

Several studies examine the impact of institutional trades on price movements and volatilities (Keim and Madhavan 1995, Chiyachantana *et al.* 2006). In an empirical study of trades of institutional investors in international stocks across 43 countries, Chiyachantana *et al.* (2006) finds temporary volatility increase during trade execution period. These results are interpreted as the evidence of the argument that institutional trades do not destabilize international stock markets. Our results are in the same line with Chiyachantana *et al.* (2006) for the trades of institutional trades. The raw average daily volatility of pre-announcement window (-50, -3) the trades of institutional investors equals to 7.19 basis points and remains stable in the post-announcement window which equals to 7.08 basis points in post-announcement (+3, +50) post-announcement window. There are volatility spike in during the (-2, +2) announcement window where average daily volatility reaches to 8.35 basis points.

Our third classification criterion is the relationship of the trader with the company. If the trader is the member of board, top-level manager, or the shareholder represented in the management, then the trader is defined as 'related'. Institutional investors and the shareholders not represented in the management are classified under 'unrelated' category. The results of the statistical tests show that there are significant differences between the volatility impact of the trades of 'related' and 'unrelated' categories. The trades of the 'related' insider traders associate with the significantly higher volatilities in almost all pre-announcement, announcement and post-announcement categories. There are temporary significant increases in the average daily volatility around the announcement date in 'unrelated' category, however it reverts back after announcement to the average pre-announcement levels. However, the impact of the 'related' insiders persist in longer term as well. Post-announcement average daily volatility over (+3, +50) window is 11.76 basis points for the 'related' insiders category and it is significantly 1.53 basis points higher than pre-announcement (-50, -3) window.

We next classify insiders according to the percentage of share ownership after the completion of transaction. It appears that the level of share ownership affects the average daily volatility in the pre-announcement, announcement and post-announcement windows. The average daily volatilities in the (-2, +2) announcement window reaches to their peak level in almost all of the categories and this level is significantly higher than the long-term pre-announcement levels. Interestingly, the transactions of the traders with the share ownership of more than 25 percent (which includes two categories) do not have lasting effect on the average daily volatilities. However, volatility increase in the post-announcement period after the transaction of the shareholders with share ownership between 5 and 25 percent and this increase becomes persistent over the longer term. These results show that market attaches more information content to the actions of the larger shareholders' transactions and rapidly adjusts the prices.

Trade volume is also an important factor that is expected to affect the magnitude of the average daily volatilities during and after the insiders' announcement. Barclay and Warner (1993) argue that most of the cumulative stock price changes occur through medium-sized trades and informed traders camouflage their trading by focusing on medium-sized trades. They call this joint-hypothesis as stealth-trading hypothesis. To study the effects of the trading volume on the stock price volatilities, we scale trade volume to the total equity of the stock. If trade volume standardized by equity is less than 1 percent, it is classified under large trades category, otherwise as small trades category.

Research findings suggest that trading volume significantly affects the magnitude of stock price volatilities. Though, the average daily volatility in (-50, -3) pre-announcement window was almost equal in large and small trades categories, the difference between them reached to 4.81 basis points in announcement window in favor of large trades category and gradually decreased to 0.60 basis points in (+3, +50) post-announcement window. The differences in volatilities between large and small groups are statistically significant in all pre-announcement windows except (-50, -3) window, announcement window, and all post-announcement windows except (+3, +5) window. The volatility effect of the large trades spikes in the (-2, +2) announcement window and volatility increase remains persistent in the post-announcement period. However, no significant changes are observed in the small trades category in the (-2, +2) announcement window and (+3, +50) post-announcement window.

To see whether the volatility effect of insider trading varies with the liquidity of securities, we classify stocks into two categories based on their coverage in ISE-30 and ISE-100 indexes separately. ISE-30 is composite index that covers largest 30 stocks in Istanbul Stock Exchange, whereas ISE-100 compromises 100 largest stocks. Our results suggest that the differences in the volatility effects of the insiders' trades are statistically significant between stocks covered and uncovered stocks in ISE-30 in pre-announcement, announcement and post-announcement windows. While volatility of individual liquid stocks covered in ISE-30 are constantly lower than the volatility of the stocks not covered in ISE-30 in pre-announcement and post-announcement periods, stocks covered in ISE-30 reacts to the insiders trading announcement dramatically and average daily volatility of these stocks reaches to the maximum level of 22.11 basis points. The volatility increase remains persistent in low-liquid stocks not covered in ISE, while it is longer term (+3, +50) post-announcement window average daily volatility is 1.01 basis points higher than the average daily volatility in (-50, -3) pre-announcement window and the differences in the volatilities are statistically significant.

The classification of the traded stocks into five industry groups, including manufacturing, service, technology, financial, and mutual funds industries shows significant differences in average daily volatilities among the stocks belonging different industries in pre-announcement, announcement and post-announcement windows. Volatility increases remains persistent in the manufacturing industry over the (+3, +50) post-announcement window which reaches to the 12.76 basis points which is significantly higher than the average daily volatility in (-50, -3) pre-announcement window. Changes in the average daily volatilities in (-2, +2) announcement window is significantly higher than its level in (-50, -3) pre-announcement window for financial and mutual funds industries. The results imply that industry is one of the important factors affecting the magnitude of the volatilities.

The technical trading strategy itself whether it is momentum (buying past strong performers and selling past weak performers) or contrarian (buying past weak performers and selling past strong performers) strategy may stabilize or exacerbate price movements. Avramov *et al.* (2006) provide evidence from US market that contrarian strategies decrease volatility, whereas contrarian trades increase volatility. In this study, we divide our sample into two categories based on the momentum or contrarian strategy that insiders follow. Our results are in the same line with the findings of Avramov *et al.* (2006). While average daily volatilities significantly increase in both insiders' trades which follow either contrarian or momentum strategy in the announcement window, the increase in the average daily volatility remains persistent in the contrarian strategy. Average daily volatility in the trades with contrarian pattern reaches to the 10.52 basis points in (+3, +50) post-announcement window which is significantly higher than its pre-announcement level. Though, volatility also increase in the trades with the momentum pattern, this increase is not statistically significant.

Conclusion

In this study, we examine the impact of the insiders' trades on the stock prices volatility in an emerging market setting. We have employed several pre-announcement, announcement and post-announcement windows to evaluate the impact of the insiders on the average daily volatilities. Our results indicated that insiders' trading increase the volatility of the stocks in the trading announcement and post-announcement windows. Market reacts asymmetrically to the buy and sell decisions which is consistent with the asymmetric volatility hypothesis. Sell decisions increase the volatility of the stocks dramatically, whereas the effects of the buy decisions over the volatility is negligible. Trader type and trader's relationship with the company also affects the volatility. More the trader is involved with the company, more the volatility of the stock prices becomes persistent. Consistent with the stealth trading hypothesis of Barclay and Warner (1993), we find negligible effects of the small-sized trades on the volatility, while volatility changes greatly after large-sized trades. The impact of the insiders' trades is larger in the stocks with the smaller capitalization. Insider traders who follow contrarian strategy also increase the stock price volatility significantly after the insiders' trades. Concluding, our results imply that insiders destabilize the market.

References

Avramov, D., Chordia, T., and Goyal, A. (2006). 'The impact of trades on daily volatility', *The Review of Financial Studies*, Bol. 19 (4), pp. 1241-77.

Ausubel, L. M. (1990). 'Insider trading in a rational expectations economy', *American Economic Review*, Vol. 80 (5), pp. 1022- 41.

Bekaert, G. and Wu, G. (2000) 'Asymmetric volatility and risk in equity markets', *Review of Financial Studies,* Vol. 13 (1), pp. 1-42.

Barucci, E., Bianchi, C. and Manconi, A. (2006). 'Internal dealing regulation and insiders' trades in the Italian financial market' *European Journal of Law and Economics,* Vol. 22 (2) pp. 107-19.

Benabou, R. and Laroque, G. (1992). 'Using privileged information to manipulate markets: Insiders, gurus, and credibility', *Quarterly Journal of Economics*, Vol. 107 (3), pp. 921-58.

Betzer, A. and Theissen, E. (2007) 'Insider Trading and Corporate Governance: The Case of Germany', *European Financial Management*, Forthcoming.

Bhattacharya, U. and Daouk, H. (2002). 'The world price of insider trading', *Journal of Finance*, Vol. 57, pp. 75-108.

Bhattacharya, U., Daouk, H., Jorgenson, B. and Kehr, C. H. (2000).'When an announcement is not an announcement: The curious case of an emerging market', *Journal of Financial Economics*, Vol. 55 (1), pp. 69-101.

Bris, A. (2005). 'Do insider trading laws work?', *European Financial Management*, Vol. 11 (3), pp. 267-312

Chakravarty, S. and McConnell, J.J. (1999). 'Does insider trading really move stock prices?', *Journal of Financial and Quantitative Analysis,* Vol. 34 (2), pp. 191-209.

Cheuka, M. Fan, D. K. and Sob, R. W. (2006). 'Insider trading in Hong Kong: Some stylized facts', *Pacific-Basin Finance Journal*, Vol. 14 (1), pp. 73-90.

Chiyachantana, C.N., Jain, P.K., Jiang, C. and Wood, R. A. (2006). 'Volatility effects of institutional trading in foreign stocks', *Journal of Banking and Finance*, Vol. 30 (8), pp. 2199-2214.

Cinar, E M. (1999). 'The issue of insider trading in law and economics: Lessons for emerging financial markets in the world', *Journal of Business Ethics*, Vol. 19 (4), pp. 345-53.

Damodaran, A. and Liu, C.H. (1993). 'Insider trading as a signal of private information', *Review of Financial Studies,* Vol. 6, pp. 79-119.

Del Brio, E. B., Miguel, A., and Perote, J. (2002). 'An investigation of insider trading profits in the Spanish stock market', *Quarterly Review of Economics and Finance*, Vol. 42, pp. 73-94.

Demirag, I. and Serter, M. (2003). 'Ownership patterns and control in Turkish listed companies', *Corporate Governance: An International Review*, Vol. 11 (1), pp. 40-51.

Du, J. and Wei, S. (2004). 'Does insider trading raise market volatility?', *The Economic Journal*, Vol. 114, pp. 916-42.

Fidrmuc, J., Goergen, M. and Renneboog, L. (2006) 'Insider trading, news releases, and ownership concentration', *The Journal of Finance,* Vol. 61 (6), pp. 2931-73

Finnerty, J. E. (1976). 'Insiders' activity and inside information: A multivariate analysis', *Journal of Financial and Quantitative Analysis*, Vol. 11, pp. 205-16.

French, K. R., Schwert, G. W. and Stambaugh, R. (1987). 'Expected stock returns and volatility', *Journal of Financial Economics*, Vol. 19, pp. 329.

Glosten, L. R., Jagannathan, R. and Runkle, D. E. (1993). 'On the relation between the expected value and the volatility of the nominal excess returns of stocks', *Journal of Finance*, Vol. 48, pp. 1779-1801.

Jaffe, J. (1974). 'Special information and insider trading', *Journal of Business*, Vol. 47, pp. 410-28.

Keim, D. B. and Madhavan, A. (1995) 'Anatomy of the trading process empirical evidence on the behavior of institutional traders', *Journal of Financial Economics*, Vol. 37 (3), pp. 371-98

Leland, H. E. (1992). 'Insider trading: Should it be prohibited?', *The Journal of Political Economy*, Vol. 100 (4), pp. 859-87.

Lin, J. and Howe, J. (1990). 'Insider trading in the OTC market', *Journal of Finance*, Vol. 45 (4), pp. 1273-84.

Makino, S., Beamish, P.W. and Zhao, N.B. (2004). 'The characteristics and performance of Japanese FDI in less developed and developed countries', *Journal of World Business*, Vol. 39, pp. 377-92.

Odean, T. (1998). 'Volume, Volatility, Price, and Profit When All Traders Are Above Average', *The Journal of Finance*, Vol. 53 (6), 1887-1934.

Seyhun, H.N. (1986). 'Insiders' profits, costs of trading, and market efficiency', *Journal of Financial Economics*, Vol. 16 (2), pp. 189-212.

Wu, G. (2001). 'The determinants of asymmetric volatility', *Review of Financial Studies*, Vol. 14 (3), pp. 837-59.

Part 2
REGIONAL ISSUES

Chapter 5

Guidelines for Corporate Behaviour: Origins, Current Stage, and Future Tendencies of Polish Corporate Governance Code

Maria Aluchna and Izabela Koladkiewicz

Abstract

The paper presents the process of building code of best practice from the perspective of emergence of corporate governance system in Poland observed within the transition reforms. It aims at the analysis of the code characteristics relating to suggested guidelines and challenges identified in Polish public companies listed on the stock exchange and problematic practice adopted by corporate bodies or dominant shareholders. Thorough the analyzed period of 1989-2007 Polish companies, investors and regulators have faced different problems and challenges in line with the reforms progress, corporate governance system development, introduction of worldwide recognized standards and law harmonization after the EU accession. Hence, best practice and corporate governance recommendations which should reflect the current stage of a country development have been changed respectively. The paper analyses the origin of corporate governance reforms and the emergence of the best practice code, discusses characteristics of there main codes formulated in 2002, 2005 and recently in 2007 as well as attempts to answer the question on future tendencies and development directions of the Polish code.

Introduction

Formulating guidelines for corporate behaviour and various initiatives of standard setting for companies have always been an important element of economic and social systems development. Such initiatives are crucial in the area of corporate governance where investor protection and stable rules of the game do not only provide for sound governance structure and efficiency but also assure development conditions, stability and low risk levels. The importance code of corporate governance code became even more visible after devastating corporate scandals which ruined investment and pension plans of millions and destroyed the confidence in markets and institutions. Codes of best practice are undoubtedly an essential part of the development process of transition economies creating market economy rules and providing sound structure for social and economic progress.

This paper discusses the creation process of best practice code in Poland from the perspective of corporate governance development and transition to market economy. The main goal is to present how recommendations of the code corresponded with different stages of corporate governance development and how they referred to the main problems and challenges faced by public companies listed on Warsaw Stock Exchange. Hence, the paper analyses guidelines of codes formulated in Poland in 2002 and 2005 as well as it identifies main future tendencies discussing the new code which recommendation starts binding January 1st, 2008. Apparently, the set of recommendations related to ownership structure, board practices and procedures, executive compensation and corporate transparency are not able to solve all corporate governance problems in Poland as they should accompany strong institutions (securities and exchange commission, stock exchange), law in action and court system. These recommendations however set standards for listed companies, change business practice and outline directions for future development.

The paper is organized as follows. The first section presents the process of Polish corporate governance emergence within transition reforms, pointing at initial problems, current characteristics and challenges. The origin of corporate governance code is discussed in the second section. The third section analyses guidelines for corporate behaviour formulated in the 2005 code, whereas recent changes of the code recommendations binding from January 1st, 2008 are discussed in the fourth chapter. The fifth section identifies the practical compliance of public companies listed on Warsaw Stock Exchange with the recommendation of the corporate governance code. The final remarks are presented in conclusion section.

The Emergence of Polish Corporate Governance

Creating Corporate Governance within Transition Reforms
Corporate governance constitutes the crucial structure for the control over companies becoming a condition for efficient performance. As Estrin (2001) states the development of corporate governance structures depends upon two processes:

1.   Restructuring of existing activities and

2.   Reallocation of resources that relates to market structure, law and institutions.

Before 1989 Poland experienced communist regime and central planning based on state ownership and reallocation of resources conducted by ministries. The disappearance of the central plan in 1990 meant that the regulatory function over companies which used to be fulfilled by the state must have been taken over by institutions of private property, set of institutions ensuring enforceable allocation of responsibility (commercial codes, collateral, bankruptcy), institutions that control and monitor the behaviour of these who hold the property of others (banking regulators, stock markets, security regulators), whole set of expectations about agents' behaviour (Murrell, 1992). However, the development process proved to the complex and consisted of three main phases identified by Aoki (1996):

- Socialist regime characterised by state ownership, continuous discretion of the state, directors appointment by the state organ controlled by the party;

- Transition regime means that all enterprises are transformed into corporations (corporatisation or commercialisation) but their ownership structures is in the process of being defined whereas the state looses its discretionary power to appoint and dismiss the management of the enterprises. There is still however no definite power to replace state;

- Post-transition regime characterised by state, where the corporate governance structure has been well defined, the share ownership structure has become stable and management teams are chosen through the process defined by the corporate law. There is a credible mechanism operating to replace poorly performing managers.

The development of corporate governance and changes within the control structure is truly a difficult and complicated process (what can be even now observed in developed countries which introduce many regulations towards increased transparency). The development of corporate governance in transition economies required implementing new laws and institutions that supported by business practice, know how and social capital would be able to play allocation, evaluation and decision making functions. Some researchers however viewed these reforms in a pessimistic way due to the lack of the minimum of market economy institutions which could provide fundaments for further reforms (Frydman and Rapaczynski, 1996).

Majority of researchers and practitioners agreed upon the significant importance of corporate governance reforms and its role for further growth and development of economic as well as social systems in Poland. Therefore, corporate governance development was recognized as crucial and belonged to the second type of transition reforms agenda which referred to rebuilding institutional framework, large-scale privatization, the development of a commercial banking sector and effective tax system, labour market regulations and institutions related to the social safety and establishment and enforcement of a market-oriented legal system and accompanying institutions (Svejnar, 2001). More precisely, the reforms aimed at shifting assets of state owned enterprises into private hand via various privatization schemes, setting laws required for corporate activity, restructuring financial system (banks and pension funds) and creating capital market. However, little research (Pistor et al, 2000) maintains that reformers in transition economies did not have any particular corporate governance model in mind while reforming law on books. The regulations were strengthen in all directions and the international comparison of corporate governance structure shows that transition economies have creditor indices highest worldwide and shareholder rights indices second highest, after common law countries, worldwide. As a matter of fact the initial plan assumed to create more Anglo-Saxon like governance structure which proved to impossible due to the weakness of law in action and court system and inexperienced institutions (stock exchanges, securities and exchange commission). Therefore despite successful and complex reforms some authors (Dzierzanowski and Tamowicz, 2000) claim there was no coordination towards development of corporate governance structure which may now result in some dysfunctions and incoherence.

Comparative analysis of corporate governance system reveals different models worldwide such as the Anglo-Saxon model or German bank based system. Due to the specific economic and legal situation also transition economies reveal their own specificity of corporate governance system. First of all, it must be realized that the structure of corporate governance results from the reform decisions made during the transition process, referring particularly to macroeconomic policy, privatization programs, financial system liberalization, bank restructuring, laws introduced, foreign direct investment inflow. Hence, the shape of corporate governance system in a given transition country results from the political economy - the role of different interest groups that pressured for given regulations and legal provision (for instance the rights for managers to buy out the previously state owned companies in Russia and Ukraine which led to the emergence of oligarchs). Despite reforms efficiency of institutional order and corporate governance in transition economies is still lagging behind the level of developed economies. Therefore, shape, efficiency and stability of corporate governance are heavily rooted in the developed institutional order, i.e. institutions and regulations that built framework for corporate activity (for instance strength of stock market, stability of banking system). Secondly, corporate governance as its challenges in a given transition economy varies significantly between companies depending on their owner (state or private), origin (commercialized, private or privatized), status and role in the economy (strategic vs. less important). Thirdly, generally speaking corporate governance is based mostly upon internal mechanisms, i.e. hierarchies such as ownership structure and board, whereas external mechanism, i.e. markets such as stock market, market for corporate control are weaker and do not play important governance functions. In particular, ownership concentration in CEE countries is highly concentrated as a result of weak investor protection (investors want to secure their position in the company buying larger stakes of shares), civil law and catch up stages of transition economies. Boards of companies in transition economies are dominated by representatives of shareholder and creditors, the participation of representatives of workers (usually in state owned or commertialised companies),whereas the presence of independent directors is marginal. Moreover, owners vary in terms of type and origin insiders do have strong position in Russian companies, investment funds appear to be relatively strong in the Czech companies, whereas strategic investors play important role in Poland and Hungary. Additionally, foreign investors usually held ca. 30% of share of publicly listed companies. And finally, compensation of executives is usually tied to size of companies and less to the corporate performance.

The Initial Stage of Corporate Governance Reforms

One of the most pivotal events in the foundations of the corporate governance system in the transformation process on the way from central planning to market economy starting with 1989 was the Act on the Privatization of the State Enterprises passed in July of 1990. According to this Act each joint stock company created as a result of the commercialization of state enterprise had a legislative obligation to establish a supervisory board. This provision introduced into Polish companies of the supervisory board as a monitoring body on a grand scale. Over the next few years the supervisory board became an integral component of the governance structures of Polish joint stock companies. The privatization of Polish state enterprises based on the relevant legislation took on several possible directions: direct privatization, indirect (capital) privatization, and through the Mass Privatization Program (PPP). The additional component of transition agenda included so called founding privatization which involved the development of conditions for business operations by new companies established after 1989.

The foundation of the stock market appeared as the second crucial event in the development of Polish system of corporate governance. The legal framework for the stock market was created by the Act on Public Trading in Securities and Trust Funds, passed in March of 1991. On April 12, 1991 the Minister of Ownership Transformation and the Minister of Finance representing the State Treasury signed the founding act of the Warsaw Stock Exchange (GPW). The first session of the stock exchange took place with the participation of seven brokerage houses and listed shares in five companies Tonsil, Prochnik, Krosno, Kable, and Exbud. It took place on April 16, 1991. Sessions were held once a week.

The number of companies listed on Warsaw Stock Exchange was (and still is) rising from year to year (see Table 1). In line with this growth the ownership concentration of listed companies increased significantly becoming the centre of corporate governance problems. This should not come as a surprise since the early 1990s was a time of initial experiments in building relations among company bodies - the general shareholder meeting, supervisory and management boards - as well as relations between the dominant shareholder and minority shareholders. Hence, facing abuse of investor rights, inefficient court system and awkward practices investors could protect themselves only by concentrating power and control, i.e. holding dominant stakes. Key problem areas of the governance of companies listed on the Warsaw Stock Exchange at that time included:

1. Conflicts among shareholders and especially between majority and minority shareholders (typical operations on the part of the majority shareholder that infringed against the interests of minority shareholders included self-dealing transactions, tunnelling, and distracting value);

2. Poor protection of minority shareholders rights;

3. Dysfunction of the general shareholder meeting as the most important body of the company (during 1990s general shareholder meetings were often the venue

for conflicts and disputes between the majority and minority shareholders where a typical example was calling of numerous recesses which made the passing of resolutions important to the company impossible);

4. Weak and often politically-oriented supervisory boards;
5. Poor transparency of companies on the market and poor or totally nonexistent investor relations.

Table 1. The Warsaw Stock Exchange over the Years 1991 - 2007

Year	Domestic company equity (PLN million)	Number of companies	Stock turnover (PLN million)	Securities turnover (PLN million)	Contract turnover volume	WIG rate of return (%)
July 2007	565,221	316	293,498	2,291	4,716,120	26.30
2006	437,719	284	334,539	5,536	6,386,046	41.60
2005	308,418	255	191,096	5,507	5,378,517	33.66
2004	214,313	230	118,518	8,353	3,609,125	27.94
2003	140,002	203	79,774	12,674	4,231,949	44.92
2002	110,565	216	63,662	4,131	3,175,890	3.19
2001	103,370	230	80,443	5,133	3,754,854	-21.99
2000	130,085	225	169,096	4,590	1,516,042	-1.30
1999	123,411	221	88,974	4,766	207,372	41.30
1998	72,442	198	62,338	8,581	24,320	-12.80
1997	43,766	143	52,342	13,488	—	2.30
1996	24,000	83	29,895	16,219	—	89.10
1995	11,271	65	13,671	19,276	—	1.50
1994	7,450	44	23,420	3,300	—	-39.90
1993	5,845	22	7,873	557	—	1,095.30
1992	351	16	228	21	—	13.20
1991	161	9	30	—	—	-8.09

Source:
http://www.gpw.pl/gpw.asp?cel=informacje_gieldowe&k=1&i=/statystyki/ opis_statystyka&sky=1, visited August 12, 2007.

Current Characteristics and Challenges

The current stage of the development of Polish corporate governance results from the transition reforms (privatization, development of financial market, legal reforms) and the harmonization process with the European Union. It is heavily rooted in the privatization process and the development of entrepreneurial spirits (newly established companies). The general characteristics of Polish corporate governance includes the following features:

- Ownership concentration public companies listed on Warsaw Stock Exchange reveal significant concentration of ownership and control: the biggest shareholder holds more than 50% stake in 75% companies out of which 27% companies are the cases of more than 75% stake of the biggest shareholder, and the median size of the biggest voting block is 33% or 39.5% and of the second accounts for 10.4% (for more data see also Aluchna, 2007). Such significant ownership concentration leads to dominant-minority shareholders conflicts, abuse of minority rights and lower liquidity and efficiency of stock market;

- Dominance of insiders as shown in Table 2 below executive is at the same time the dominant shareholder in 28% of sample companies. This phenomenon results from the development of newly founded companies where the first generation, i.e. the founders manage and still control companies;

Table 2. The Dominant Shareholder Identity of WIG (Warsaw Stock Exchange index) Companies (Average 1997-2004)

Dominant shareholder identity	Number of companies	Structure
Domestic company	19	21%
Foreign company	12	13%
Executive	25	28%
Privat e investor	6	6%
Bank	4	4%
Other financial institution	15	17%
State	8	9%
Employees	1	1%
Total	90	100%

Source: Aluchna M. (2007)[1]

- Growing role of pension funds in line with pension system reforms created open pension fund accumulate substantial funds (ca. 3 bln euro per year) and are obliged to invest some of these funds in share of public companies. Therefore, pension funds become an important player in ownership structure and set standard of corporate governance practices (see 'other financial institution' in Table 2);

---

[1] *Struktura własności a efektywność przedsiębiorstwa. Przypadek polskich spółek giełdowych* [Ownership structure and company performance: The case of Polish listed companies], Collegium of Management and Finance Working Papers, Warsaw School of Economics, p. 73.

- Growing popularity of stock market as shown in Table 1 above Warsaw Stock Exchange experiences substantial growth in the post-accession period due to the development of the economy and optimism on capital market accompanied by mentioned inflow of capital and the growing public awareness of the investor capitalism;
- Role of the state despite successful transition reforms the state still possesses shares in almost every second largest industrial company, among which many belong to the biggest Polish ones. Some of them are listed on Warsaw Stock Exchange and experience control or at least influence executed by the Ministry of Treasury. The state criticised for adoption of 'political key' in the process of supervisory board member appointment (practice popular no matter what party is ruling), decided to formulate code of best practice for corporate governance in companies with stake held by Ministry of Treasury;
- Low transparency the analysis of the last 10 years of Polish corporate governance system reveals tremendous progress in all areas. Researchers and practitioners point out growing shareholder awareness, improved board efficiency, development of formal procedure and increase corporate disclosure. However, research conducted by Pajuste (2004) indicate that in terms of transparency Polish (as well as Bulgarian) companies are ranked in the last place.

It is worth mentioning that various privatization schemes and firm development paths resulted in different current characteristics of companies listed on Warsaw Stock Exchange. Hence, these companies characterized by different origin and experience reveal their specific sets of problems and weaknesses. For instance, significant ownership concentration and dominant shareholder practices abusing minorities take place mostly in companies privatized within the case by case scheme to foreign investors. Dominant position of insiders (mostly CEO) either in terms of ownership structure and control rights executed from preferred shares or in terms of proportion of affiliated board members (friends, relatives) appears to be characteristic for companies founded after 1989 where powerful founders exert control. Interestingly such 'control model' in many case proves to outperform other companies. At the same time problems of Ministry of Treasury influence in company supervisory board refers only to several companies in 'strategic' sectors such as oil or mining characterised by significant state ownership.

Additionally, current challenges of corporate governance system and code of best practice refer to the development of Warsaw Stock Exchange in term of number of listed companies. This element requires taking into account vast range of companies types and origin (large and small, privatized and newly founded, domestic and international) which means the need of guidelines of corporate behaviour adjusted to the specificity of various companies. Moreover, the process of setting standards and formulating corporate governance best practice needs to follow the recommendations prepared by European Commission. The biggest challenge for public companies listed on Warsaw Stock Exchange refers to the number of independent directors on board and creating board committees (audit, nomination and compensation) under the assumption of vast proportion of independent directors as well as to improvement of corporate transparency.

The Origins of a Corporate Governance Code

The late 1990s saw the growing wave of problems and the increase of awareness and questions relating to corporate governance among individual market participants as well as various institutions at the Polish stock market. The national debate resulted in several institutional outcomes first, Corporate Governance Forum was established at the end of 1998. The Forum aimed at promoting corporate governance initiatives and ideas among participants of the Polish stock market organizing conferences and workshops[2] and it led to the emergence of Best Practice Committee in May of 2001. The Committee is made up of well known Polish lawyers (Prof. Grzegorz Domanski and Prof. Stanisław Soltysinski) as well as representatives of such institutions as Polish Confederation of Private Employers (Henryka Bochniarz, President), Polish Institute of Directors (Krzysztof A. Lis, President), Warsaw Stock Exchange (Wieslaw Rozlucki, President), and Ministry of the State Treasury (Jacek Socha, Minister of the State Treasury). The primary goal of the Committee was to undertake the work on "best practice" encompassing principles of the behaviour of company bodies and the members of those bodies as well as the relations between majority and minority shareholders. The main objective in preparing best practice was to 'civilize' corporate behaviour.

The first version of Polish corporate governance code is dated on February 2002. "Best Practices in Public Companies 2002" ("Best Practices ...", 2002) was developed by the Best Practices Committee (KDP). The Best Practices Council encompassing selfgoverning and stock market-related institutions was established at the same time and intended to involve other participants in the stock market in discussions on proposed recommendations and guidelines while simultaneously formulating principles of corporate governance. The primary interested parties - the companies themselves - also took part in discussions. All listed companies received the first version of the "Best Practices in Public Companies 2002" code. Unfortunately, companies participation in the debate was disappointingly minimal. According to one of stock market experts involved in preparing the above document companies did not fully understand the idea behind these actions. Stock market authorities would have wished that companies reacting to "Best Practices in Public Companies 2002" would have undertake efforts to conduct independent and critical analyses of their own corporate practices. The results of such analyses could then be used as a starting point for a true in-house dialogue on the topic of best practices of main corporate bodies. This dialogue should involve members of the management

---

[2] The first public discussion on domestic models of owner supervision took place in January of 1999. This was during the 1st Corporate Governance Forum. The Forum was organized by Institute for Business Development (IRB) in cooperation with Warsaw Stock Exchange, and Securities and Exchange Commission, Polish Confederation of Private Employers, Polish Business Council, Association of Stock Issuers, the National Securities Deposit, Association of Investment Fund Societies in Poland, Chamber of Brokerage Houses, Retirement Society Chamber of Commerce, Union of Polish Banks, and Union of Private Investor Brokers and Advisors www.gov.pl

board and board of supervisors as well as the general shareholder meeting. Unfortunately, companies appeared to be very passive as they simply used to forward the "Best Practices in Public Companies 2002" document to their lawyers requesting the legal review of this document. According to experts such reaction narrowed to merely the legal perspective demonstrated the lack of understanding of the concept of best practice in its broader context which focuses not only the proper building of relations among corporate bodies and its shareholders but also the structuring relations with other participants in the securities market.

The final version of the "Best Practices in Public Companies 2002" document which took into account comments received from the stock market appeared in July 2002. Management Board and Council of the Warsaw Stock Exchange approved this document in fall 2002 what resulted in the obligation for listed companies to submit for the very first time a statement on observance of corporate governance recommendations by July 1, 2003. This declaration is to be updated each year by July 1.

The worldwide experience demonstrates that developing corporate governance code is only the first step in building best practices with respect to the corporate bodies, practice of these bodies members as well as the behaviour of majority and minority shareholders. The primary goal of developing such a document is as a response to pathologies in corporate governance as well as the continuous reaction to emerging problems. The Polish case seems to follow this well known path of development. The new corporate governance challenges revealed worldwide which are in fact answers to the crisis caused by creative accounting of Enron and other known corporations as well as new problems emerging on the Polish capital market, led in July 2004 to discussions on a new set of guidelines known as "Best Practices in Public Companies 2005" ("Best Practices ... 2005"). The Best Practices Committee released the "Best Practices in Public Companies 2005" document in October 2004 and submitted it to the stock market authorities in November. According to the new document companies had to submit corporate governance statement regarding recommendations of "Best Practices in Public Companies 2005" starting from July 1, 2005.

Concluding this historical overview of the Polish best practices in public companies it is worth to mention that the content of the code generally follows the current practice for implementing corporate governance codes as initiated by the Cadbury Commission in 1992 in the UK[3]. The development of such codes is among basic reforms presently undertaken throughout the world. These codes are treated as

---

[3] For example, Great Britain: The Cadbury Report with the Code of Best Practices of the English Cadbury Committees (1992), Greenbury and Hampel Reports (1995 and 1998), and the Turnbull ReportInternal Control Guidance for Directors on the Combined Code (1999); France: The French Viénot Reports I and II (1995 and 1999); United States of America: "Statement on Corporate Governance" as developed by the American Business Roundtable (1997), and the Millstein Report (1998); Germany: The Berlin Incentive Group German Code of Corporate Governance, and the paper of the German Grundstazkommission for Corporate Governance (spring, 2002); Switzerland: Swiss Code of Best Practice.

non-binding sets of principles, standards, and best practices (known as soft law) formulated and issued by collective bodies referring to internal governance mechanisms in companies (Weil, Gotshal, and Manages, 2002, p. 1). The main goal of such initiatives is to create a framework for attracting new capital and thus expanding potential for procuring resources by the company. Various types of institutions including government and quasi-government organisations, committees established by state and stock market authorities, associations including representatives of the world of science and business as well as associations of directors are involved in this process. Apparently, investors play an important role in these initiatives (Weil, Gotshal, and Manages, 2002, p. 2). Additionally, international institutions such as the World Bank, OECD and the International Monetary Fund take part in the development of best practice codes. For example, best practice principles developed by the OECD in 1999 became a reference point for individual states of their own policy in this field. (Tricker R. I., 2000a, pp. 2-6; Nobel P., 2002) Polish authors of best practice codes for companies listed on Warsaw Stock Exchange also could refer to this works.

The Polish "Best Practices in Public Companies 2005" Corporate Governance Code: Characteristics

Principles of the "Best Practices in Public Companies 2005"[4]

The document "Best Practices in Public Companies 2005" approved by the authorities of the Warsaw Stock Exchange as well as the earlier "Best Practices in Public Companies 2002," referred only to public listed companies and belonged to soft law. Companies followed its recommendations on voluntary basis according to the worldwide known and accepted comply or explain rule. As signalled above, each company listed on Warsaw Stock Exchange is obliged to file the annual statement on observance of the best practice principles by July 1 each year. In this declaration, company must comment each point of the "Best Practices in Public Companies." The declaration is in tabular form consisting of three columns. The first column contains all the principles. The company must present a oneword declaration (yes or no) as to whether or not it intends to apply the given principle in the second column. The company can deliver comments related to the way in which the given principle is observed or why it is not observed in the third column. The corporate governance statement must be attached to the annual report and be submitted using the EMITENT system as well as made public. Such policy intends to allow investors to learn more about the corporate governance practices applied by the given company.

---

[4] At the moment of preparing this article, companies listed on the Warsaw Stock Exchange were subject to the "Best Practices in Public Companies 2005."

Main Components of the "Best Practices in Public Companies 2005"

The Polish "Best Practices in Public Companies 2005" corporate governance code encompasses 48 principles that constitute the following five sections:

1. General Principles (IV)
2. Best Practice of General Shareholder Meeting (principles 117)
3. Supervisory Board Best Practices (principles 1831)
4. Management Board Best Practices (principles 3240)
5. Best Practices in Relations with External Individuals and Institutions (principles 4148)

The "General Principles" section contains 5 general principles relating to company objectives, relations between company majority and minority shareholders (the principles of majority rule, minority protection, honest intentions and care against any abuse of power), the scope of judicial supervision, and the requirement to guaranty independence of expert opinions hired by the company (especially with respect to expert services in the form of certified auditors, financial and tax consulting and legal services).

The section focusing on "Best Practices of General Shareholder Meeting" is made up of 17 principles referring to conducting the meeting. The principles touch upon the following matters:

- The venue and time for organizing general shareholder meetings to assure for participation of as large group of shareholders as possible,

- Terms for demanding the calling of a general shareholder meeting as well as its cancellation, and principles of calling recesses during sessions,

- Terms of introducing modifications for a session's agenda and conditions for participation of shareholder representatives,

- General shareholder meetings bylaws, defining principles of managing sessions and undertaking resolution,

- Method of appointing the chairman of the general shareholder meeting and his/ her role in managing the session,

- Presence of members of the supervisory board and the management board and their role in the general shareholder meeting, as well as the right of shareholders to demand explanations, and

- Terms for passing a resolution regarding desisting from the examination of matters specified in the session agenda.

The "Supervisory Board Best Practices" section encompasses 14 principles (principles 1831). Their analysis demonstrates the importance of the independence of board members. The proposed best practices for supervisory boards not only specify the number of its members, but also the types of resolutions that require the consent of the majority of independent board members. Moreover, the information by board members of the emergence of any conflict of interest as well as the public disclosure of information regarding links of members of the supervisory board with specified shareholders (especially the majority shareholder) is a matter of importance. The principles of best practices of supervisory board also delve into matters of board bylaws, remuneration for board members, the building of information flow channels between the supervisory board and the management board, the manner in which board sessions are to be conducted and their accessibility by management board members.

"Management Board Best Practices" principles (principles 3240) mainly concentrate on such issues as:

- Taking care by of company interests and the reconciling of those interests with those of various shareholders (majority shareholders, minority shareholders, and employees),
- Informing the supervisory board by executives (management board) of the emergence of any conflict of interest or the potential for its emergence,
- The loyalty of board members with respect to the company,
- Remuneration for members of the board, and
- The development of generally accessible board bylaws.

The last part of the Polish "Best Practices in Public Companies 2005" code contains 8 principles regulating the relations of the company with external institutions and persons - "Best Practices in Relations with External Individuals and Institutions." Best practices in this area include:

- Assuring for the independence of certified auditors,

- Access by stock market participants to corporate documents such as the statutes, bylaws of the general shareholder meeting, supervisory board, and management board, and

- Building the information policy guarantying cohesive and reliable information regarding the company as well as access to declarations regarding application by the company of principles of corporate governance best practice.

Changes in Polish "Best Practices": Main Trends
The Years 2002-2005

As mentioned above, the Polish code of corporate governance best practices characterises continuous change. The main reason behind these changes is not only the need to react to new problems appearing on the Polish capital market, but also an answer to what is happening in the area of corporate governance worldwide. Additionally, corporate governance code is an important factor for increasing stock market competitiveness attracting not only domestic but also foreign investors[5].

The first modification of the Polish code of best practice took place after the implementation of the initial document"Best Practices in Public Companies 2002." "Best Practices in Public Companies 2005" resulted from of wide ranging consultations in the business, investor and regulator communities and took into account practical experience as well as the opinions and suggestions of market participants collected over the two year period. Additionally, the code focused on recommendations of the European Commission (Preamble to "Best Practices in Public Companies 2005"). The modifications in set of guidelines encompass a total of 10 principles from sections IIV. The major change refers to more details and precision in corporate governance practice. Table 3 presents that most changes relate to supervisory board operations as well as the building relations with external persons and institutions by the company.

Table 3. Principles Modified in "Best Practices in Public Companies 2005"

Section	Principle
II. General Assembly of Shareholders Best Practices	9, 14
III. Supervisory Board Best Practices	18, 20, 27, 28
IV. Management Board Best Practices	39
V. Best Practices in Relations with External Individuals and Institutions	42, 43, 44

Source: Own studies.

"Best Practices in Public Companies 2005" delivered mostly the reaction to supervisors and executives compensation. The reason behind the changes was the corporate practice in compensation policy. The new guidelines introduced regulations that required setting remuneration on the basis of transparent procedures and

---

[5] Research conducted by McKinsey Company shows that investors are willing to pay a premium in the case of companies that are seen as entities with good corporate governance standards. On average, this premium amounts to 12%14% in North America and Western Europe, 20%25% in Asia and South America, and over 30% in Eastern Europe and Africa (Spira L. F., 2002).

principles as well as disclosure of remuneration of all members of the supervisory and management boards as well as the individual remuneration of the individual members including principles of its establishing (principles 27 and 39) in the annual report.

"Best Practices in Public Companies 2005" also included proposals for changes with respect to the structure of the supervisory board. Principle 28 which referred to the development of board bylaws, included a provision on appointing two committees (audit and remuneration) within board structure. At the same time, the bylaws should define the tasks of these committees. The same principle also defined the procedure for appointing the audit committee: "The composition of the audit committee should consist of at least two independent members and at least one holding qualifications and experience in accounting and finance."

Tasks for the audit committee are also defined by principle 43 (in the new version of Best Practices from 2005) which states that the committee should prepare for the supervisory board a list of entities that could be selected to serve as certified auditor. Also worth adding at this point is the fact that the remaining principles 42 and 44 relating to selection and actions of the certified auditor were also modified to provide greater precision of what is understood as a change in certified auditor (it relates not only to a change of entity, but also of the person conducting the audit) as well as the defining of who can fill the function of certified auditor in special cases.

The characteristics of modifications introduced in "Best Practices in Public Companies 2005" should also discuss changed principle 20 which regulates issues of the independence of supervisory board members. The 2005 code added the possibility of the company to apply independence criteria as formulated by European standards the Commission Recommendations on strengthening the role of nonexecutive and supervisory directors.

Moreover, due to the concentrated ownership structure of companies listed on Warsaw Stock Exchange the recommendation suggesting at least one half of the independent directors in the supervisory board was modified. According to the new recommendation, in cases of companies with a dominant shareholder holding over 50% of votes, the supervisory board should have at least two independent members.

The new recommendations on "Best Practices of General Shareholder Meeting" allow to notice a significant improvement in the meeting practices. Recommendations included requirements to explain the absence of the supervisory board member at the general shareholder meeting as according to principle 9 directors should take part in these meetings. Furthermore, 2005 code clarified conditions required for passing a resolution eliminating an item from the agenda of the session or desisting from discussing a given point of the agenda if proposed by a shareholder (principle 14).

What Will Tomorrow Bring? … Best Practices Anno Domini 2007

In line with the main goal, the code of best practices is a living document reacting to challenges and needs of the stock market. Hence, Warsaw Stock Exchange launched discussion on a new document on corporate governance principles at the end of 2006. This initiatives resulted in the draft "Best Practices for Companies Listed on the Warsaw Stock Exchange" submitted for public consultation in April of 2007. On July

4, 2007, the Board of Warsaw Stock Exchange approved new best practice principles known as "Best Practices for Companies Listed on the Warsaw Stock Exchange." The new document shall come into force as of January 2, 2008 (www.gov.pl).

The proposed formula for the new principles of corporate governance differs from those of earlier best practice codes (2002 and 2005). The main differences include changes in the structure of the document and in the number of principles, the different character of individual parts of the set of principles, the selection of issues for regulation and methods of principles implementation, application and then execution (Sobolewski L., 2007). In its new form, the Polish code of best practices consists of three sections:

- Part I Recommendations A "soft" area (10 principles), including a ban on preferred shares and transactions with related entities,
- Part II Principles implemented by the management board (5 principles), and
- Part III Principles addressed to members of the supervisory board and shareholders (17 principles), including guidelines relating to independent members of supervisory board and its committees.

A novelty introduced by "Best Practices for Companies Listed on the Warsaw Stock Exchange" in the shaping of best practice is stressing issues related to communications with investors and corporate disclosure. New matters in this sphere include recommendations referring to:

- The application of modern technologies for communications and disclosure (part I),
- Preparing corporate website of defined content (part II),
- Justification of draft of general shareholder meeting resolutions,
- An obligation to facilitate media presence at general shareholder meeting (part III),
- An obligation to report on a daily basis on infringements against parts II and III, and
- An obligation to prepare an annual report on the state of corporate order as required by parts II and III.

The second set of new issues introduced by the "Best Practices for Companies Listed on the Warsaw Stock Exchange" concentrates on corporate decisions important from the investors perspective as well as the manner in which they are undertaken and announced. Such decisions include the issue of stock, the decision defining the day of rights to dividends becoming effective as well as the date and terms of disbursal.

In addition to the above mentioned novelties, the new set of recommendations also refers to classic questions of corporate governance where the authors suggest the following:

- The independence as well as competencies and experience of all members of the supervisory board are a value (part I),
- The presence of at least two independent directors in the supervisory (independent from the company and its related parties as well as according to the European Commission criteria),

- At least one independent director in the audit committee as well as in the nomination and remuneration committee,
- The establishing of committees may be waived in the case of boards with only a minimum number of members as defined by the Code of Commercial Companies (*i.e.* five).

Recommendations proposed in the new set of best practices relating to independent members of supervisory boards are based on the assumption that companies shall adopt these guidelines conditional to the importance of this subject as well as their diversity (size: large, medium, or small and their origin: Polish or foreign).

Additionally, 2008 code provides a modification to the "comply or explain" rule referring to its application. "Best Practices for Companies Listed on the Warsaw Stock Exchange" introduce the principle with respect to parts II and III as well as the obligation to report infringements (incidents or states). Moreover, information regarding the lack of application is no longer formally neutral in light of the principles of creating corporate order.

Theory and Practice: The Corporate Approach to Best Practices

Stock market statistics on statements regarding observance corporate governance guidelines shown in Table 4 demonstrate that all companies listed on the stock market submitted declarations in which they present their approach to the "Best Practices in Public Companies 2005" document. Out of 317 listed companies listed on Warsaw Stock Exchange as of July 31, 2007, only 4 declared the lack of observance of the code principles.

Table 4. Declarations on Compliance with the Principles of Corporate Order: Statistics, Data as of July 31, 2007

Total companies	317
Number of companies that failed to provide the declaration	0
Number of companies that observe none of the principles	4
Number of companies that declare a meeting of the principles	313

Principle	Number of Companies Embracing the Principle	Number of Companies Not Complying with the Principle (excluding companies that have declared non observance of the principles)
General Principles		
I.	312	1
II.	304	9
III.	311	2
IV.	312	1
V.	313	0
General Assembly of Shareholders Best Practices		
1.	312	1
2.	287	26
3.	309	4
4.	304	9
5.	309	4
6.	285	28
7.	306	7
8.	312	1
9.	267	46
10.	301	12
11.	311	2
12.	312	1
13.	305	8
14.	263	50
15.	310	3
16.	299	14
17.	303	10
Supervisory Board Best Practices		
18.	297	16
19.	291	22
20.	95	218
21.	310	3
22.	309	4
23.	307	6
24.	256	57
25.	304	9
26.	287	26
27.	280	33
28.	92	221
29.	301	12
30.	296	17
31.	307	6

Management Board Best Practices		
32.	311	1
33.	307	6
34.	312	1
35.	312	1
36.	300	13
37.	309	4
38.	301	12
39.	280	33
40.	296	17
Best Practices in Relations with External Individuals and Institutions		
41.	312	1
42.	289	24
43.	149	164
44.	302	11
45.	310	3
46.	301	12
47.	279	34
48.	311	2

Source: http://www.gpw.pl/gpw.asp?cel=spolki&k=75&i=/spolkigieldowe/
corporate/statystyka&sky=1

A more detailed analysis of data shown in Table 4 reveals that companies had the greatest difficulties in compliance with principle 20 (218 companies not complying), principle 28 (221 companies not complying), and principle 43 (164 companies not complying). These principles refer to independent directors on the supervisory board (principle 20), establishing of the audit committee and remuneration committee within the board (principle 28), and the role of the audit committee in selecting a certified auditor (principle 43).

The main reasons behind the failure to observe these principles result from the concentrated ownership structures where the dominant shareholder exert its influence over the composition of the supervisory board and is not interested in the increase in the role of independent directors. A disdain for creating audit and remuneration committees may stem from not only a failure to observe the principle of supervisory board independence, but also its size. According to requirements stipulated by the Code of Commercial Companies the minimal number of supervisory board members in a capital company amounts to five persons. In the case of such a board it is difficult to imagine the establishing of committees. Such a supervisory board is not rare among Polish listed companies where a significant number belongs to the small and medium enterprise sector.

The analysis of the raw data presented in Table 4 may lead to the impression of broad acceptance by the companies of the proposed recommendations. However, recent studies conducted by M. Jerzemowska and her team have shown that reality is not that optimistic. The analysis of the declarations regarding observance of code principles demonstrates the frequent use of such formulas as "yes, but," or "no, but" next to the "yes and no" answers. This signifies the partial meeting of the "Best Practices in Public Companies 2005" recommendations by listed companies. At the same time, the lack of precise corporate statements makes impossible to evaluate the actual level of compliance to the code guidelines. Such corporate practice may point to a need to reformulate the principles so as to make them more univocal and lucid (Campbell K., Jerzemowska M., Najman K., 2006, pp. 369370).

This situation also signals the need to strengthen the efficiency of mechanisms for monitoring of corporate best practice statement and making companies responsible for submitting false information in this respect. According to the ROSC report, such mechanisms include:

- Shareholders (the issues of following best practice recommendation should be discussed by the general shareholder meeting),
- Independent supervisory board members (they should conduct analyses of the correctness of the company declaration),
- Independent certified auditors (in spite of the fact that such activities are not a part of their responsibilities, performance of audits of financial reports may include an overview of certain aspects of the code of best practice),
- Warsaw Stock Exchange (this body is capable to fine a listed company if it fails to submit the obligatory declaration of best practice),
- The Securities and Exchange Commission (this body can conduct investigations on stock exchange fraud).

Among sanctions for submitting false declaration on observance of the principles of best practice are (the ROSC report):

- On the part of shareholders the right to recall members of the supervisory board during the general shareholder meeting, both ordinary and extraordinary,
- On the part of Warsaw Stock Exchange (GPW) the ability to remove a company from trading if it fails to submit the obligatory declaration on observance of best practice or submits a false declaration, whereas accusations of providing false information in the declaration may be examined by the Stock Exchange Court which may punish the company with a fine of up to PLN 100,000,
- In the case of the Securities and Exchange Commission (KPWiG) the ability to investigate issuers for fraud and accuse companies and persons who are responsible.

Summary

Polish experience in the field of developing the corporate governance code presented above demonstrates that suggested recommendations are answers to problems appearing on the stock market and attempt to meet stock investor expectations.

The Polish case illustrates the process of setting best practice guidelines in line with existing conditions. The paper aimed to discuss the continuous evolution of problems in Polish corporate governance some problems and hence recommendations disappear, whereas others appear. Public companies listed on

Warsaw Stock Exchange were dominated by problems linked to the functioning of the general shareholder meeting over the initial years of its operations. Pathologies observed in this area became a sign of the times. Participants of the Polish stock market learnt everything from scratch making many mistakes, as is typical of any learning process. The effects of such learning became visible with time and the new recommendations of 2007 known as "Best Practices for Companies Listed on Warsaw Stock Exchange" already stress other issues. Questions related to company communications with investors and the corporate disclosure as well as decision making process so crucial for investors are now in the centre of code attention. The above direction of change the rise in the value of information should not be surprising. It corresponds with Warsaw Stock Exchange goal as approved in 2006 which refers to "the creation of a regional, Central European centre for trading in financial instruments, with Warsaw Stock Exchange as the leading component of such a centre" (www.gov.pl).

Regardless of time passing by, a lot of attention and concern in the recommendations on corporate governance still remains linked to the presence of independent members on supervisory boards. It may be assumed that this is the successive typical calling card of our times. The beginning of 21st century was marked by numerous corporate scandals which significantly affected many countries and in several cases resulted in corporate bankruptcies and shareholder litigations. As result deep corporate governance reforms became the essential initiatives worldwide and the importance of independent directors appears the most frequently stressed component.

In conclusion, it is worth to quote Sue Rutledge, World Bank Regional Coordinator for Corporate Governance and her opinion referring to the assessment of implementing best practice and corporate governance reforms in Poland made in December of 2005. She stated "Poland is at the advanced state of corporate governance dialog and reform. These recommendations would further strengthen corporate governance practices. With the increasing role for private pension funds, corporate governance should be an important priority for further reform." (http://www.worldbank.org.pl)

References

Aluchna M. (2007) *Mechanizmy corporate governance w spółkach giełdowych* [Corporate governance mechanisms in public listed companies], Warsaw.

Aluchna Maria, *Struktura własności a efektywność przedsiębiorstwa. Przypadek polskich spółek giełdowych* [Ownership structure and company performance: The case of Polish public listed companies] Collegium of Management and Finance Working Papers, Warsaw School of Economics, 2007.

Aluchna M., Gruszczynski M. (2007) "Challenges of Corporate Governance in Poland" in *Corporate Governance: Issues and Challenges*, Nova Publishers.

Campbell K., Jerzemowska M., Najman K. (2006) "Wstępna analiza przestrzegania zasad nadzoru korporacyjnego przez spółki notowane na GPW w Warszawie w 2005 r." [Preliminary analysis of the observance of corporate governance principles by companies listed on the Warsaw Stock Exchange in 2005], in Rudolf S. (Editor), *Tendencje zmian w nadzorze korporacyjnym* [Tendencies for change in corporate governance], Łódź

University Press, Łódź, pp. 357372.

Dzierżanowski M., Tamowicz P. (2001) *Własność i kontrola polskich korporacji* [Ownership and control of Polish corporations], Instytut Badań nad Gospodarką Rynkową Market Economy Research Institute], Gdańsk, http://www.pfcg.org.pl/pfcg/download/dopdf.pdf.

Estrin S. (2001) "Competition and corporate governance in transition," William Davidson Working Paper, No. 431, http://eres.bus.umich.edu/docs/workpap-dav/wp431.pdf.

Frydman R., Rapaczynski A. (1996) "Overview of Volumes 1 and 2," in Frydman R., Gray C. W., Rapaczynski, A. (Editors), *Corporate Governance in Central Europe and Russia*, Vol. 1, Central European University Press, Budapest, 1996.

Koładkiewicz, I. (2002) Nadzór korporacyjny w Narodowych Funduszach Inwestycyjnych [Corporate Governance in National Investment Funds in Polish], monograph, LKAEM Publisher, Warsaw.

Koładkiewicz, I. (2001) "Building of a Corporate Governance System in Poland: Initial Experiences." Corporate Governance. An International Review, Vol. 9, No. 3, July 2001

Murrell P. (1992) "Evolution in Economics and in the Economic Reform of the Centrally Planned Economies," in Clauge C. C., Rausser G., *The Emergence of Market Economies in Eastern Europe*, Blackwell Cambridge, http://www.bsos.umd.edu/econ/murrell/papers/czep.html .

Nobel P. (2002) "Corporate Governance and the Role of the Independent Audit: Maintaining Diversity within the Framework of International Standards and Principles," conference materials for the 2nd European Conference on Corporate Governance: Can Europe Build on its Diversity to Develop the Corporate Governance System of the Future, Brussels, November 27-29, 2002.

Pajuste A. (2004) "What Do Firms Disclose and Why? Enforcing Corporate Governance and Transparency in Central and Eastern Europe", *Beyond Transition: The Newsletter about Reforming Economies*, The World Bank, December.

Pistor K., Raiser M., Gelfer S. (2000) "Law and Finance in Transition Economies," *Economics of Transition*, Vol. 8, pp. 325-368.

Raport dotyczący przestrzegania norm i kodeksów (2005) [Report on the observance of standards and codes, ROSC]. *Ocena nadzoru korporacyjnego w kraju* [An assessment of corporate governance at home], Poland, June

Securities and Exchange Commission (2003) "Prawa i obowiązki akcjonariuszy spółek publicznych" [The rights and obligations of public companies], group work, Warsaw

Sobolewski L. (2007) "Listed on WSE: Corporate Governance" presentation for the 24th Corporate Governance Conference: Listed on WSE: ład korporacyjny 2007 r. [Corporate order 2007], Warsaw, Giełda Papierów Wartościowych [Securities Exchange], March 5, 2007.

Spira L. F. (2002) "The Role of the Audit Committee: The Gap Between Expectations and Reality," conference paper for the 2nd European Conference on Corporate Governance: Can Europe Build on its Diversity to Develop the Corporate Governance System of the Future, Brussels, November 27-29, 2002.

Svejnar J. (2001). "Transition Economies: Performance and Challenges," William Davidson Working Paper No. 415, http://eres.bus.umich.edu/docs/workpap-dav/wp415.pdf.

Tricker R. I. (2000b) "Editorial: Corporate Governance: the Subject Whose Time Has Come," *Corporate Governance: An International Review*, Vol. 8, No. 4, pp. 289-298.

Weil, Gotshal, and Manages LLP (2002) "Final Report and Annexes IIII: Comparative Study of Corporate Governance Codes Relevant to the European Union and Its Members States."

Dobre praktyki w spółkach publicznych w 2002 [Best practices in public companies 2002].

Dobre praktyki w spółkach publicznych w 2005 [Best practices in public companies 2005]. http://www.gpw.pl/gpw.asp?cel=spolki&k=7&i=/spolkigieldowe/corporate/lad&sky=1 &sky=1, visited 14.08.2007.

Chapter 6

Corporate Governance and Corporate Social Responsibility of Public Listed Companies in Malaysia[1]

Roshima Said, Hasnah Haron, Yuserrie Hj Zainuddin,
Daing Nasir Ibrahim and Saiful

Abstract

In 2004, the government has launched the National Integrity Plan (NIP) which is aimed at promoting an accountable and corrupt-free society. Under the National Integrity Plan one of the problems affecting integrity of the private sector is corruption. Therefore it is very important that good management practices be adopted. To achieve this, there should be a proper monitoring and enforcement of these practices. Realising the seriousness of this issue, in the 2007 budget speech, the Prime Minister has stressed the importance of Corporate Social Responsibility Reporting. This task requires companies to disclose their Corporate Social Responsibility activities in the annual report. In the context of the private sector, NIP has identified that enhancing corporate governance and business ethics will ensure that stakeholders' interest will be looked after and at the same time good ethical companies will contribute to a higher quality of life of the community.

This study therefore examines whether good corporate governance have a positive influence on the level of Corporate Social Responsibility in Malaysian Public Listed Companies. Annual reports of 100, 2005 Malaysian Public Listed Companies were examined. It was found that the level of CSR and the corporate governance index was 8.8% and 57.24% respectively, which can be considered to be at a low level. Human Resource theme has the highest number of disclosure, followed by community, product, environment and energy. The study found that better corporate governance will lead to a higher corporate social responsibility.

---

[1] The chapter is from research funded Institute Integrity Malaysia and Malaysian Accountancy Research Education Foundation (IIM-MAREF)

Introduction

The Honourable Dato' Seri Najib Tun Razak, Deputy Prime Minister of Malaysia in his keynote speech at the Corporate Social Responsibility (CSR) Conference held on 21 June 2004 had expressed his belief that CSR is able to help improve financial performance, enhance brand image and increases the ability to attract and retain the best workplace. This will eventually contribute to the market value of the company.

Prior to the above statement made by the Deputy Prime Minister, earlier on 23 April 2004, the Malaysian Prime Minister, Datuk Seri Abdullah Ahmad Badawi had announced the National Integrity Plan or known in Bahasa Malaysia as "Pelan Integriti Nasional" (PIN). The 152 pages document is a comprehensive blueprint that entails the long-term strategy to be introduced which is aimed at promoting an accountable and corrupt-free society. Under the National Integrity Plan one of the problems affecting integrity of the private sector is corruption. Generally, the private sector is the "giver" while public officials were the "receivers". Both of these activities are termed corruption. Therefore it is very important that good management practices be adopted. To achieve this, there should be a proper monitoring and enforcement of these practices. Realising the seriousness of this issue, more recently in the 2007 budget speech, the Malaysian Prime Minister has also stressed the importance of Corporate Social Responsibility Reporting. This task requires companies to disclose their Corporate Social Responsibility activities in the annual report.

In the context of the private sector, PIN has identified that enhancing corporate governance and business ethics are the priority target for the year 2008. Good corporate governance will assure that financiers get back their investments with maximum value added. At the same time good ethical companies will contribute to higher quality of life of the community. Therefore, the current investment trend is that investors will take into account the social, environmental, and ethical issues in investment selection process (Masley, 2000 as cited by Van De Velde, Vermeir & Corten, 2005) before any decision is made. The above contention is supported by Webley and More (2003) who found out that enterprises committed to ethical behavior performed better financially over the long term. This is in comparison with enterprises that are slacking in commitment. Many other studies have also supported the contention that investors value more highly risky companies if compared to the ones that are less exposed to social, environment and ethical risks.[2]

The Government's incentive to further promote corporate social responsibility (CSR) among public listed companies (PLC) is very encouraging. The honourable Dato' Seri Najib Tun Razak, Deputy Prime Minister of Malaysia, in his keynote speech at Corporate Social Responsibility Conference on 21 June 2004 had made it clear that CSR helps improve financial performance, enhance brand image and increases the ability to attract and retain the best workplace, contributing to the market value of the company. This statement is consistent with the study done by Csrnetworks (2006) which is one of UK's leading CSR consultancies showed that engaging in Corporate Social Responsibility will lead to better financial performance,

---

[2] http://www.domini.com/Social-Screening/Non-US-Operations/index.htm

access capital, reduced operating costs, enhanced brand image and reputation, increased sales and customer loyalty and increased productivity and quality.

The deliberation on the issue of Corporate Governance is further discussed by the Chairman of Bursa Malaysia Berhad, Tun Dzaiddin. In his keynote address, entitled "Corporate Governance - Sustaining the Momentum" at the Asian Corporate Governance Conference 2005 in Kuala Lumpur he acknowledged and heightened the awareness and appreciation for good corporate governance practices. To him it has evolved from prescribed practices to mandatory and obligatory practices. Many countries and companies have voluntarily adopted the frameworks and principles of corporate governance to remain relevant and competitive. What we all need to collectively do now is to keep this momentum going. In sustaining the momentum, according to him, he has advised to continuously focus on raising the standards of corporate governance, encourage shareholders' activism as an effective check and balance mechanism, and to publicize good corporate governance initiatives and success stories. As a final initiative in sustaining the momentum for corporate governance he has also encouraged companies and markets to publicize their corporate governance efforts to the domestic and international investors. In doing so, it will raise the profile of the company or market.

"In Malaysia, some companies have already done so through bagging awards for good and exemplary levels of corporate governance practices. Now, large companies are emphasizing on social and environmental initiatives on their websites and in their annual reports."

Corporate Social Responsibility (CSR) covers three key areas namely: environmental performance, economic performance and social performance. Environmental issues include the impact of production processes, products and services on air, land, biodiversity and human health. Economic performance, covers wages and benefits, productivity, job creation, outsourcing expenditures, Research and Development investments, and investments in training and other forms of human capital. Social performance includes traditional topics such as health and safety, employee satisfaction and corporate philanthropy, as well as more external topics such as labour and human rights, diversity of the workforce and supplier relations. CSR therefore focuses beyond financial (economic performance) as the bottom line figure. It also looks at how the company has performed in terms of its environmental and social performance. Hence, CSR essentially constitutes Triple Bottom Line.

Table 1: The Penetration of CSR Reporting in Asia

Country	% of CSR activities in the Top 50 Companies per Country
India	72%
South Korea	52%
Thailand	42%
Singapore	38%
Malaysia	32%
Philippines	30%
Indonesia	24%
Seven Country Mean	41%
UK	98%
Japan	96%

Source: Chamber, Moon and Sullivan (2003)

Chambers, Moon and Sullivan (2003) have investigated CSR reporting in seven countries. This is done through analysis of the websites of the top 50 companies in Asia. This study investigates the penetration of CSR reporting within countries; the extent of CSR reporting within companies and the waves of CSR engaged in. The findings in Chambers, Moon and Sullivan (2003) showed that, there are fewer CSR companies in the seven selected Asian countries as compared to UK and Japan companies. The mean for the seven countries studied, show a score of 41% which is under half the score for the UK (98%) and Japan companies (96%). From the above table, Malaysia showed fewer CSR companies as compared to Singapore, Thailand and South Korea.

Previous studies revealed that Corporate Social Disclosures in Malaysia is generally still low (Foo & Tan,1988; Nik Ahmad & Sulaiman, 2004; Too Shaw Warn, 2004; Ramasamy & Ting, 2004). Another study by Longo, Mura, and Bonoli (2005) has found that in most Italian small medium enterprises, there are concerns for social responsibility because of the ethical motivation of the top management of the companies. Top management of these companies have found that with social responsibility reporting, the market share and company's image will improve.

ACCA (2002) emphasized that among the driving forces for environmental reporting in Malaysia are the introduction of the *Malaysia Code on Corporate Governance* listing requirements, the National Annual Corporate Award (NACRA) and ACCA Award named as Malaysian Environmental Reporting Award (MERA), recently in year 2004 changed to Malaysian Environmental and Social Reporting Award (MESRA). These evidenced local encouragement and motivations for Malaysian companies to report environmental information. It can be seen that the introduction of Malaysia Code on Corporate Governance was one of the drivers for environmental reporting in Malaysia. Corporate governance is the process and structure that used to direct and manage the business and affairs of the company towards enhancing business prosperity and corporate accountability. Thus, this study will look into the governance structure that will enhance the extent of corporate social disclosure among public listed companies in Malaysia. The study also revealed that there is a positive relationship between corporate governance index (CGID) and

Corporate social responsibility disclosure (CSRD). Better corporate governance will lead to higher companies concern on corporate social responsibility.

Research Objectives

The main objective of this paper is to ascertain the relationship between the level of corporate governance index and corporate social responsibility disclosure of Malaysian PLCs for the year ended 2005. Other objectives of the study were to gauge the level of CGID (Corporate Governance Index) of Malaysian PLCs., to determine the level of CSRD of Malaysian PLCs. and to investigate the location of CSRD for the Malaysian Public Listed Companies for the year ended 2005.

Definition of Key Terms

Corporate governance

Corporate governance can be defined as a system by which corporations are directed and controlled (Toksal, 2004). In this study, corporate governance will be measured by an index comprising board matters (39 items), nomination matters (17 items), remuneration matters (29 items), audit matters (25 items), and communication (4 items). Those measurements are adopted from Standard and Poor's (2002) as well as based on part 1 and 2 of Malaysian Code of Corporate Governance.

1. **Board matters index disclosure** measures independence of board, disclosure of directors' detail such as previous employments, and educational qualification, CEO-chairman separation, frequency of board meeting, and attendance of board meeting.

2. **Nomination matters index disclosure** measure existence, independence and activities of nomination committee.

3. **Remuneration matters index disclosure** measures independence of remuneration committee, frequency and attendance of remuneration committee meeting, and disclosure of director remuneration.

4. **Audit matters index disclosure** measures independence of audit committee, frequency of audit committee meetings, attendance at audit committee meetings, and task of audit committee.

5. **Communication matters index disclosure** measures effectiveness of a company communication with shareholders, such as board committee and external auditor present in annual general meeting of shareholders and availability of company's annual report in web site.

Corporate Governance index disclosure (CGID) is an overall score of all the 5 dimensions mentioned above.

CSR

CSR comprised five themes. They are (1) community, (2) human resource (3) product (4) energy and (5) environment (Hackston & Milnes, 1996).

Corporate Social Responsibility Disclosure provides information to the public regarding companies' activities with community, environmental, its employees, its consumer and energy usage in the companies. CSRD are categorized as voluntary disclosures since it is not required by any financial disclosure, accounting standards, the Stock Exchange rules and regulations, and the Companies Act in Malaysia.

CSRD can be defined as the provision of financial and non-financial information relating to an organization's interaction with its physical and social environment, as stated in annual report or separate social reports (Hackston & Milne, 1996). Corporate Social Disclosure includes details of the physical environment, energy, human resource, products and community involvement matters.

According to Gray et al. (2001), social and environmental disclosure can be typically be thought of as comprising information relating to a corporation's activities, aspirations and public image with regard to environmental, employee, consumer issues, energy usage, equal opportunities, fair trade, corporate governance and the like. Social and environmental disclosure may also take place through different media such as annual report, advertising, focus group, employee councils, booklets, school education and so forth.

This study will follow the definition used by Hackston and Milne (1996), because it covers the five themes that can be found in company's annual report in Malaysia which were environment, human resource, energy, community involvement and products.

Themes of CSR

CSR provides information regarding a company's activities in relation to environment, energy, human resource, product, and community involvement. CSR disclosures include details of the physical environment, energy, human resources, products and community involvement matters (Hackston & Milne, 1996). They are as follows:

1.   Environment

The environment theme is disclosures that explain whether listed companies' corporate activities will have an impact on the environment. This include for example compliance with environmental laws, regulations and policies , availability of environmental Programs , protection of the environment, conservation of natural resources, e.g. recycling glass, metals, oil, water and paper etc.

2. Community

The community theme involves corporate social activities which are related to the society. This theme include disclosures such as donations of cash, products or employee services to support established community activities, community outreach programs, funding scholarship programs or activities, aiding disaster victims or medical research etc

3. Human Resources

The human resources theme includes information affecting the employee in raising the productivity of the companies. This include the existence of employee training & development programs, complying with health and safety standards and regulations, improvements to the general working conditions, conducting research to improve work safety etc.

4. Energy

This theme includes information on how companies generate their energy resources efficiently such as the need to conserve water, indirect materials or supplies, R&D on energy savings, train employees or stress on waste material recycling activities (papers, stationeries, direct materials, etc

5. Product

The product theme includes include statement or information whether companies' product meet safety standards, information on developments related to the company's products, research on product safety/quality, Verifiable information that the quality of the firm's product has increased (e.g. ISO 9000) etc.

The CSRD score or index was developed by adding all the items covering the five themes, which were Environment, Community, Human Resource, Energy and Product.

Literature Review

Corporate governance can be defined as a system by which corporations are directed and controlled (Toksal, 2004). The control mechanism of managers' behaviour can be divided into internal and external mechanism. The internal mechanisms refer to management-discipline instruments which include voting rights, firm provision on management liability, effectiveness of board of directors, and incentive based compensation. On the other hand, the external mechanisms refer to market-based control such as equity, product, and managers market. According to Tosksal (2004), BOD, audit committee, disclosure quality, legal system, takeover market, and product market are important elements of corporate governance mechanism.

The Bursa Malaysia CSR Framework defined Corporate Social Responsibility as open and transparent business practices that are based on ethical values and respect for the community, employees, the environment, shareholders and other stakeholders. This CSR framework was designed to deliver sustainable value to society at large. CSR supports Triple Bottom Line Reporting which emphasizes the economic, social and environmental bottom-line wellness.

Corporate Social Responsibility Disclosure provides information to the public regarding companies' activities with community, environmental, its employees, its consumer and energy usage in the companies. Corporate Social Disclosure are categorized as voluntary disclosures since it is not required by any financial disclosure regime, accounting standards, the Stock Exchange rules and regulations, and the Companies Act in Malaysia.

Corporate Social Disclosure can be defined as the provision of financial and non-financial information relating to an organization's interaction with its physical and social environment, as stated in annual report or separate social reports (Hackston and Milne, 1996). Corporate Social Disclosure includes details of the physical environment, energy, human resource, products and community involvement matters. CSR basically covers three key areas and they are environmental performance, economic performance and social performance. The environmental issues of CSR include the impact of production processes, products and services on air, land, biodiversity and human health. Economic performance reporting covers wages and benefits, productivity, job creation, outsourcing expenditures, R&D investments, and investments in training and other forms of human capital. Social performance include documenting of traditional topics such as health and safety, employee satisfaction and corporate philanthropy, as well as more external topics such as labour and human rights, diversity of the workforce and supplier relations. To be more specific, CSR provides information regarding a company's activities in relation to environment, energy, human resource, product, and community involvement. CSRD include details of the physical environment, energy, human resources, products and community involvement matters (Hackston & Milne, 1996). CSR can be defined as the provision of financial and non-financial information relating to an organization's interaction with its physical and social environment, as stated in corporate annual reports or separate social reports. (Guthrie & Matthews, 1985). In this we follow the definition by Hackston and Milne (1996), because it captures the areas that form the themes within CSRD which is applicable in Malaysia. CSR can be classified as: (1) environment, (2) human resource,(3) energy,(4) community involvement and (5) products. Ho (1990) showed that the most social responsibility disclosure related to community involvement, human resource, product improvement, energy and environment.

Foo and Tan (1988) found that corporate social reporting in Singapore companies is higher than Malaysian companies. Hackston and Milne (1996) tested the corporate social responsibility disclosure content of the 50 largest companies listed on the New Zealand Stock Exchange and found that most companies disclose information related to human resources, environment and community. They found that companies' positive CSR disclosure averaged about three quarters of an annual report page. Meanwhile, Deegan and Gordon (1996) also found that most companies disclose social responsibility information in qualitative form within the companies' chairman's report, managing director's report or equivalent.

Guthrie and Parker (1990) found that the maximum number of negative disclosure is 85 words or about five lines. Only 14 companies out of the entire sample did disclose any negative environmental disclosure. Further, the overall difference between the extent of positive and negative disclosures found that of the 71 firms that disclosed environmental information, 70 firms provide significantly more positive than negative information. The maximum level of environmental information is 1049 words or about two pages.

In their study in Australia, there does appear to be a significant increase in disclosure practices from 1988 to 1991. The increase in reporting was positively associated with the increase in environmental group membership (Lehmann, 1983 & 1992). Further, the highest levels of reporting seem to relate to the years where the mining, steel and oil industries were criticised by environmental groups. The disclosures were made as a reaction to these criticisms.

Guthrie and Parker (1990) found that 85% of US companies disclosed some form of corporate social information. Energy and product themes were also found to receive more attention in the US compared to other countries surveyed. This perhaps can be linked to regulations that require these disclosures. Meanwhile Vives (2006) found that human resource and working environment are more commonly disclosed compared to community involvement and environmental practice.

Nik Ahmad and Sulaiman (2004) examined the extent and type of voluntary environmental disclosures in the annual reports of Malaysian companies in selected industries. They also attempt to identify the factors, which motivated management to disclose environmental-related information in annual reports among 140 companies on the Main Board of the Kuala Lumpur Stock Exchange for the year ended 2000. The two sectors selected for the study were construction and industrial product. They used content analysis to analyze the environmental disclosures. The second part of their study involved a mail questionnaire survey on the companies in the sample. The questionnaires were answered by four distinct groups comprising the accountants and financial controllers, assistant managers/managers/general managers in accounting and finance, company secretaries and others. They found that only 27.54% of the annual reports examined contained some environmental disclosures while 72.46% did not have any environmental disclosures. They concluded that the level of current environmental reporting and disclosures in Malaysia appears to be low and restricted to very general, ad hoc statements on environmental matters.

Shaw Warn (2004), examined the significance of firm characteristics and management attributes on the level of social reporting of Malaysian listed companies and also investigated whether the types of industry sector have an influence on the categories of social reporting, such as environmental, energy, "human resource and management", products and customers", and community services. The study used content analysis to measure the corporate social disclosure. The contents of each annual report are compared to the items on the checklist. If items on the checklist can be found in the annual report, a score of "1" is given. If it is not found, then a "0" score will be given. Total scores derived from the checklist will be the "Disclosure Index". She used three types of reporting, comprising qualitative reporting, quantitativenon monetary item and quantitative-monetary item. Different type of reporting will be assigned different score ranging from zero to three. The sample consisted of 105 Malaysian public listed companies. The companies were categorised into primary, secondary and tertiary. Among the eight determinants that had been tested, only three independent variables were found to be significantly associated with level of social reporting, size of the corporations, directors' serving non-profit organizations and frequency of board meeting. Industry sector had no significant influence on the overall level of CSR but it affected the categories of CSR. Overall, this study found that corporate social reporting in Malaysia is at a very low level, with a mean Disclosure Index of 0.03 out of 1.00.

Eng and Mak (2003) examined the impact of ownership structure and board composition on voluntary disclosure. Specifically, this paper examined the association between ownership, board composition and voluntary disclosure. Ownership structure is characterized by managerial ownership, block holder ownership and government ownership, and board composition is measured by the percentage of the independent directors. Voluntary disclosure is proxies by an aggregated disclosure score of non- mandatory strategic, non-financial and financial information by developing a disclosure index. The sample for this study included both financial and non-financial firms that listed on the Stock Exchange of Singapore (SES) as at the end of 1995. Based on a sample of 158 Singapore listed firms, they found that lower managerial ownership and significant government ownership are associated with increased voluntary disclosure. Total block holder ownership is not related to disclosure. An increase in outside directors reduces voluntary disclosure. They also found that larger firms and firms with low debt have greater disclosure.

Bhimani and Soonawalla (2005) argued that corporate governance guidelines are now more than simply optional and voluntary reporting measures for companies. Corporate Social Reporting debates show similar progression toward standardized reporting and it is likely that corporate performance reporting underpinning stakeholder value creation will move in this direction. The argument presented here is that corporate conformance and corporate performance are linked as they are essentially different ends of the same continuum (continuous) rather than dimensions operating on independent organizational planes. Recognizing this, will allow companies reporting, whether mandatory or voluntary, to adopt a more comprehensive and integrated approach in considering disclosure issues as part of corporate responsibilities. It has long been recognized that analyzing association between economic performance, environmental performance, and disclosure produces mixed results unless management strategy and governance structure is also assessed in terms of its effects on such associations.

Coffey and Wang (1998) analyze the board diversity and managerial control as predictors of corporate social performance. In their study, they used corporate philanthropy (charitable contributions as reported by Council on Economies Priorities and was measured as a percentage of pre-tax earnings) as a measurement for corporate social performance, and board composition (age of board members, number of years served and size of the board), board diversity (% of insiders on the board and % of women on the board) and managerial control (% of total stock owned by inside board members and ratio of stock owned by outside to inside board members). They found that the ratio of insiders to outsiders on the board (measurement for board diversity) was positively related to charitable to charitable contributions and the percentage of stock owned by insiders (measurement for managerial control) is positively related to charitable giving.

Haniffa and Cooke (2005) has examined whether the extent of Corporate Social Disclosure in the annual reports of Malaysian listed companies changes over time and whether there is an association with three groups of variables: culture, corporate governance and firm specific. Content analysis is used to examine the extent of Corporate Social Disclosure and they found two cultural, three corporate governance practices and four of the control variables to be significant determinants that help explain variability incorporate Social Disclosure practice of Malaysian companies in both years of 1996 and 2002. They also found that, there is a significant relationship between executive directors and chair with multiple directorships with Corporate Social Disclosure indicates that those who are aware of the business environment make disclosure decisions for a purpose. Furthermore, they found a significant relationship between Corporate Social Disclosure and foreign shareholders indicates that Malaysian companies use Corporate Social Disclosure as a proactive legitimating strategy to obtain continued inflows of capital and to please ethical investors.

Mohd. Ghazali and Weetman (2006) delved to what extent ownership structure, board structure and industry competitiveness statistically significant in explaining the extent of voluntary disclosure in annual report of Malaysian companies included in 2001 Bursa Malaysia, subsequent to the Asian crisis. To explain the ownership structure, they used variables which were ownership concentration, number of shareholders, director ownership and government ownership. Three directorship variables were considered in this study which was the proportion of family members on the board, independent non-executive directors and independent chairman. A checklist of 53 items had been developed based on past studies, adjudication criteria developed by the KLSE for the KLSE Corporate awards. The mandatory items were excluded from the checklist. Additionally, they referred other recommended disclosures contained in the Samples annual Report prepared by the Malaysian Institute of Accountants and PriceWaterhouseCoopers in Malaysia. Expert opinions from investment analyst and a senior official from the KLSE were gathered to refine the list so that it will reflect voluntary items that were considered important for disclosure in a Malaysian corporate annual report. The regression analysis was used to analyze the data and the findings implied that director ownership and family domination on the board are strong determinants of voluntary disclosure, while government ownership, new governance initiatives and industry competitiveness are not significant in pointing companies towards grater transparency.

Theory underlying CSR

Moir (2001) argued that the analysis and explanation of corporate social responsibility can be based on three theories i.e. stakeholder, social contract, and legitimacy theories.

Stakeholder theory

Moir (2001) suggested that the stakeholder theory is the basic theory that can be used to explain those groups to whom the firm should be responsible. The theoretical thrust underpinning the research on Corporate Social Responsibility in Malaysian companies needs to be situated within the stakeholder theory. Three main reasons support this point of contention. First, the stakeholder theory is based on the "stakeholder" conception, rather than the "stockholder" conception, supports the notion of companies' responsibility towards societies, and particularly, the dynamic thrusts of CSR activities, which are punctuated within the web of dynamic relationships between companies and the stakeholders. Second, as the stakeholder theory offers a relatively new conception of the nature of a corporation (i.e. a stakeholder corporation vs. a stockholder corporation) from corporate governance point of view, this research provides an opportunity for the advancement of new findings through the relationship between Corporate Governance and Corporate Social Responsibility. Third, the nature of business organisations today is very much intertwined within the social-economic-web of networks

Social contract theory

Moir (2001) argued that corporate social responsibility is a part of how society implicitly expects business to operate. Donaldson and Dunfee (1999) developed an integrated social contract theory as a way for managers to take decision in ethical context. They classified social contract as macro-social and micro-social. A macro-social contract in the context of communities, for example, will be an expectation that business provide some support for local community and the specific form of involvement would be the micro-social contract.

Legitimacy theory

Legitimacy theory suggests that organizations disclose information as a means of establishing or protecting the legitimacy of the organization in that they may influence public opinion (Hackston & Milne, 1996). Suchman (1995) identified three legitimacy organizations i.e. pragmatic, cognitive, and moral. He also identified three key challenges of legitimacy management; those are gaining, maintaining, and repairing legitimacy. Hogner (1982) supported legitimacy theory based on the result of his study on disclosure of information by American companies.

Theoretical Framework

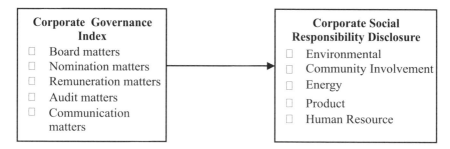

Figure 1: Conceptualisation of the relationships between corporate governance and Corporate Social Responsibility Disclosure

Hypotheses Development

CG Disclosure and Corporate Social Responsibility
The stakeholder theory states that the governance of the company will be responsible to look after the best interest of the stakeholders. Thus proper governance that is in place will lead to a more socially responsible company. Hanifa and Cook (2005) found that chairs with multiple directorships is positively significant related to CSR. Their study also showed that the proportion of independent non executive-directors have a negative and significant influence on CSR. The more the companies conform to the best practices of corporate governance, the better will of independent non executive-directors negatively significant influence CSR. Bhimani and Soonawalla (2005) have shown that corporate conformance and corporate performance are linked. The more the companies conform to the best practices of corporate governance, the better the disclosure of their corporate responsibilities. Prior to the above, Coffey and Wang (1998) found that the ratio of insiders to outsiders on the board was positively related to charitable contributions and the percentage of stock owned by insiders is positively related to charitable giving. Based on the literature, the study hypothesises that,

H1:   There is a positive relationship between CGID and the level of CSR
H1a: There is a positive relationship between board matters index disclosure and the level of CSR
H1b: There is a positive relationship between nomination matters index disclosure and the level of CSR
H1c: There is a positive relationship between remuneration matters index disclosure the level of CSR
H1d: There is a positive relationship between audit matters index disclosure and the level of CSR
H1e: There is a positive relationship between communication matters index disclosure and the level of CSR

Sample

The samples for this study comprises of Malaysian companies that are listed on the main board of Bursa Malaysia. Only 6 industries (construction, consumer product, industrial product, plantation, properties, trading and services) were selected as they had the largest number of companies. Finance industry was omitted. Total of the 6 industries is 360. Stratified proportionate random sampling technique was used.

Table 2: Sample of Companies

Industry	Number of companies	Companies selected
Construction	35	20
Consumer product	90	27
Industrial product	156	52
Plantation	44	21
Properties	106	33
Trading and services	143	47
Total	**574**	**200**

Based on Roscoe's rule, it is ideal that for every item investigated, 10 sample sizes are needed. 5 items for CGID and 1 item for CSRD, 50 samples are needed for the study. Annual reports for 100 PLCs as at 2005 were examined to measure the CGID and CSRD. Both variables use a checklist to measure the level of disclosure.

Measurement of variables

Dependent Variable

Level of CSRD

The study used the five themes to measure the Corporate Social Disclosure from various locations in annual report such as Chairman /CEO Statement, Notes to the Account, Corporate Governance Statement, Director's Report, Calendar Events, Corporate Achievements, CSR Stand Alone Report and Internal Control Statement.
The numbers of items used in the checklist are as shown in Table 3 below:

Table 3: The five themes of CSR

Themes	Total Items
Environment	20
Community	13
Human Resource	36
Energy	15
Product	16
Total Items for five themes	**100**

The CSRD was developed by adding all the items covering the five themes, which were Environment, Community, Human Resource, Energy and Product.

This CSRD was developed by using the dichotomous, which the scores of "1", if the company disclose the items and "0", if it is not.

The process will add all the scores and equally weighted. The scores will be calculated as follows:

$$CSRD\,j = \frac{\sum t = 1 \; Xi\,j}{nj}$$

Where:

  CSRD j= Corporate Social Responsibility Disclosure Index
  nj= Number of items expected for the company nj≤100
  Xij = of "1", if the company disclose the items and "0", if it is not disclosed

Level of CSRD Percentage

The score for each theme is computed by the number of items reported under that theme and divided by the total number of items for all themes. The total number of items for the five themes totalled 911. Items for human resource, community, product, environment and energy totalled 484, 153, 135, 104 and 35 respectively.

Independent variable

Corporate Governance

The measurement of this index is based on the criteria of Standard and Poor's Index for Malaysia and part 1 and part 2 of Malaysian Code of Corporate Governance (MCCG). 114 items were decided as the potential scores for corporate governance index.

In this study, corporate governance will be measured by an index consisting of: (1) board matters (2) nomination matters (3) remuneration matters (4) audit matters and (5) communication. This measurement was adopted from Standard and Poor's (2002) and was adapted based on part 1 and 2 of Malaysian Code of Corporate Governance.

1 point will be given for each of 114 items that disclosed by company's annual report. Corporate governance index Disclosure (CGID) will be calculated as follows:

$$CGID_{it} \quad = \quad (\sum_{i=1}^{n} GID_{it})/PI$$

where:

  $CGID_{it}$: corporate governance index for company i at period t
  GID_{it} : corporate governance items disclosed by company i at period t
  PI : potential items should be disclosed by the company i

Table 4: CG Dimensions

Dimensions	Items
1. Board matters index	39 items
2. Nomination matters index	17 items
3. Remuneration matters index	29 items
4. Audit matters index	25 items
5. Communication matters index	4 items

Result

Descriptive statistics of Corporate Social Responsibility Disclosures (CSRD)

CSRD Themes
Descriptive statistics on CSRD was performed on the 100 sample. Results are as follows.

Table 5: Descriptive statistics of CSRD themes

	N=100 Companies			
Themes	Minimum	Maximum	Mean	Std. Deviation
CSR	.00	.41	.0887	.07901
Environment	.00	.70	.0520	.13650
Community	.00	.69	.1177	.19171
Human Resource	.00	.56	.1344	.08887
Energy	.00	.40	.0233	.06987
Product	.00	.63	.0844	.12257

As shown in Table 5, Human Resource theme has the highest number of disclosure for 100 companies. This is contributed by the information on existence of employee training and development programs, provision or benefits of Employee Share option Scheme (ESOS) and information on staff cost. The result is consistent with the study done by Manaseh (2004) and Tan (2006). The community theme is ranked second for the number of disclosures for 100 companies. This is contributed by the information on the availability of community outreach programs, donations of cash, products or employee services to support established community activities, events, organizations and education.

Table 6: Level of Percentage of Disclosures by Themes

Theme	No. of Items	Percentage	Rank
Human Resource	484	53.13	1
Community	153	16.79	2
Product	135	14.82	3
Environment	104	11.42	4
Energy	35	3.84	5
Total	911	100%	

Level of percentage of disclosure of the various themes is as shown in Table 6;

Human Resource has the highest disclosure and Energy the lowest disclosure.

Location of CSRD

Table 7 - Location of CSRD for 100 Companies

LOCATION/THEMES	Environment	Community	HR	Energy	Product	Total
Chairman /CEO Statement	42	84	63	10	91	290
Notes to the Account	0	2	323	1	3	329
Corporate Governance Statement	0	2	15	0	0	17
Director's Report	0	0	42	0	0	42
Calendar Events	10	62	21	4	11	108
Corporate Achievements	13	9	24	5	23	74
CSR Stand Alone Report	46	45	36	6	10	143
Internal Control Statement	3	2	18	0	25	48

Table 7 showed that the highest disclosures were found in the notes to the account. This is followed by Chairman/CEO Statement and then the CSR stand alone report. CSR stand alone report can be found in a separate section in the annual report. Although most of the disclosures are in the notes to the accounts, but it is predominantly the Human Resource theme that are disclosed there. The second most popular location that the companies explained their CSRA is in the stand alone report. All the 5 themes of CSRA can be found there. Community themes are mostly found in the Chairman/ CEO statement.

Descriptive Statistics of Corporate Governance Index Disclosure (CGID)

Descriptive statistics on the 5 themes and CGID were performed. As can be seen from Table 8, the two dimensions of CGID that had the highest mean are Communications and audit matters.

CGID Dimensions

Descriptive statistics on the 5 themes and CGID were performed. This study investigated the level of CGID of Malaysian public listed companies. As shown in Table 8, this study found that corporate governance index for 100 Malaysian public listed companies vary range from 45.83% to 89.75%, with the overall CGID of 57.24%. In context of individual dimension of corporate governance index, communications ranked the highest followed by audit matters.

In context of individual dimension of CGID, communications matters index ranked the highest followed by audit matters index. There is not much dispersion in the results with highest dispersion in nomination matters index. Results should therefore be interpreted with caution. Communication matters index range is between 50% and 100% with mean of 90% and standard deviation 16%, reflecting that most of Malaysian PLCs have good relationship with investors. Audit committee matters index also is in good condition, where the range is between 62 and 92% with a mean 87% and standard deviation 8%. It means that most of Malaysian PLCs have followed part 1 and 2 of the MCCG rule on audit committee. Related to board matters index, nomination matters index, and remuneration matters, index, we concluded some Malaysian PLC's have given more attention and some Malaysian PLC's are not concerned on the issues. There is a wide variation between minimum and maximum index disclosure as shown by the standard deviation.

Table 8 - Descriptive Statistics of Corporate Governance Index Disclosure (CGID) and CGID Dimensions

Dimensions	100 sample				
	Minimum	Maximum	Mean	Std dev	Rank
Communications index	.50	1.00	.8975	.15527	1
Audit matters index	.68	.92	.8704	.07694	2
Board Matters index	.33	.82	.5277	.08771	3
Nomination Matters index	.00	.88	.4712	.21714	4
Remuneration matters index	.07	.83	.4583	.15005	5
CGID (114 items)	.13	.82	.5724	.11239	

The Relationship between CGID and CSRD

H1:   There is a positive relationship between CGID and the level of CSRD.
        H1 was conducted for the 100 sample size. The tests were run at once, as there is enough sample size.

CGID and CSRD

H1:   There is a positive relationship between CGID and the level of CSRD.
H1a: There is a positive relationship between board matters index and the level of CSRD
H1b: There is a positive relationship between nomination matters index and the level of CSRD
H1c: There is a positive relationship between remuneration matters index and the level of CSRD
H1d: There is a positive relationship between audit matters index and the level of CSRD
H1e: There is a positive relationship between communication matters index and the level of CSRD

Table 9 - Regression results of the 5 dimensions of CGID and CSRD

Independent Variables	N=100 Companies					
			CSRD			
	CGID		Model 1 (all dimensions run at once)		Model 2 (two dimensions – Board matters and nomination matters)	
CGID (Overall)	0.143	1.790*	-		-	
Board matters			-0.104	-1.510	-0.131	-1.445
Nomination Matters			-0.101	-1.855*	-0.066	-1.786*
Remuneration Matters			0.071	0.873	Not applicable	
Audit Matters			-0.135	-0.921	Not applicable	
Communication			0.008	0.150	Not applicable	
R- Square	0.032		0.080		0.067	
F-Stat	3.205		1.618		3.464	
Prob. F-Stat	0.077		0.163		0.035	
DW	1.912		1.852		1.805	

*sig at 10% Level, ** Sig at 5% Level *** sig at 1% level

CG1D was found to be significantly related to CSRD. Therefore, H1 is accepted. However, the model was only able to explain 3.2% of the variance in CSRD.

However, when all dimensions were run all at once to test for H1a to H1e, the model was not significant. Several tests were done on combinations of CGID dimensions until a significant model was found. The final significant model (represented by Model 2, in Table 9) was determined and it comprise of two dimensions of CGID (Board matters index and Nomination matters index). It was found that only nomination matters index have an influence on the CSRD. This means to say that companies that have an active and independent nomination committee will tend to also report a higher level of CSR. The explanatory power of the model is only 6.7%, which is very low.

Discussion and Conclusion

Recapitulation of the Findings of the Study

The study was undertaken using both the secondary and primary data. CSR was measured both using secondary (CSRD) data and CGID was measured using the secondary data from annual reports. The two "main research questions" of the study were answered using secondary data of CSR (CSRD) and CGID.

Main Research Questions
What is the relationship between the level of CGID and level of CSRD of

Malaysian PLCs?

The findings from the 100 sample size showed that even though CGID has indicated a significant and positive influence on CSRD, the model was only able to explain 3.2% of the variance of CSRD. It was also found that when all the dimensions of CGID were run all in one go, the results exhibit that the model was not significant. On the other hand when the stepwise regression was applied, it was found that the model of CGID to CSRD was only significant when only the Board and Nomination matters were considered. Results from the test also indicated a positive and significant influence of nomination matters on CSRD. However, the model was only able to explain 6.7% of the variance of CGID.

Other Research Questions

What is the level of CGID of Malaysian PLCs?

CGID (Corporate Governance Index Disclosure) used in the study refers to the 114 items adapted from Standards and Poors (2002) and part 1 of the MCCG. It comprises 5 dimensions or matters:

1. Board matters index relates to whether the companies have an independent and active board and whether the company disclose the BOD's detail of previous employments, and educational qualification and whether the companies have a separation of CEO and chairman.

2. Nomination matters index relates to whether the company has an independent and active nomination committee.

3. Remuneration matters index relates to whether the company has an independent and active remuneration committee. The index also sees as to whether the remuneration of BODs members is disclosed.

4. Audit matters index relates to the company having an independent and active audit committee and the tasks of the audit committee is disclosed appropriately in the annual report.

5. Communication matters index relates to whether the company has an effective communication with its shareholders. One of the ways of measurement of effective communication is as whether the company has its annual report on its website.

As can be seen in Table 8, based on the 100 companies' annual reports, the overall level of CGID is 57.24%. The level of disclosure for each of the matter is 89.75% for communications matters, 87.04% for audit matters, 52.77% for Board matters, 47.12% for Nomination matters and 45.83% for Remuneration matters.

What is the level of CSRD of Malaysian PLCs?

From Table 5, it can be seen that the level of CSRD for 100 Malaysian PLCs is very low with only 8.8%. Human Resource theme has the highest number of disclosure, followed by community, product, environment and energy. As shown in Table 6, the level of percentage of disclosure by themes are 53.13% for human resources, 16.79% for community, 14.82% for product, 11.42% for environment and 3.84% for energy. These results are consistent with the study done by Manaseh (2004) and Tan (2006). From Table 9, the level of CSRD of 30 Malaysian PLCs is 15.50% which although still on the low side is much higher that CSRD for the 100 companies (8.8%).

Where are the CSR normally disclosed in annual reports of PLCs?

As can be seen in Table 7, the highest CSRA were disclosed in the notes to the account. This is followed by Chairman/CEO Statement and then the CSR stand alone report. CSR stand alone report can be found in a separate section in the annual report. Although most of the disclosures are in the notes to the accounts, but it is predominantly and bias towards human resource theme. The second most popular location where the companies explain their CSRA is in the stand alone report. All the 5 themes of CSRA can be found there. Community themes are mostly found in the Chairman/ CEO statement.

Summary of Hypotheses

H1: There is a positive relationship between CGID and the level of CSRD	Accepted
H1a: There is a positive relationship between board matters index and the level of CSRD	Rejected
H1b: There is a positive relationship between nomination matters index and the level of CSRD	Accepted
H1c: There is a positive relationship between remuneration matters index and the level of CSRD	Not applicable
H1d: There is a positive relationship between audit matters index and the level of CSRD	Not applicable
H1e: There is a positive relationship between communication matters index and the level of CSRD	Not applicable

The level of CSRD for 100 Malaysian PLCs is very low with level of disclosure of 8.8%. Human Resource theme has the highest number of disclosure, followed by Community, Product, Environment and Energy. The level of percentage of disclosure by themes are 53.13% for Human Resource, 16.79% for Community, 14.82% for Product, 11.42% for Environment and 3.84% for Energy. The result is consistent with the study done by Manaseh (2004) and Tan (2006). The low level of energy theme being disclosed is consistent with the study conducted by Nik Ahmad and Sulaiman (2004).

CGID

CGID for 100 Malaysian public listed companies vary 45.83% to 89.75%. The overall CGID is at 57.24%. With respect to the individual dimensions of corporate governance index, communications matters index was found to rank the highest followed by audit matters index. There is not much dispersion in the results with highest dispersion found only in nomination matters. Results should therefore be interpreted with caution.

Communication matters index range between 50% and 100% with an average mean of 90% and a standard deviation of 16%. This reflects that most of Malaysian public listed companies do communicate effectively with their shareholders. Audit matters index range between 68% and 92% with an average mean of 87% and a standard deviation of 8%. Related to board matters index, nomination matters index, and remuneration matters index, it can be concluded that some Malaysian PLC's have given more attention to the matters compared to some others as there is a wide standard deviation on these indices.

Studies from Standard and Poors and CGFRC (2004) showed that the CGID for the 50 largest capitalizations of Malaysian PLCs is between 36% to 82% with a mean of 57% and standard deviation 10%. Since, there is no profound differences between the result in maximum and mean index between this study and previous studies, it can be concluded that there is no improvement in CGID of Malaysian PLCs for the period during 2002 to 2005. The minimum index of this study was also found to be lower than the previous studies. This could be because of the different sample sizes used in this study as compared to the previous studies. It can be concluded that there is room for Malaysian PLCs to improve their CGID.

This study also revealed that there is a positive relationship between CGID and CSRD. Better corporate governance will lead to higher companies concern on corporate social responsibility. The result of this study supported the previous studies on the positive relationship between corporate governance characteristics and voluntary disclosure and corporate social disclosure (see Arifin, 2002; Haniffa & Cooke, 2002, 2005; Eng & Mak, 2003; Lian Kee, 2003).

Implications of the study

The level of CGID in Malaysian PLCs is still at a very low level. The average level of CGID of Malaysian PLCs is 57.24%. Malaysian PLCs place importance to effective communication with shareholders and having an effective audit committee. Level of CGID pertaining to communication matters and audit matters is 90% and 87% respectively. The minimum level of CGID in Malaysa is lower if compared to previous studies. Governments need to take actions to improve the CGID of Malaysian PLCs.

There is a positive relationship between CGID and CSRD. Therefore, by improving the CGID of any Malaysian PLCs would lead to an increase in the CSRA. Thus, this would exhibit that the Malaysian PLCs is more socially responsible.

This study has proven that the stake holder's theory can be used to relate CG to CSRD. The study has also proven that CG is positively and significantly related to CSRD. Also the study has shown that BOD should not be encouraged to have unethical orientations as this would weakened the relationship of CG to CSR.

Suggestions for Future Research

The study has shown that annual reports are not the only means of disclosure. Hence, studying other forms of disclosure could possibly complement and add-value to any investigation on the nature and extent of CSR disclosure through annual reports in future.

While this research does not delve into the gap between performance and disclosure, it is obvious that future research on CSR disclosure should investigate on this situation further. Based on the limitations of the study, future researchers on similar topic are recommended to make improvement in certain area. First of all, there is a need to investigate the changes of corporate social disclosure and its relationship to corporate governance using the time series. A study of more than one year will be necessary to examine a trend or pattern of corporate social disclosure. The research approach could possibly utilize a qualitative research approach such as in-depth interviews, case studies, in combination with survey questionnaire.

Other than annual reports, there are other forms of communications that can be investigated together with annual report such as environmental reports submitted to Department of Environment, companies' websites, newspapers, magazines etc.

The future researcher may add more sample size in order to make a generalized and solid conclusion.

References

ACCA (2002). The State of Corporate Reporting in Malaysia. Malaysia, the Association of Chartered Certified Accountants, ACCA Malaysia Sdn. Bhd.

Arifin. (2001).The effect of firm's characteristics on the level of voluntary disclosure practices in the annual report of Indonesian companies listed in the Jakarta Stock Exchange. *Unpublished Ph.D Thesis Universiti Sains Malaysia.*

Bhimani, A. and Soonawalla, K. (2005). From conformance to performance : The corporate responsibilities continuum. *Journal of Accounting and Public Policy 24, 165-174*

Chambers, E, Moon, W.C.J. & Sullivan, M. (2003). CSR in Asia: A Seven Country Study   o f CSR Website Reporting. *Research Paper Series conducted at International Centre for Corporate Social Responsibility.* Retrieved July 18, 2006, from http://www.nottingham.ac.uk/business/ICCSR/pdf/ResearchPdfs/092003.PDF

Coffey, B.S. and Wang. (1998). Board Diversity and Managerial Control as Predictors of Corporate Social performance. *Journal of Business Ethics: Oct 1998, 17,14, 1595-1603*

Csrnetworks.(2006).The top ten benefits of engaging Corporate Social Responsibility. Retrieved March 19, 2006, from http://www.csrnetwork.com/downloads/OpinionWhyBother.pdf

Deegan, C & Gordon, B. (1996). A study of the environmental disclosure practices of Australian corporations. *Accounting and Business. 26*; 187-199

Eng,L.L. and Mak, Y. T. (2003). Corporate governance and voluntary disclosure. *Journal of Accounting and Public Policy,22 (4),* 325-345 .

Foo, S, L & Tan, M, S. (1988). A comparative study of corporate social reporting in Malaysia and Singapore. *Singapore Accountant, august,* 12-15.

Gray, R., Javad, M, Power, D. & Sinclair,D.(2001). Social and Environmental Disclosure and Corporate Characteristics: A Research Note and Extension. *Journal of Business & Accounting, 28(3) & (4)*

Guthrie, J & Mathews, M. R. (1985). Corporate social accounting in Australia;. *Research in Corporate Social Performance and Policy, 1; 251-277*

Guthrie, J. and Parker, L. (1990). Corporate social disclosure practice: A Comparative International Analysis. *Advances in Public Interest Accounting, 3, 159-176.*

Hackston, D & Milne, M. (1996). Some determinants of social and environmental disclosures in New Zealand Companies. *Accounting, Auditing and Accountability Journal,9*; 77-108

Haniffa, R.M and Cooke, T.E. (2002). Culture, Corporate Governance and Disclosure in Malaysian Corporations. *Abacus, 38(3),* 317-348

Haniffa, R.M.& Cooke, T.E. (2005). The Impact of Culture and Corporate Governance on Corporate Social Reporting. *Journal of Accounting and Public Policy, 24,* 391-430

Ho, S, K. (1990). Corporate social responsibility disclosure in Malaysia. *Akuantan Nasional, January;* 4-9.

Hogner. R, H. (1982). Corporate Social Reporting: Eight Decades of Development at U.S. Steel. *Research in Corporate Social Performance and Policy, 4*; 243-250.

Lehman, C (1983). *Stalemate in corporate social responsibility research.* American Accounting Association Public Interest Section, Working Paper.

Lehman, C. (1992), *Accounting's Changing Role in Social Conflict* (London: Paul Chapman).

Lian Kee, P. (2003). Factors affecting the variation in corporate voluntary disclosure level: Evidence from the annual reports of Malaysian companies. *Unpublished Ph.D Thesis Universiti Sains Malaysia.*

Longo, M., Mura, M & Bonoli, A. (2005). Corporate social responsibility and corporate performance; The case of Italian SMIs. *Corporate Governance: The International Journal of Effective Board Performance, 5*; 28-42.

Mohd. Ghazali, N.A. and Wheetman,P. (2006). Perpetuating traditional influences: Volntary disclosure in Malaysia following the economic crisis. *Journal of International Accounting, Auditing and Taxation, 15*, 226-248

Moir, L. (2001). What do we mean by corporate social responsibility? *Corporate Governance, 1*; 16-22

Nik Ahmad, N.N. and Sulaiman, M. (2004). Environmental Disclosures in Malaysian Annual Reports: A legitimacy perspective. *International Journal of Commerce & Management, Vol. 14 No. 1,* 44-58

Ramasamy, B & Ting H, W. (2004). A comparative analysis of corporate social responsibility awareness: Malaysia and Singapore firms. *The Journal of Corporate Citizenship, 13;* 109-123

S&P and CGFRC. (2004). Corporate governance disclosure in Malaysia. *Working paper of NUS Business School, National University of Singapore.* www.cgfrc.nus.edu.sg

Shaw Warn, T. (2004). Determinants of Corporate Social Reporting in Malaysia. *Unpublished Thesis Master of Science in Accounting.* Universiti Putra Malaysia

Suchman, M. C. (1995). Managing legitimacy: Strategic and institutional approaches. Academy of Management Review, 20(3), 571-610.

Toksal. M. A (2004). The Impact of Corporate Governance on Shareholder Value. *Doctoral dissertation of Universitat Zu Koln.*

Tun Dzaiddin, Chairman of Bursa Malaysia Berhad. Keynote address titled "Corporate Governance- Sustaining the Momentum" at the Asian Corporate Governance Conference 2005

Van De Velde; E., Vermeir; M & Corten, F. (2005). Finance and accounting: Corporate social responsibility and financial performance. *Corporate Governance, 5*; 129-138

Vives, A. (2006). Social and environmental responsibility in small and medium enterprises in Latin America. *The Journal of Corporate Citizenship, 21*, 39-50.

Webley, S and More, E. (2003). Does Business Ethics Pay? Ethics and Financial Performance. Institute of Business Ethics, London.

Chapter 7

Culture and Corporate Governance: The Turkish Case

Mustafa A. Aysan

Abstract

The concept of "Corporate Governance" is new for the Turkish business firms and managements. The reason for this late recognition in Turkey, was the delayed development of the competitive liberal economy, private initiative, private enterprise and managements.

The country had initiated economic development with state-owned enterprises (the SOE's) which were under the management of central government departments that had created a bureaucratic organization for managing and auditing the SOE's. In spite of a fairly liberal law for encouraging private industry and initiative (Law for the Encouragement of Industry of 1927), new private investments in industry were not many. With low economic growth rates, with an uneducated and untrained population, almost no capital accumulation, backward technology and a mainly agricultural economy, people did not have incentives for private investments. 1950 was marked with the first multi-party democratic elections changing political power to a political party with a pledge to transfer economic power from SOE's (better known in Turkey as the SEE's) to liberal markets and private enterprise. However, the new liberal governments increased the dominance of the SEE's in the economy over the two decades following 1950. During these decades, "Corporations", "holding companies", "public disclosures of financials", "capital markets", "stock exchanges", "financial intermediaries" etc., were not very well known by the under-developed Turkish Financial Markets.

High annual inflation rates of the 1970's (15 % in 1970 going up to 110 % in 1980 as measured by the CPI) and very high interest rates with annual rates on government bonds ranging from 15% in 1970 to 100 % in 1979) which worked against political and economic stability did not let private enterprise flourish. There were a few success stories of private initiative, but 98 % of all enterprises remained very small with less than 10 employees.

Corporate Governance can be defined as an approach of public responsibility to business management aimed at re-organizing the relationship of the society with the private corporate sector. This relationship had to be based on trust, ethical behavior, moral values and confidence created by the transparency of real financial results, accountable and responsible business managers and members of the Board of Directors of corporations.

Unfortunately, huge business scandals of the late 1990's, shocked the world financial markets of the developed countries, almost suddenly and wiped out the public trust in private enterprise and capitalism, built-up over the centuries. In Turkey where private enterprise was less developed, the emergence of the 2001 recession following a 35 year period of high inflation, resulted in the bankruptcies of 22 banks, a loss of some 50 billions of US Dollars, also resulted in a weakening of confidence which was barely developing form 1980 to 2000.

The Accounting profession also suffered from this loss of public trust, the undisputed base of the profession all over the World, The dissolving of Arthur Andersen in 2002, which was originally considered the "ethical conscience" of the profession, was also a blow to the assumed integrity, independence and ethical behavior of the accounting profession.

The concept of Corporate Governance developed recently was considered as a way to restore the public confidence and trust in private enterprise, tarnished by the corporate scandals of the last decade over the world.

In Turkey, following the enactment of the Capital Markets Law (1982) and the establishment of the Capital Markets Board (1983) a rapid improvement was reached at the degree of financial disclosure and the implementation of the international accounting standards. At the end of the first half of 2007, there were some 350 companies quoted at the Istanbul Stock Exchange (modernized in 1985) observing international accounting and financial reporting requirements. Capital Markets Board enlisted its first "Principles of Corporate Governance" in July 2003, based on a "comply or explain non-compliance" rule, for companies quoted at the ISE. These principles were heavily influenced by the OECD guidelines for Corporate Governance.

As the Turkish companies were mostly family firms dominated by founders and/or their immediate relatives, the owners and the managers were not yet used to the principles of Corporate Governance.

The purpose of this chapter is to investigate into the relationship of the Turkish Business Culture and the state of implementation of principles of Corporate Governance in quoted and non-quoted companies of Turkey. In addition, relationship of cultural characteristics of the Turkish Society will be investigated and analyzed for determining whether these characteristics were supporting or against the development of Corporate Governance implementations in quoted and non- quoted companies in Turkey.

Finally the chapter will try to develop some recommendations for improving the implementation of Corporate Governance principles in Turkish, private, government and municipal enterprises.

Introduction: Purpose, Scope and Methodology

The purpose of this chapter is to search for the basic characteristics of the intricate relationships between the Turkish Corporate Culture and the degree of implementing the principles of Corporate Governance in Turkish companies. The search will necessarily include the degree with which the Turkish private, government, municipal, quoted and non-quoted companies, have observed and implemented the concepts and principles of Corporate Governance. Also, the discussion will try to lead the reader to decide whether the Turkish Corporate Culture supported the creation and adoption of the concepts and principles of Corporate Governance in Turkey.

For achieving the objectives, the chapter will treat the issues and problems related to the topic in five sections.

The introductory first section will try to define the objectives, scope and the methodology utilized in the study. The objective of the chapter is established as, "studying the existing literature on corporate culture and specifically the Turkish Corporate Culture, to determine if the corporate culture is supporting the principles of corporate governance."

The second section will try to review the main cultural characteristics of Turkish Society, as indicated by previous research and social studies. This discussion of previous studies on the cultural characteristics of Turkish Society will necessarily end up with some speculations on the future directions of the intricate influences of cultural developments on company owners, managers, management systems, financial disclosures and transparency of business firms in Turkey. This section will also deal with the responsibilities of private business firms to the society and to the confidence of the society in business firms.

The third and the fourth sections will concentrate on a review of the Turkish corporate culture with the purpose of measuring the impact of the latter on the practices of the Turkish business firms related to their approaches to the management of their businesses.

The Fifth Section will summarize the definitions, objectives, principles and practices of corporate governance. This section had to depend heavily on the previous work on the definitions, concepts, principles and practices of corporate governance as they were developed following business scandals of the late 1990's. The model of corporate governance developed by the Turkish Capital Markets Board (TCMB) will also be summarized in this section.

Section Six will try to estimate some future developments in the economic and social environment in Turkey and the resulting changes on the future of corporate culture and practices of corporate governance in the Turkish business firms. This section will try to define the possibilities for reform in legal, social and economic areas recommendations.

Culture and its Expected Influence on the Practices of Corporate Governance

Culture, in a sociological context, is defined as "the concepts, habits, skills, arts,

---

[1] Webster's New World Dictionary, The World Publishing Company, New York, 1957.

Another definition of the term, lists the different demonstrations of culture in a sociological context:

- "The totality of socially transmitted behavior patterns, arts, beliefs, institutions, and all other products of human work and thought, from one generation to the next;
- Those patterns, traits and products considered as the expression of a particular period, class, community, or population: like Japanese culture; the culture of poverty, Turkish culture, etc.;
- Those patterns, traits and products considered with respect to a particular category, such as a field, subject or mode of expression: musical culture, oral culture, etc.;
- The predominating attitudes and behavior that characterize the functioning of a group or organization;
- Development of the intellect through training and education;
- Enlightenment resulting from such training and education".[2]

The American Heritage Dictionary gives the following refinement on "Corporate Culture".

"The application of the term "Culture" to the collective attitudes and behavior of corporations arose in business jargon during the late 1980's and early 1990's. From business usage, the term spread to popular use in newspapers and magazines. Some usage panelists object to it. But over 80 percent of panelists accept the sentence, "The new management style is a reversal of GE's traditional corporate culture, in which, virtually, everything the company does, is measured in some form and filed away somewhere". Ever since C.P. Snow wrote of the gap between "the two cultures" (the humanities and science) in the 1950's, the notion that culture can refer to smaller segments of society has seemed implicit. Its usage in the corporate world may also have been facilitated by increased awareness of the importance of genuine cultural differences in a global economy, as between Americans and the Japanese, that have a broad effect on business practices."

"Corporate Culture" in this chapter is used in the above meaning of the Heritage Dictionary.

For our purpose here, "culture" consists of four elements passed on from generation to generation by learning:

- Values, ideas about what in life is important;
- Norms, methods or sanctions of enforcing values;
- Institutions, structures of a society within which values and norms are transmitted;
- Artefacts, things or aspects of material culture derived from a culture's values and norms.

---

[2] American Heritage Dictionary of the English Language, Fourth Edition, Houghton Mifflin Co., 2006 (Google, www.dictionary. reference.com

Culture is used to mean the characteristics "the world view" (Concéption du Monde) of a certain society or a group within the society, like "civilized", "primitive" or "tribal" cultures.

The term "Corporate Culture" is used to define the sub-culture within the general characteristics of an overall culture. Corporate Culture, to be extensively used in this chapter, is aimed to mean "the distinct and defined social characteristics within the context of an organization or a workplace."

Assuming that the above definition is accepted, I should like to suggest that the following methodology be adopted: Assuming that organizational culture is difficult to define and change at short notice, we should concentrate on the practical consequences of the impact of social culture on the behavior of business firms.

According to this methodology, for changing the cultural characteristics of on organization, a plan for change must be made and carefully implemented in specific situations:

- Formulating a clear strategic vision for changing the values, norms and symbols must be made;
- Displaying the commitment of top management, including the managing partner(s) and the leaders;
- Changing behavior at the top, to form a model at the top willing to change;
- Selecting and socializing newcomers (employed with a mission for the planned change) and terminating the domination of the deviants, if any, who refuse to make the organizational change;
- Developing ethical and legal sensitivity, towards deviations from the plan;
- Repeating actions which represent firmness on the necessary follow-up and corrective actions required by the priorities of the action plan;
- Allowing for enough time for assimilation, with no hasty implementations, and patient and enduring insistence on firm steps over time.

Especially in a country like Turkey, where corporate culture is slow to accept the principles and practices of Corporate Governance, the above methodology for implementations in actual managerial situations seems to be a necessity. Prof. Gert Hofstede, who conducted the most comprehensive comparative research on the cultural characteristics of different countries, tried to measure the impact of societal culture on the values of people in the work place.[3]

Using a huge database on employee values accumulated by the International Business Machines (IBM), the giant computer company of the USA, Prof. Hofstede, tried to determine the cultural characteristics of different nations on specific dimensions:

---

[3] www.geert-hofstede.com/hofstede-turkey.shtml
Essential publications of Professor Hofstede are also listed at his web site:
"Culture's Consequences, Comparing Values, Behaviours, Institutions and Organizations Accross Nations" , Newbury Park, CA: Sage Publications; Second Edition, Febr.2003
"Cultures and Organisations: Software of the Mind: Intercultural Cooperation and Its Importance for Survival." New York, McGraw-Hill-2004.

1. ***Power Distance Index (PDI)***: PDI was used to indicate the extent to which the less powerful members of organizations (like the junior members of the family) accept and expect that power is distributed unequally. This measure assumed that a society's level of inequality was endorsed by the followers, as much as by the leaders. In this context higher power distance index meant more inequality and vice versa.

2. ***Individualism (IDV)***: IDV, was used to show whether individuals were loosely tied to each other, as opposed to collectivism, in which individuals were more integrated in groups. In individualistic societies, people were assumed to be self-centered and cared only for themselves and the members of their immediate families. Whereas in collectivist societies, people were integrated into strong, cohesive groups, families were larger (included uncles, aunts, parents, children) and very loyal to each other in the families.

3. ***Masculinity (MAS)***: The MAS index referred to the roles between the genders, whether groups were dominated and managed by men or women. Masculine (dominated) countries were more assertive and competitive; feminine (dominated) countries were deemed to be more caring and modest.

4. ***Uncertainty Avoidance Index (UAI)***: UAI, was used to refer, ultimately to man's search for truth. Some societies had more tolerance for uncertainty and ambiguity, while some societies felt more uncomfortable in unstructured situations. Uncertainty avoiding cultures tried to minimize the possibility of such situations by strict laws and rules, safety and security measures and on the philosophical and religious level by a belief in absolute truth. Members of uncertainty avoiding societies were more emotional and motivated by inner nervous energy. Uncertainty accepting cultures were more tolerant of opinions different from what they were used to; they tried to have as few rules as possible and on the philosophical and religious level they were relativist and allowed for many currents to flow side by side.

5. ***Long-term Orientation (LTO)***: This dimension was created in the Far East (Chinese) to refer to societies with long-term orientation dominated by values of thrift and perseverance. Societies with short-term orientation were deemed to be dominated by values of respect for tradition, fulfilling social obligations and protecting one's "face".[4]

---

[4] Far a more comprehensive discussion of Hofstede's cultural indices and their influences on accounting, financial reporting and corporate culture please refer to: "International Accounting and Multinational Enterprises, 4th edition." By: Lee H. Radebough and Sidney J. Gray. John Wiley and Sons, Inc. New York. Pp.73-84. "Culture, Social Values and counting-Simmental

The Characteristics of Turkish Culture in General and Their Impact on Turkish Corporate Culture

According to Hofstede Turkish Society was classified as follows:

- 60% of the working population believed that power was unequally distributed, i.e. had higher scores on the PDI, indicating that in Turkish Society, the majority of the working population believed that power was mostly unequally distributed. Juniors tended to accept the power of the seniors as granted, rather than disputing senior dominance.

- Turkish working population measured as low as 30% on the IDV index, meaning that members of the Turkish Society were mostly not individualistic; most of the members of the Turkish Society wished to be integrated into groups, i.e. more inclined to collectivist as opposed to individualistic behavior.

- The Turkish working population believed that the dominance of masculine values was 40%, as opposed to feminine values (60%) in the society. This meant that the Turkish society was less assertive and competitive and was more caring and modest.

- Members of the Turkish Society wanted to avoid uncertainty, mostly (80%). The risk appetites of the working population in Turkey were indeed, low.

- Long-term Orientation, the LTO, was not measured.

According to these evaluations, Turkish People were mostly inclined to:
- Accept the superior power of the persons high in hierarchy in organizations; they would be more inclined to obey the orders of the "boss". They would not tend to disobey the orders of the superiors; and less inclined to question their powers;
- Be unwilling to take initiative for new ventures by themselves; they tried to shy away from taking individualistic initiative, i.e. more reluctant to lead and more inclined to follow the leader. They would be more inclined to obey the norms of the group, rather than taking initiative for changing them;
- Be less assertive and competitive, and more modest and caring. And hence the Turkish society will be characterized by masculine dominance (superiority of the father over children, husband over wife and sons over daughters in families);
- To avoid uncertainty as much as possible with low risk appetites.

To summarize, the Turkish working population was fairly low (30%) on the individualistic attitudes (the lowest on this index was China) than citizens of the Anglo countries (82-85%) and hence less inclined to enter into new ventures by themselves. This characteristic of the Turkish people was in line with their high score on Uncertainty Avoidance, indicating their unwillingness to speculate with new ventures; 80% of them would avoid speculative decisions under uncertainty. One would expect Turkish people would measure high on the Power Distance Index, but they measured not very high on PDI (60%) meaning that they would be more tolerant to hierarchal powers of the superiors. However, Turkish working population scored Low (40%) on the masculinity index, meaning that they would be more conservative and had high inclinations for secrecy.

With the above characteristics, Turkish business was characterized by the abundance of small family companies (99% of business firms employed less than 250 persons and/or had annual sales below 20 million US dollars (25 million TRY). These family SME's did not have their financials open to public, about half of their employees were off-the records and did not have social security coverage. Most of these small firms were reluctant to join forces by mergers and acquisitions (M+A) and would manage their businesses like their families. Therefore, they would be less willing to organize their firms in accordance with the requirements of the Principles of Corporate Governance.[5] In many cases, cash-flows of the firm and the family; cash balances of the firm and the dominant share holder were difficult to separate from each other.

Implementation of the Principles of Corporate Governance was delayed to the last few years, because Turkey was dominated by State Owned Enterprises (the SOE's), better known in Turkey as the State Economic Enterprises (the SEE's). The SEE's were organized, managed and audited by the "state" as tools of the policy of "statism" of the Atatürk era, the period of 1920-1940.[6]

---

[5] For more information on the dominant structural characteristics of Turkish firms, the following publications in Turkish are available:

Aile İşletmeleri Kongresi, I ve II (Congress of Family Companies, I and II) Istanbul Kültür Üniversitesi, İstanbul 2004 and 2006. (Both publications include research papers on family companies) KOBİ'ler ve Verimlilik Kongresi, I ve II. (Congress of SME'S and Efficiency I and II) Istanbul Kültür Üniversitesi, İstanbul, 2004 ve 2006.

"Kurumsal Yönetim ve Risk", the Turkish text of the present author, Istanbul, 2007.

[6] For more information on the economic and social developments of this period, please refer to the following publications:

Morris Singer, "The Economic Advance of Turkey, 1938-1960, Turkish Economic Society, Ankara 1977. pp.77-175 "The Economy of Turkey", World Bank Mission Report, The Johns Hopkins Press, 1951.

Bernard Lewis, "Modern Türkiye'nin Doğuşu", Çeviri: Metin Kıratlı, Türk Tarih Kurumu, Ankara, 1970. "The Emergence of Modern Turkey, Oxford University Press, 1961.

"Türkiye'de Devlet İşletmeciliği" of the present author, İstanbul Üniversitesi İşletme Fakültesi, İstanbul, 1973. Second Paper of the Book is in English, "On Measuring Perfomance in Government Companies, The Turkish Experience. Pp.75-103

Although the SEE's were established mostly in the 1930's to be managed as "independent" organizations, by their "Board of Directors" and audited by a newly established government unit,[7] they were in reality managed by the bureaucrats of the ministries, "related" to the enterprises. They were larger firms with better strategic plans, policies and organizational structures and managed more rationally than private enterprises, but were dominated by civil servants of the central government departments and politicians forcing the SEE's into irrationalities at an increasing pace, starting with the introduction of the multi-party political system in 1946. All of the efforts for improving the governance of the SEE's were eliminated under political interferences overriding the managements. Through the years the SEE managements existing in 2007 were still under political influences and in serious need of implementing the principles of corporate governance.[8]

Following the disappointments and losses that investors of the developed markets had suffered in the late 1990's, the interests of the international investor turned to emerging markets, like Turkey. Turkey as one of the most promising financial emerging market economies attracted the interests and investments of international investors in a much larger scale than in previous years. Higher growth and increased profitability, attracted investors to the Turkish financial markets to push portfolio investments to Turkey from negative annual amounts until 2002 to about 7.4 billions USD by 2006.

Foreign direct investment (FDI) increased from 1,1 billion USD in 2002 to 20,0 billion USD in 2006.[9]

This shift in the interest of the global investors to Turkey, increased the demand for the implementation of the principles of corporate governance in the larger corporations of the country,[10] especially those quoted at the Istanbul Stock Exchange (the ISE). The initiative of the Capital Markets Board (the CMB) for publishing a set of "Principles of Corporate Governance" in July 2003, was a quick response to the demands of financial investors of international markets.

The above definitions of cultural developments indicate that "culture" is related to a society's accumulated knowledge, know-how and traditions at a certain time. In this context, the Turkish Culture can be characterized by the following special characteristics:

- Male dominance;
- Dominance of "The Father" and the elderly in the family;
- Strong ties to traditional values;
- High propensity to consume;

---

[7] The SEE Audit Board (Yüksek Denetleme Kurulu), established by Law in 1938.
[8] "OECD Guidelines on Corporate Governance of State- Owned Enterprises", TUSIAD - OECD joint publications. Also available at: www.oecd.org/dof/corporate affairs.
[9] "Yıllık Ekonomik Rapor-2007", T.C.Maliye Bakanlığı, Ankara 2007.p.146. Also available in English at http://www.sgb.gov.tr and the websites of the MOF, the Turkish Treasury and the Central Bank.
[10] "Corporate Governance in Turkey An Investor Perspective", The Institute of International Finance, Inc, TASK Force Report April 2005, Istanbul, www.iif.com

- Patient endurance under adversity;
- Respect for elders, in general;
- Female subservience;
- Mother-centered households;
- Son-birth adored;
- Etiquette is central;
- Leniency towards dates, time lines and punctuality;
- Companionship most important;
- Dominance of Islamic traditional values;
- Dominance of emotional (less national) traditional relationships among individuals as apposed to national and logical relationships on scientific evidence.

Professor Hofstede had classified Turkey within the "Near Eastern" group of countries with Arab Countries, Greece, Iran and Yugoslavia.[11] According to this classification referred to by Radebaugh and Gray,[12] Corporate Cultures of the Anglo-Saxon countries, were more receptive to professionalism (i.e. believe and rely on Judgments of professionally educated talent), more tolerant towards more room for flexibility in implementations. This type of culture was different from Less Developed Latin, Near Eastern and similar countries who are inclined towards more uniformity and stricter statutory controls.[13] According to these authors Turkish Corporate Culture should be inclined to accept more uniformity, more statutory controls and less tolerant to flexibility provided by professionalism. Also, peoples of the Near Eastern countries including Turkey, would be classified as more conservative, less transparent (i.e. more inclined for keeping the secrecy of financial information of companies), more inclined to pessimism (i.e. less optimistic).[14]
For a more comprehensive discussion on the influences social/cultural characteristics of societies on corporate culture and their impact on practices of financial transparency "Gray's model offers statistically significant explanatory power".[15] Using Gray's accounting values of Professionalism, Uniformity, Conservatism and Secrecy developed from Hofstede's cultural characteristics of Individualism, Uncertainty Avoidance, Power Distance and Masculinity,[16] Salter and Niswander try to link Culture, Societal Values and the Accounting Subculture.[17]

---

[11] Geert Hofstede, "Culture's Consequences: International Differences in Work-Related Values, Beverly Hills: Sage, 1980.p.336.
[12] Op.cit.p.72
[13] Op.cit.p.81
[14] Op.cit.p.82
[15] Stephen B. Salter and Frederick Niswander, "Cultural Influence On the Development of Accounting Systems Internationally: A Test of Gray's (1988) Theory". Journal of International Business Studies; Second Quarter 1995; 26,2; AB/ INFORM Global. Pg.379-397.
[16] Defined in the previous discussion.
[17] Op.cit.pg.383

Consequently, Salter and Niswander would expect Turkish accounting practices to be more conservative (less willing to change), more inclined to secrecy (less transparent), less receptive to professional judgment (more receptive to statutory controls), more demanding for uniformity (less flexible and less receptive to new ideas) according to their classification and interpretation of basic cultural characteristics of societies. These basic characteristics of the Turkish working population can be used to explain the reasons for the lack of less transparent business firms, fairly reluctant for implementing principles of corporate governance.[18]

In fact, following the financial scandals of the late 1990's[19] of ENRON, WorldCom, Global Crossing, Quest, Adelphia, Xerox, Tyco, etc., the integrity of the auditors and the interrelationships between the accounting profession and countries social values and cultural characteristics were almost the dominant topics of all conferences and discussions on the accounting profession.[20] Discussions were concentrated mostly on the social and institutional aspects of accounting and the responsibilities of auditors to the public and financial community over the world.[21] The discussion on social responsibilities of auditors, had already started in the 1980's.[22]

As the implementations of the principles of corporate governance depended heavily on the availability of timely and dependable financial information to the public at large, societies are demanding a public service from the profession, for which it is not well-equipped, yet.[23]

However, "A new era in corporate governance" is in full swing[24] following the "Enron Phenomenon".[25] Public disclosure of financial information will have to be extended to all companies, listed and unlisted, large or small, in all countries, for changing the economic and business environment to be more receptive to the implementations of corporate governance.

---

[18] Serdar Paksoy and Elvan Aziz, "Corpoarete Governance in Turkey", Discussion Paper, Paksoy and CO. İstanbul. Also available from e-mail; admin@Paksoy-Law.com

[19] "Accounting Education: What Can We Learn From Recent Corporate Scandals" W. Steve and Conan C. Albrecht, 2005 Discussion Paper.

[20] Samuel A. Piazza, Jr. and Robert G. Eccles, "Building Public Trust The Future of Public Reporting", John Wiley and Sons, NY, USA.2000.

[21] Jean-Guy Degos, "Is the Future of Accountancy Compatible with Accounting of the Future, University of Montesquieu, Bordeaux, 2007. www.igdegos.wandoo.fr.

[22] Antony G. Hopwood and Peter Miller, "Accounting As Social and Institutional Practice". Cambridge Studies in Management, 1994.

[23] Robert E. Litan and Peter J. Wilson, "The GAAP-Gap-Corporate Disclosure in the Internet Age." Brookings Institute, 2000 Washington DC.

[24] Robert F. Felton, "A New Era in Corporate Governance" Mc Kinsey and Co. Seattle, 2004.

[25] For more information on Enron, the following publications should be consulted:
Loren Fox, "ENRON The Rise and Fall", John Wiley and Sons, Inc.2003. New Jersey,USA.
Mimi Swanta with Sharon Watkins, "Power Failure, The Inside Story of the Collapse of Enron, Doubleday, Random House, Inc. 2003. NY. USA.

The Main Characteristics of Turkish Business Firms: The Turkish Corporate Culture

A recent OECD report[26] on corporate governance in Turkey, defined the characteristics of Turkish corporate culture as follows:

"The corporate governance landscape in Turkey is characterized by concentrated ownership, often in the form of family-controlled, financial industrial groups. Free floats are often low, pyramidal structures are common and there is a high degree of cross-ownership within some company groups. Controlling shareholders often play a leading role in the daily management and strategic direction of publicly held companies. An organized equity market is a relatively recent phenomenon, with the Istanbul Stock Exchange (ISE) being established only in 1985. From the mid 1980's until 3-4 years ago, economic conditions were difficult for companies. Thin markets, relatively few active institutional investors and an unpredictable macro-economic environment limited incentives for companies to adopt good corporate governance practices. More recently, however, the return of foreign investors, greater opportunities for Turkish Companies to do business abroad and increasing competition for foreign capital appear to be encouraging more companies to make good corporate governance practices a competitive advantage.

Upon the above background the CMB, has issued "Corporate Governance Principles" in July 2003 for companies quoted at the ISE, on a "comply or explain" basis. Although complete compliance is not mandatory, companies had to state reasons for non-compliance in the "Corporate Governance Compliance Report" section of the Annual Reports and reasons for non-compliance, in case they chose not to disclose.

It is widely expected that there will be rapid growth in Turkey in the coming decade for improving on the practice of corporate governance fueled by demands among companies for foreign financing to expand their businesses. Since debt and equity financing from international financial markets increased at a very fast rate in the last decade, Turkey and its institutions needed to improve the implementation of the principles of corporate governance as fast as possible. Foreign debt financing grew from 130 billion USD in 2002 to 208 billion USD in 2006. Foreign debt of private companies increased from 43 billion USD in 2002 to 120 billion USD in 2006.[27]

The following recent developments will support wider implementation and more disciplined and responsible treatment of serious and advanced principles of corporate governance:[28]

---

[26] From "Corporate Governance in Turkey- A Pilot Study" ISBN-92-64-02863-3, OECD, 2006. p.11

[27] Yıllık Ekonomik Rapor, 2007 of the Ministry of Finance, Ankara, 2007.

[28] Please note that Foreign Direct Investment to Turkey had grown from 1.1 billion USD in 2002 to 20 billion in 2006; Portfolio investments from -593 million USD to 7.4 billion USD in the same period.

- The authorities (the CMB, the Union of Chambers of Certified Public Accountants of Turkey the TURMOB, the Turkish Accounting Standards Board the TASB, the Ministry of Finance the MOF) have already adopted, or are introducing, high quality corporate governance, accounting auditing and financial reporting standards.
- Transparency and periodic availability of financial information of companies have improved significantly in recent years, in spite of some room for more improvement.
- A major revision of the Turkish Commercial Code (TCC) which is intended to bring significant accounting and auditing standards and improved disclosure rulings for all corporations in Turkey, is under discussion at the parliament, and is expected to be enacted in 2008.
- Widespread implementation of some important corporate governance principles had already started in companies listed at ISE, following the publications of the CMB principles as recently as in 2003.
- A recent study[29] indicated that most important corporate level factors when selecting emerging market companies in which to invest were, "Distinction between company and family interests", "Clearly defined governance arrangements", and "Accuracy of financial reporting".[30] The same study referred to the most important institutional factors as, "Enforceability of legal rights", "Quality of economic management" and "Independence of judiciary / quality of the legal system."
- The low ability of the Turkish Economy for attracting Foreign Direct Investment (FDI)[31] has improved considerably in recent years following the serious economic depression of 2001, which decreased the GNP by 9.4%.[32] However, the country's GNP increased by an average of 7.4% per year over the five years from 2002 to 2006. This period was also marked with the reduction of the annual rate of inflation (measured by the CPI) from 34.5% in 2002 to 9.7% at the end of 2006.
- PricewaterhouseCoopers survey of 2001 indicated Turkey to be one of the four countries in the world, with a minimum degree of transparency, a rather detrimental corporate characteristic apposing the implementation of the principles of corporate governance. The transparency situation has probably improved slightly in the last five years to the end of 2006.[33]

---

[29] Melsa Ararat & Mehmet Uğur, "Corporate Governance in Turkey: an overview and some policy recommendations, Corporate Governance, Vol.3 No: 1, 2003 pp. 57-75. ISSN 1472-0701. Istanbul.

[30] Melsa Ararat & Mehmet Uğur referred to the "McKinsey Emerging Market Investor Opinion Survey" of 2001 of the mentioned consulting company.

[31] Melsa Ararat & Mehmet Uğur, op. cit. p.62

[32] Turkish lira was devalued by 26% in Jan-Apr.2001. The Central Bank has stated that the economy had grown at an average annual growth of 7% from 2002 to 2006 with an average inflation of 13,4 % and a drop in the government bond interest rate from 70% to 22%, and USD price dropping from 1,7 YTL to 1,20 YTL in July 2007.

[33] Ararat & Uğur, op. cit.

The Corporate Governance Model Recommended by the CMB for Listed Companies in Turkey

The Corporate Governance Model, recommended for listed companies in Turkey on a "comply or explain reasons for non-compliance" basis, is similar to the OECD model represented by the Principles of Corporate Governance recommended for member countries. In fact the recommendations of the Turkish CMB were prepared in line with the OECD Principles[34] originally published in July 2003 and amended in Feb. 2005.[35] CMB Recommendations were grouped in 4 sections:
1. Facilitating the usage of share-holders rights;
2. Providing Public Disclosure and Transparency;
3. Protecting rights of other stakeholders;
4. Assuring the Implementation.[36]

The implementation of the recommended principles indicated to an increasing acceptance among the listed companies, the total number amounted to only 353 companies in the middle of 2007. The degree of acceptance of the large corporations (i.e. listed companies) started as early as Nov.2004, the date at which the "Survey of the CMB on the Degree of Implementation of the Recommended Principles of Corporate Governance" was carried out. The questionnaire of the survey was e-mailed to all of the 303 companies listed at the ISE on July 26, 2004, one year after the implementation of the principles. Answers of 248 companies were processed and findings were published.[37]

Findings indicated that practices were at the initial stage of compliance.

However, even if complete compliance was achieved, the majority of Turkish companies composed of SME's and family companies, would be left out of the scope of CMB recommendations.

The basic characteristics of the Turkish business culture summarized above combined with dearly needed improvements in the economic and legal social structure in the country had created a business community dominated by very small companies. In fact, the latest statistics on the size of companies in Turkey[38] indicated to an economy dominated by tiny companies.

---

[34] The Principles of Corporate Governance of the OECD were assumed, accepted and published by the Corporate Governance Association of Turkey in January 2005.

[35] The CMB Recommendations on Corporate Governance were approved at the July 4, 2003 meeting of the board and published.

[36] For more information on the interpretations and the degree of implenentation in the OECD Countries, please refer to the following evaluations:
Charles Oman, Steven Fries and Willem Buiter, "Corporate Governance in Developing, Transition and Emerging Market Economies", Policy Brief No:23, OECD, 2003
"Kurumsal Yönetim Derneği Ekonomik İşbirliği ve Kalkınma Örgütü Kurumsal Yönetim İlkeleri", Kurumsal Yönetim Derneği, Ocak 2005, Yayın No: KYD-Y/2005-01-01 www.tkyd.org Grant Kirkpatrick, "Improving Corporate Governance Standards: The Work of the OECD and the Principles", OECD.2004

[37] Available at CMB web-site: www.spk.gov.tr

[38] Classified as a fast growing and volatile emerging market economy, Turkey is estimated to have a population of 73 million with a total GNP of 400 billion US dollars (560 billion YTL) in 2006. Per capita GNP reached 5500 USD (7300 YTL) (On purchasing power parity (PPP) scale, per capital GNP was around 8500 USD or 10.000 YTL) Please refer to www.treasury.gov.tr for further details.

The Size of Companies in Turkey
(As measured by the number of employees)

	No. of Employees	% of Total	Cumulative %
Tiny	0	1.38	1.38
Micro	1-9	94.94	96.32
Small	10-49	3.09	99.41
Medium	50-250	0.48	99.89
Large	251+	0.11	100.00
Total		100.00	

Source: 2. Kobiler ve Verimlilik Kongresi (Second Congress on SME's and Efficiency, Kongre Kitabı, ISBN-975-6957-51-4, İstanbul Kültür Üniversitesi, 2005 pp.XXII.

Many government departments had projects aimed at improving performances of SME's, and SME definitions and classifications.[39] The above classification is based on the Government Decree published on Nov.18, 2005 for reducing SME classifications.

As indicated by the above figures the great majority (almost all) of firms in the Turkish economy were family SME's. Even the 1000 largest company listing of the Istanbul Chamber of Industry (The ISO), only 560 firms employed more than 250 persons.[40]

In addition, only 702 firms out of 7507 firms covered by the sect oral studies of the Central Bank of Turkey had turnovers of 40 million Euro (or 70 million YTL) and about 40% of the 353 firms quoted at the Istanbul Stock Exchange were family SME's.

The Statistical Institute noted that out of the total of 800,000 companies registered in Turkey, only about 1000 of then employed more them 250 persons.[41]

The number of SME's was large but they were low in productivity. Firms having less than 250 workers had a share of only 45.6% in total employment, a share of a tiny 6.5% in total fixed investment and a share in the production of added value at only 37.7%. Their direct share in exports was only 8.8%.

Smallness and less organized managements of the majority of firms in Turkey, expanding implementations of corporate governance in the country seemed almost impossible for the SME's. Even in the area of larger enterprises, 40% of companies were family businesses.

---

[39] Different organisations have different classifications in Turkey: KOSGEB (Küçük ve Orta Ölçekli Sanayi Geliştirme ve Destekleme İdaresi Başkanlığı), Halk Bankası, Eximbank, Hazine Müsteşarlığı, Dış Ticaret Müsteşarlığı, Devlet Planlama Teşkilatı, Türkiye İstatistik Kurumu, Kredi Garanti Fonu, Sanayi ve Ticaret Bakanlığı all have measures of "smallness" for business firms.
[40] See Güler Aras: "Basel II Sürecinde Kobi'ler için Yol Haritası" (The Road Map for the SME's in the Context of Basel II), Deloitte and Touche Danışmanlık, Türkiye, İstanbul, 2007.
[41] Please refer to the Central Bank website at www.tcmb.gov.tr for more information.

The total number of family business firms in Turkey measured slightly over 90% of the total like in the USA.[42] Shares of family firms were also high in other countries: 99% in Italy,[43] 80% in Germany and Mexico and 75% in Australia and Chile.

As a result of smallness, dependence on the leader(s) and families, no plans for succession, only 6%[44] of business firms in Turkey could survive with the fourth generations of families. Observations and case studies on business failures indicate to some weaknesses of the family SME's in Turkey:

- Management practice was not participative but authoritative;
- Family and the firm leadership were represented by the same person(s), in most cases;
- Leaders and the able family members were also executives of the firm;
- Major share holder(s) is the top manager of the firm, and share ownerships and the executive managements were not separated;
- Leaders (and the single owner) made quick decisions and changed them on short notice, without consultations with professionals;
- The "boss", in the majority of cases, was cognizant of his superior abilities, liked his ideas much more than competitors and /or executives did not feel in search of the "best practices";
- Intuitive decisions dominated in companies, with less attention to long-range rational planning;
- The "boss" tended to make all the strategic decisions and did not want any "interference" from outsiders;
- Personal accounts of the bosses were mixed up with the accounts of the business;
- Employees of the firm were selected in accordance with informal relationships of the boss, rather than on the professional competence of individuals;
- Management of the family was mixed with the management of the family company;
- "Succession" of the boss and indeed of the other key individuals in the business was ignored.

Because of the characteristics of the Turkish family companies and basic intrinsic values of the Turkish corporate culture, a recent OECD report [45] had the following judgment on the possibilities of improving implementation of the principles of corporate governance in Turkey:

1. "The Turkish corporate sector is dominated by family controlled, complex financial industrial company groups, usually comprising both publicly and privately held companies. Pyramidal structures are common and there is often a high degree of cross ownership within the groups. Controlling shareholders

---

[42] KOBİ FİNANS, Journal Published by Finansbank. Although 90% is given in the journal, the percentage of family companies should be higher among private companies.
[43] Kobifinans, op.cit.
[44] Op.cit.
[45] "Corporate Governance" in Turkey- A Pilot Study", ISBN-92-64-02863-3, OECD, 2006.

often hold shares with nomination privileges and/or multiple voting rights. "Approximately 30 % of ISE-listed companies... had "flotation ratios" of less than 25 % as of the end of 2005"

2. "In Turkey, ... comprehensive and systematic studies of board structures and decision-making processes are rare."
3. However, the OECD report has depicted the following structure for "holding company"[46] boards:
    *   A formal, statutory board whose members are elected by share holders;
    *   A "designated" board member to whom the controlling shareholders entrusted principal day-to-day responsibility for overseeing the group's operations;
    *   An extended executive committee consisting of top management;
    *   "The "designated" board member, commonly known as the "Murahhas Aza"[47] often (but not always) is a member of the family that controls the corporate group";[48]
    *   Majority of board members are often "dependent" on the major shareholder or the family.
4. "A corporate culture and capital markets are relatively recent phenomena ... as the significant state involvement in the economy confirmed through the 1970's.

Beginning in the 1980's, a trend toward liberalization started to expose Turkish companies to global competition while providing some of them with opportunities to attract foreign investment. Following the establishment of a regulatory framework for the capital markets in the early 1980's the ISE opened in 1985.

However, "An era of macro-economic instability distorted incentives" as..."From the mid 1980's until recently, inflation usually exceeded 60 % per year. High levels of government barrowing crowded out private debt and equity financing in combination with unpredictable[49] tax administration and poor enforcement, companies had incentives to conceal profits and organize their own captive sources of finance by establishing or acquiring banks. "The business environment has improved significantly since the 2000-01 crisis..."After contracting by almost 7.5% in 2001, real GDP growth has increased every year at an average of 7.1%.

---

[46] As the majority of corporations in Turkey are family companies consisting of a group of companies headed by a holding company, the above judgment of the report defines the dominant company structure of the Turkish quoted ISE corporations as well as unquoted closed private corporations.

[47] Can best be defined as "Board Member with Executive powers".

[48] Many family corporations, often would have more than one "Murahhas Aza" with designated executive powers in separate functional areas.

[49] And high corporation tax rates.

Consumer price inflation fell from 54% in 2001 to 8.2% in 2005[50], the consolidated budget deficit fell from 16.3% of GDP in 2001 to an estimated 2.1% in 2005,[51] and public sector debt dropped from 106% of GDP in 2001 to an estimated 74% in 2005[52]

The Corporate Governance framework has improved in a major way in recent years.

"The principal sources of general mandatory corporate governance standards are the joint stock companies provisions in the TCC,[53] the CML[54] and subordinate instruments published under CML, generally in the form of CMB[55] communiqués."

"The ambitions and comprehensive CMB Principles adopted in 2003[56], are the principal source of non-binding corporate governance standards for publicly held companies.[57] ... Listed companies must publish an annual Corporate Governance Compliance Statement ... which CMB Principles have not been adopted and the reasons for not doing so."

Against the above economic conditions, the OECD report has found that:

1. The following OECD Principles related to some shareholder rights were Fully Implemented. Detailed information in the report indicate that shareholders receive relevant and timely information[58] can participate in shareholders meetings elect and remove board-members, share in profits, participate in changes in the by-laws, participate in issuing new shares, have equal rights for shares of the same class.

2. The following OECD Principles related to shareholder rights were only:
   • Shareholders rights to transfer shares, to ask questions place items on the agenda and propose resolutions, to vote via representations;
   • Stakeholders, rights for participating in corporate governance, for having access to relevant, sufficient and reliable information;
   • Disclosures on company objectives and risk factors on employees and other stakeholders;
   • Accountability of external auditors to shareholders;
   • Ethical standards related to executives.

---

[50] And to 7.7% in 2006, estimated to fall to 7% for 2007.
[51] And to less than 1,0 % in 2006, but is estimated to grow to around 4% in 2007.
[52] And 65% in 2006 and estimated to grow to around 70% in 2007.
[53] Turkish Commercial Code.
[54] Capital Market Law.
[55] Capital Market Board.
[56] And revised in 2005 to adapt to the OECD principles.
[57] For improvements for unlisted companies we will have to wait until the TCC will be completely changed in 2008. (A new draft designed by a group of specialists over 2003 to 2006 was presented to the parliament at the end of 2006.)
[58] The numbers relate to the list of "OECD Principles of Corporate Governance".

The following OECD Principles related to shareholder rights, stakeholder rights, responsibilities of the board were Partly Implemented:

- Transparency and enforceability of legal framework, division of regulatory responsibilities, and the adequacy of the authority, integrity and resources of regulatory bodies;
- Shareholders right for participation in decisions relating to extraordinary transactions, and effective participation in key corporate governance decisions;
- Adequate disclosure of capital structures and arrangements allowing certain shareholders to obtain a degree of control disproportionate to their equity ownership;
- Rules governing acquisitions of corporate control;
- Ability of shareholders to consult each other on issues relating to basic shareholder rights;
- Protecting minority shareholders from abusive actions by controlling shareholders, and insider trading;
- Disclosure rules of material interests of board members add key executives.
- Rules related to employee participation;
- Quality standards of accounting and financial and non-financial disclosures;
- Independence, competency and qualifications of external auditors;
- Regulations related to the behavior of the Board and its members.[59]

The above-mentioned OECD report indicated that a few of the OECD Corporate Governance Principles were "Not Implemented". Those were related to:

Institutional investors acting as fiduciaries should disclose:[60] and the framework on the roles of financial analysts, rating agencies, brokers and others.

The above findings of the OECD Pilot Study indicate that possibilities for improving practices of corporate governance in Turkey is indeed immense as many new codes and regulations will have to be introduced and implemented as the country approaches membership in the EU. For purposes of improving the corporate culture for enhancing corporate governance practices by companies, a priority list for improvements should be established. Naturally, responsibility for the results achieved will fall on the Governments of the Future. The following suggestions for improvements are aimed to help the researchers and decision makers of the future who will carry the responsibilities of the outcomes.

Cooperation among universities and academicians, non-governmental agencies and researchers in government departments seems to be needed for covering these wide areas of research.

---

[59] "Corporate Governance in Turkey: A Pilot Study", ISBN-92-64-02863-3 OECD 2006, P.27-30

[60] The principle is not enacted in any ruling of either the Turkish Commercial Code, The Capital Markets Law or in any regulation related to these basic laws and hence is not known in Turkey. The new bill aiming to change the TCC, will bring the concept to the Turkish legal system, if enacted.

The OECD Pilot Study, summarized the policy options for enhancing practices of corporate governance in Turkey for improvements to:

- "Increase the potential for market disciplinary forces to operate effectively;
- Enhance standards addressing risks associated with prevailing ownership and control structures;
- Introduce a risk-based approach to supervision, regulation and enforcement;
- Enhance remedies, enforcement mechanisms and adjudicative procedures;
- Centralize the financial reporting standard setting process and active full alignment with the International Financial Reporting Standards, the IFRS's;
- Restructure and deepen the audit oversight process;
- Strengthen the capacity and accountability of key regulators".[61]

Following is a discussion on possible areas of improvement for enhancing corporate governance practices within the Turkish corporate sector.

Areas for Improvement for Enhancing Corporate Governance in Turkish Business Firms

As indicated by the above discussion on the characteristics of the Turkish corporate environment, corporate culture in Turkey does not give strong support to enhancing corporate governance implementations in the business firms of Turkey in some members of the European Union and OECD countries.[62]

Corporate governance regulations in the ISE-listed companies had just been started. Institutional investors having more sophisticated standards of disclosure, shareholder and stakeholder rights, responsibilities of directors and managers, accountability, etc. not effective by implemented. Most of the shareholders of small denominations were in general, not very effective for exercising their minority interests. The fatherly dominance of the majority owner/corporate leader/dominant CEO shadowed and governed over the firm and the family.

Although some significant improvements could be achieved, especially in the last two decades, for enhancing financial disclosure standards relating to ownership and control of listed companies, additional improvements were needed to bring financial disclosures, financial audits and reporting to international standards. However, the real and greater disclosure problem relating to SME's and family companies also needed practical solutions. Auditing and disclosure requirements for family SME's were seriously underdeveloped. Even for listed companies, the improvements related to full implementation of the CMB Principles had not yet been achieved. Disclosures for most related party transactions, timeliness of financial reporting systems were yet to be improved to the requirements of the IOSCO Principles.[63] Internal reporting and information provided for BOD's and managements

---

[61] Op.cit.p.31-32
[62] "Corporate Governance- A Survey of OECD Countries," ISBN 92-64-10605-7- OECD, 2004.
[63] Principles for financial auditing and reporting requirements of the International Organisation of Securities Commissions.

were not yet fully developed to satisfactory levels. However, as reviewed above, improvements in this area were started vis-à-vis the international standards and directed to more effective implementation.

As far as the family SME's did not have a formal and distinct organizational structures and integrated financial reporting systems for enlightening the decision makers for rational decisions, a research on existing practices for determining a long range action plan for improvements seemed a necessary. Practices of other countries should also be studied for the purpose of improving the Turkish practices.[64]

Although a risk-based approach to supervision, regulation and enforcement have been achieved for banks and other financial institutions in the last decade, improvements for non-bank, non-listed and non-financial private corporations needed improvements at the basic levels. Thanks to the efforts and rulings of the Banking Regulation and Supervision Authority (the BRSA), major improvements were achieved towards improving the risk-based approaches to supervision, regulation and enforcement towards financial disclosure standards for financial corporations open to public, towards better internal and external auditing practices, and towards enhancing corporate governance practices. Lacking was a comprehensive risk-based strategic plan of the CMB, for better coordination among regulatory bodies such as CMB, the BRSA, ISE management and the Ministry of Finance (MOF). Also needed were incentives for IPO's, offerings of shares to the public, improved practices of corporate governance, quality of disclosed financial information, improved legal framework for large, small, publicly held or family-owned corporations.

Furthermore, more enforcement power will have to be developed for all regulatory bodies.

Centralizing the financial standard setting process and better implementation of the IFRS were needed. The "Audit Oversight" concept was not yet known to the business community. The enforcement of educational and training requirements of internal and external auditors, were needed. An "Audit Oversight Body" could be established and provided with powers to "clean the market from bad apples", i.e. to screen out incompetent and unethical auditors. Governments will have to plan for the establishment of such a body, independent of the MOF, the CMB, the corporation, political interference and the like.

Turkish Society and Corporate Culture did not support the development of corporate governance practices and implementations in Turkey needed the following measures:

• Changing social and business environments for supporting corporate governance implementations in small, medium and large business firms in Turkey;

• Introduce inducements for business firms to be organized as joint-stock corporations (Societé Anonyms) even if they do not think of being listed at a stock

---

[64] "International Experts Meeting on Corporate Governance of Non-Listed Companies", Meeting Materials on the experiences of 36 countries are available from the OECD. The actual Round Table Meeting was held in Istanbul Turkey during 19-20 April 2005, in Istanbul, Turkey.

exchange;

- Governments and municipalities should organize their enterprises in the form of corporations and should open those corporations for listing at the ISE;
- Introduce inducements for business combinations, mergers and acquisitions;
- Introduce inducements for Initial Public offerings of shares and enlarging percentage of shares for free-floats at the ISE;
- Introduce inducements and facilitations for re organizing companies and public ownership of companies;
- Discourage the formation of business establishments in other legal forms than corporations with shares open to public;
- Training and education of future business managers should be aimed to carry factual business cases to the educational programs at especially the post graduate and post experience levels. Universities should be induced to establish "Case Research and Development Centers" to develop case studies to be used for training in post-graduate programs. Corporate Governance Learning Programs based on actual business cases should be developed by business schools for utilizing in class discussions and e-learning programs;
- Soon after scandals were publicized in 2000, Stock Markets in the USA crashed and stock prices fell at a very fast pace until 2003.[65] Sweeping reforms during the following years in almost all countries with advanced stock markets, brought complaints about the high costs of the reforms. Professor Clark of the Harvard Law School had the following judgment on the costs of the reforms:

  "… the band wagon reform measures did not come out of thin air as new inventions, nor were they arbitrary ideas. Some major reform measures were "taken off the shelf", so to speak and modified for the occasion. Accordingly, they reflected previously accumulated policy positions that were based on experience, anecdotes, general policy arguments and the outcome of long-running competitive posturing by 'good corporate governance proponents' and their targets";

- The debate on the optimum mix of measures continues in the USA and else where. As Turkey is at the beginning stages of reform, policymakers should benefit from studying the details of the debate covering social, economic and business areas of reform in other countries;
- Reforms related to improving quality of the internal and external audits in companies and improved disclosure regulations, will have an important share for the needed reforms in Turkey. In addition, in spite of the many restrictions o f recent changes in regulation, the accounting profession in Turkey needed much reform;

---

[65] Robert Charles Clark, "Corporate Governance Changes in the wake of the Sarbanes-Oxley Act: A Morality Tale for Policymakers too". Harvard Law School, John Mc. Olin for Law, Economics and Business, Discussion Paper, September, 2005. http://www.law.harvard.edu/olin center/ ISSN 1045-6333, Cambridge, MA., USA.

A research project for the needed changes in standards of accounting and the organization of the profession will have to be made for determining what-to-do and what-not-to-do with respect to measures, regulations and enforcement of standards.

Going into the details of the dearly needed reform of the profession in Turkey will divert us from our main topic here: improving practices of corporate governance in Turkey.

However, an improved accounting profession and better practices of public disclosures of financial reports of companies seem to be the necessary pillars of corporate governance. Worldwide problems of the accounting profession and the standards will have to be studied for purposes of reform, in this context.[66]

---

[66] Two fairly old publications should be studied for the purpose: Tony Tinker, "Paper Prophets- A Social Critique of Accounting" Praeger Publishers, NY.1985; Tony Tinker and Tony Puxty, "Policing Accounting Knowledge", Makus Wiener Publishers, Princeton, NY 1994.

PART 3
CULTURAL ISSUES

Chapter 8

Culture and Corporate Governance: Revisiting the Cultural Imperative

Loong Wong

Abstract

While there appears to be an emerging convergence towards best-practice standards on corporate governance, there is also the recognition that no single model of governance can exist. Many have alluded to significant cultural intransigence as an impediment to implementing consistent and effective rules and practices across countries. This paper seeks to examine the influence of culture on disclosure, transparency and enforcement practices, drawing on East Asian examples. The paper argues that prevailing legal and institutional forms in Asia mitigate against effective governance systems and practices. Relationship-based business practices further exacerbate the issue. As such, this paper suggests that cultural, historical and institutional factors and contexts are critical influential factors to consider in developing better and more effective governance practices. The paper however concludes that an uncritical acceptance of this cultural imperative is flawed and that a critical interrogation of culture and its exegesis is essential to unpack the different and contending claims of culture.

Introduction

We no longer live in the world of stable and somewhat self-contained political economic systems of the golden age of post-war capitalism. Increasingly, we have become controlled and governed by a seemingly seamless web of corporate power. There are claims that the state and national governments have become superfluous as the process of globalization takes over (Weiss, 1998). Since the 1980s, globalization as a discourse has dominated the social sciences. Used in almost magical fashion, its evocation alone renders any social/economic problem immediately explicable and obviates the need for clarification (Dicken, 2003; Hay & Marsh, 2000; Hirst & Thompson, 1999). The other word 'governance' - raised in the late 1980s and coming into greater prominence in the 1990s refers routinely to the exercise of authority within a given sphere, and is used to conjure up the idea that our era and social life is one which is ultimately shaped by management activities and that any meaningful act can consequently be determined and regulated (de Alacantra, 1998). In many ways, this emphasis on governance is understandable given the context of 'anarchic' global society and its attendant risks. The Asian financial crisis of 1997, for example, was seen as direct consequence of these twin movements. The spectacular collapses of Enron, Tyco, MCI and other organisations in the United States of America; Parmalat in Italy, BCCI and Polly Peck in the UK, and in Australia, HIH, OneTel and Harris Scarfe and ongoing concerns over NRMA, amongst others, have become critical flashpoints and represent globally 'a general crisis in corporate governance' (Bargh, Scott and Smith, 1996: 170). 'Enronitis' has occupied the attention of governments globally, resulting in new reform measures aimed at enhancing best corporate governance practice to manage risks and ensure continuing growth and economic success.

Old institutional arrangements are defunct and there was an urgent need to adopt new market competitive mechanisms for authority, guidance and socializing power to better manage new global processes. Good governance thus became the 'magic bullet' for managing turbulence, 'transitions', risks and the environment and has become mandatory in developmental aid calculations. Asia certainly has bore the brunt of these 'new governance reforms'. Once large 'reputable firms' and robust economies were found to be wanting, corrupt and lacking transparency and new corporate governance principles and practices pronounced as the elixir of the new growth agenda. This also percolated within development aid deliberations, multilateral discussions and reform packages touted the supremacy, integrity and veracity of 'western' practices. What was needed, some analysts claimed, was a liberal dose of western corporate arrangements and practices. It has been argued that the relationships between globalization, economic adjustment, economic growth and corporate governance remains underdeveloped. This claim is also a little short-sighted for it fails to appreciate, as various events in the 'west' has shown, that corporate collapses are not just a function of allegedly 'poor' corporate governance practices alone but includes many different factors - amongst other things the lack of accountability, 'inappropriate' accounting standards, poor management and the lack of effective government regulation. Significantly, it neglects history for two critical reasons 'corporate governance' has been an issue preceding the Asian financial crisis (Bargh, Scott and Roberts, 1996), and more tellingly, a 'cultural hegemony' existed, persists and remains dominant in Asian corporate practices. This is due to the colonial heritages of many Asian societies, e.g. in Singapore, Hong Kong, Malaysia, Philippines and India, where laws and statutes resemble those of their former colonial masters. In East-Asian countries, the transfusion of European ideas, laws, and practices have been significant nation-building artefacts. The single most important factor, however, has to be the growth of and the need to attract and maintain/retain international capital.

The question of which model of corporate governance to adopt is however not so apparent. Suggestions of only one approach to corporate governance are clearly not tenable. The history and genealogy of corporate governance suggests that corporate governance as a concept is ambiguous, contentious and evolutionary. Its intellectual roots, similarly, suggests that the 'one size fits all' approach is also not sustainable.

Various disciplines emphasise and privilege different approaches.

For example, there is a profound difference in corporate structures and practices between and within Europe and the USA (Hampden-Turner & Trompenaars, 1993; Thurow, 1992; Chandler, 1990; Herrigel, 1996). and lead to varying analytical insights. Moreover, differing legal systems, business cultures and corporate structures further complicate the picture (Hall & Soskice, 2001; Dore, 2000; Whitley, 1999; Albert, 1993). This is even discernible in Anglo-American and western traditions.[1]

Even the OECD (Organisation for Economic Co-operation and Development) has boldly proclaimed in the preamble to its 'Principles of Corporate Governance' that "There is no single model of good corporate governance".[2] Despite this pronouncement and recognition that there are diverse business systems, academics and analysts alike have sought to maintain the notion that there is only one route to good corporate governance. This is most marked in the literature and criticisms of corporate and corporate governance practices in developing and transitional economies. In this paper, I seek to challenge the monolithic and one-dimensional proclaimed truth of the 'one true road' to corporate governance. The paper argues that corporate governance is culturally and historically derived and focuses on control, risk management, expert knowledge and the application of this knowledge through the enactment of rules, regulations and procedures. Rooted in an idealized Anglo-American view of the world, it is however limiting and fails to consider divergent economic systems and practices. Accordingly the paper points to other possible constructions of corporate practices, in particular the cultural and institutional settings through which corporate structures and practices have evolved in different economies and societies. The paper suggests that these institutional settings have worked against the implementation of universal rules and practices across countries. Relationship-based business practices further compound the problem of governance as they are so intricately bound to cultural and political liaisons. As such, this paper suggests that to develop better and more effective governance practices, cultural, historical and institutional factors and contexts are critical influential factors. However, the paper concludes that an uncritical acceptance of this cultural imperative is flawed and that a critical interrogation of culture and its exegesis is essential to unpack the different and contending claims of culture.

---

[1] Despite claims of a growing convergence of 'global capitalism', the ways in which economic activities are organised in different economies suggest different systems of economic organisation persists and exist (Kristensen, 1997). Indeed, even in the USA, there is the recognition that American capitalism is uneven and manifests different characteristics (Hollingworth, 1991; Lindberg & Campbell, 1991; Chandler, 1990; Fligstein, 1990). Dobbin (1994) has also demonstrated the importance of state actions in the development of different economic ideologies and coordination systems. Herrigel (1996) has also shown that in Germany, different kinds of industrial order have characterised different regions of Germany and accordingly, impacted on regional forms of production and development. Lazonick, in his formulation of a more general approach to economic development and competitiveness, for example, suggests that there are at least three varieties of capitalism: proprietary, managerial and collective.

[2] www.oecd.org/daf/governance/principle.html)

The North American Hegemony: Growth and Limits

Since the 1980s, 'corporate governance' has gained greater currency. The global drive towards privatisation opened up new arenas for concern but the Asian financial crisis of 1997 propelled the idea of corporate governance to the frontline of change and soon, it dominated business discourses globally. 'Cronyistic and corrupt' Asia was beseeched to emulate the 'clean, ethical, accountable and robust' corporate systems in western societies (Backman, 1999; Delhaise, 1998) but as recent events in the 'west' have shown, the issues of the reliability, credibility and efficacy of clean and transparent corporate systems and practices are not confined to Asia but also affect advanced industrial economies in the West (Clarke, Dean & Oliver, 1997).[3]

Ronald Coase's paper 'Nature of the Firm' set the agenda for much of the reworking of corporate governance (Coase, 1937). According to Coase and his followers, the corporation is a distinct species of a firm that carried out production in modern western economies. It is also a method of raising substantial amounts of capital, enabling both an elaborate organisation and team of professional management to pursue growth economies in transaction costs. In conjunction with the growth of limited liability, corporate firms grew rapidly; management and ownership diverged and evolved into separate spheres of specialisation (Berle & Means, 1932). Via the elected board of directors, owners exercise their control internally (Fama & Jensen, 1983; Lazonick & O'Sullivan, 1996; Williams, 2000) while the market flexes its control externally. This is usually manifested in the firms' capacity to attract investment capital which rewards management efficiencies (which affects their competitiveness and survival prospects as take-over bids) and capabilities (via reward systems and also as in the articulation and circulation of management as a resource and a commodity). Auditors and other fiduciary statutes augment these control measures. Clearly, in this form, corporate governance focuses principally, if not exclusively, on the relation between shareholders and managers as a principal-agent problem (Williamson, 1996; Jensen & Meckling, 1976; Tricker, 1984, 1994). This is further reinforced by technological changes and globalization of the economy.

Corporate governance in its current form is both influenced and shaped by a North American ethos and a focus on large public-listed companies. There is the notion of a triumphalist, universalising and civilising influence of North American governance and governing practices replicated on a global scale (Fukuyama, 1992: Gilson, 1994).[4] Indeed, American legal scholars Hansmann & Kraakman have suggested that corporate governance is best exemplified in the US shareholder-oriented model which is not simply irresistible but 'has emerged as the normative

---

[3] Clarke, Dean & Oliver (1997) have consistently raised these issues of credibility and reliability pointing out that the charter of accounts and financial statements do not reflect real-time transactions.

[4] It must be pointed out that the USA does not have a uniform approach to corporate laws although much of securities regulation is federal (Jordan, 1997). States in the USA each have their own separate law jurisdiction with its own business corporations act and tend to adopt a competitive approach towards legislative control, compliance and penalties.

consensus' (Hansmann & Kraakman, 2001: 449). For these authors, the American model marked the 'end of history for corporate law', i.e. an end for continued evolution of corporate law or the advocacy of competing models of corporate governance for 'no important competitor…remain persuasive today (ibid, 454). Elsewhere, they proclaimed '(t)he triumph of the shareholder-oriented model of the corporation over its principal competitors is now assured…'(Hansmann & Kraakman, 2001: 468; see also McCahery et. al., 2002). However, this is not a shared view. As Bebchuk and Roe (1999) so perceptively and cogently argued, despite the forces of globalisation and the quest for greater global efficiency, key differences have persisted and could well continue in the future.

The evidence clearly suggests that. In the 'west', there are a range of business organisations ranging from public-listed companies to small and medium-sized enterprises and the private limited liability companies to public corporations (Hollingsworth & Boyer, 1997; Hollingsworth & Lindberg, 1985). The notion and the practices of corporate governance therefore differ accordingly (Moreland, 1995a,b); Gilson & Roe, 1993; Turnbull, 1997) but most analyses have approached the issue of corporate governance in a uncritical and undifferentiated manner, and failed to understand the different cultural logics of different businesses (Clarke & Clegg, 1999; Kristensen, 1997; Clarke & Bostock, 1994; Best, 1990; Chandler, 1990).[5]

Definitions of corporate governance clearly vary widely. Mooted originally as a response to the demand for greater business and organizational flexibility and responsiveness (Child & McGrath, 2001; Budros, 1997; Handy, 1995; Drucker, 1992), corporate governance as a concept has become rather ambiguous in both its intent and practice (Keasey, Thompson & Wright, 1997; Turnbull, 1997). As Farrar (2001:3) pointed out, 'it (corporate governance) has been used to refer to control of corporations and to systems of accountability by those in control', and is capable of being subsumed under broader concepts of contractual and social governance. It refers to legislations impacting on corporations but increasingly has become more expansive and now incorporates practices and arrangements of *de facto* control of companies, including self-regulatory codes of practices and business ethics. In a wide sense, it encompasses 'the entire network of formal and informal relations involving the corporate sector and their consequences for society in general' (Keasey, Thompson & Wright, 1997: 2). Clearly then, corporate governance is not only an evolving concept but is also tied in with the notion of corporations; their roles, objectives, functions and practices within the wider society (Branson, 2001; McDonnell, 2002; Gordon & Roe, 2004). In different regions of the world, there are deeply embedded differences regarding business values and ways of doing things, and

---

[5] For a discussion of the issues of SMEs, see Dugan, McKenzie & Patterson (2000) and Neubauer & Lank, (1998); non-governmental organisations' issues are covered in Hirshhorn, (1995); McGregor-Lowdes, Fletcher & Sievers, (1996). Public corporations and their governance are discussed fairly extensively. For some examples, see Duncan & Bollard, (1992); Collier & Pitkin (Eds) (1999); Joint Committee of Public Accounts and Audit Report (1999); Konig & Siedentopf (1988).

very different relationships with stakeholders. There exist profoundly different and contrasting views of the market in different systems and the manner in which they affect corporate behaviour and practices. Firms must adapt to multiple features of their environment (Fligstein & Freeland, 1995), and their behaviour cannot simply be attributed to agency costs alone (Fligstein, 1990; Roe, 1994; Roy, 1997). Rather, corporate governance needs to be understood in the context of a wider range of institutional domains (Aoki, 2001) Consequently, countries with identical institutions in one domain will not necessarily have identical corporate governance systems to the extent that other institutions will provide other effects.

The Problematique of Culture

Described by the late Raymond Williams as one of the two or three most complicated words in the English language, 'culture' defies easy definition. At its simplest form, it refers to the artistic and intellectual product of an elite. Popularly, it refers to a system of shared beliefs or a whole way of life. Culture is a relative new entrant in the discourse of international business and management. Earlier practitioners and 'theorists' paid very little attention to culture *per se* it was seen as the economists would have it, via the lens of the nation-state (Harbison and Myers, 1959). This was due to the dominance of economics as the new prescriptive science and concerns in international business was only glimpsed through the 'comparative advantage of nations'. Culture, if invoked, was seen as an obstacle and retardant on economic growth. In the early 1980s, the rise of Japan and the 'four Asian tigers' re-inscribed culture into the debate.[6] 'Uniqueness' and distinctive management styles and systems spawned new exercises in isolating and identifying the magic elixir of business and economic growth (Hampden-Turner & Trompenaars, 1997). This increase in magnitude as the economy became increasingly internationalised and globalised, and firms adapted and sought their competitive advantage in various locales. Because of this strategic import the need to enhance business effectiveness and outcomes - the quest for cultural literacies and competencies became an important business agenda and firms sought to cultivate and acquire these competencies. While proclaimed competencies point to the complex and multi-faceted aspect of culture, culture is categorized in terms of definable traits and characteristics of different clusters of culture. For example, in a textbook on intercultural communication, culture is defined as 'the total accumulation of identifiable groups' beliefs, norms, institutions and communication patterns' (Dodd, 1991: 41). The text then cautions that over-generalisations are a problem because they lead to stereotyping and proceeds to argue for a 'middle ground' which is described as 'central tendencies among groups of people, a modality tendency' (Dodd, 1991: 43). Having qualified the range of

---

[6] Since Pascale and Athos (1981), there have been numerous books and articles dealing with Japanese management techniques. Chen (1995) provides an introductory discussion of Asian management systems. (1992); Collier & Pitkin (Eds) (1999); Joint Committee of Public Accounts and Audit Report (1999); Konig & Siedentopf (1988).

applicability of the claims, the issue is then left alone and not dealt with in any other passage; instead the 'cataloguing of differences' begins and is reproduced and reiterated.

This anatomical and enumerative view of culture, i.e. culture is a system of beliefs, codes, values and so forth, is a static approach. It is generalistic and also clearly reductionistic and does not accord with Hofstede's own analysis. It becomes more apparent if we undertake a closer analysis of these texts. A systematic and appropriate reading of Hofstede will readily reveal that he provides an auto-critique, albeit submerged in an appendix on methodology, particularly that of abstraction and generalisation of organisational culture and national attributes. Moreover, Hofstede (1991: 171) admitted to having a 'Western' way of thinking'[7] and that most people/cultures are hybridised and that the rules of typologising are made arbitrarily in order to classify people.[8] Sadly, these qualifications aside, generalised categorisations and typologising have become the authoritative dominant discourse on doing business across cultures.

Clearly, despite himself, there is a constant ontological as well as epistemological distinction being made between cultures in Hofstede's work. It implied that there is a static core to each culture and that we can identify, know, and deal with. Although 'mental programs vary as much as the social environments in which they were acquired' Hofstede readily conceded that 'the sources of one's mental programs lie within the social environments in which one grew up and collected one's life experiences' (Hofstede, 1991: 4-5). This 'mental software', Hofstede claimed, 'is culture' (Hofstede, 1991:4). This is clearly problematic it implies a relationship between mental process and social life and that the content of each cultural (or racial) group is identifiable and particularistic. Inevitably, it creates stereotypes and enables the progenitors to accumulate and exercise knowledge and power over 'created' and identifiable cultural types. This is perhaps most apparent in its seemingly naturalising of dichotomised and polarising terms, laden with 'values', to describe cultures. In the main, this 'training' focused on an 'anthropology of manners' of determining, the cataloguing of cultural characteristics and the assembly of cross-cultural data sets (Hall, 1955; Morrison et. al., 1994, 1997).

---

[7] This 'western' mode of thinking invariably is ethnocentric and tend to see its worldview as central to all others. It is evaluative, defining and also almost always positively self-referential. Bias can therefore, be not excluded. This has prompted some intercultural theorists to warn that because of its emphasis on achieving desirable intercultural effectiveness, intercultural courses may actually augment and even enhance existing ethnocentrism, prejudice and stereotyping (Lustig & Koster, 1996; Samovar & Porter, 1991; Dodd, 1991).

[8] This 'construction' of Hofstede and his views are used to reinscribe national cultures as western/eastern, masculine/feminine, collectivist/individualist even though Hofstede's work was developed through an examination of attitudes of organisational communication in only one organisation. Not only are such linkages problematic but some of the indices used are also questionable. More importantly, the study reinforces the notion of essence which constitutes national identity which may not have any congruence with empirical realties.

The doyen of anthropologists, Clifford Geertz, has suggested that culture not just patterned conduct, a frame of mind which points to some sort of ontological status.

For Geertz, 'culture is not a power: something to which social events, behaviours, institutions, or processes can be causally attributed; it is a context' (Geertz, 1973:14; see also, Geertz, 1984). As such, culture is, public, social, relational and contextual.

Despite this, the reductionistic and functionalist view of culture persists and pervades everyday discussions of international business. But laden as they are with gross over-generalisations, they ignore the contested nature of culture nor do they acknowledge the partial and structural and cultural frameworks embedded in the proclaimed texts and programmes. As such, while cultural awareness and recognition of diversity may offer us 'the possibility of obtaining new insights and understanding of organisations and their practices' (Morgan 1993:13), the concerns of cross-cultural and international management and training texts and practices are more narrow. They seek to impose discipline, restore order and enable the 'skilled and trained employee' to manage the 'cultural conflicts' and chaos arising from transgressive international business practices. In contending that culture does not 'exist' in any of the more commonly understood forms and arguing that it is in fact an interpretative feature of our relationship with our environment, culture is not a neat and tidy package. Culture, therefore is not merely descriptive or functional but a means by which we view our world. It is 'in the eye of the beholder'.

The 'Culture' of Business

Culture is constantly evolving, interacting and shifting; it is wild, complex and diverse, problematic and unstable at the same time (Hannerz, 1992; Marcus and Fisher, 1986). This dynamic nature of culture, however, poses serious problems for the critical analysts and businesses. Participants in these business environments are not only of differing cultures but those cultures are constantly changing and are mediated as parties seek to effect some accommodation and consequently, changes in their respective positions. These changes may be superficial and may have no effect on fundamental values but this cannot be assumed (Mead 1990: 15). Recent research has pointed to divergences in economic organization in different countries (Whitley, 1999; Hall & Soskice). These researchers suggest that the key to understanding business behaviour and practices is to develop a critical appreciation of the interrelationships between market structures, the financial system and nature of corporate governance and control systems. For example, in Germany, Japan and many 'Asian' economies, there is often a long-term relationship between banks and businesses as a source of finance compared with Anglo-Saxon business systems such as the USA, Australia or the UK (Dore, 2000). It is also claimed that the former also typically displays long term webs of relationships between suppliers, customers and financiers unlike the latter. The latter, because of their emphasis on shareholder logic, generates highly formalized and elaborate internal financial control systems, giving finance a dominant role in the organization. In contrast, production and commercial functions have a higher profile in Asian and Germanic firms. Human resources management practices are also similarly affected. In Germanic and Asian countries, human resources are seen as an investment in the enterprise and they tend to emphasise employment stability for core workers whilst also committed to flexible work organizations and practices. Perhaps, the most common refrain has been the notion of concentration of ownership and control of corporate entities.

Because of its close relationship with corporate financial goals, it would be churlish and naive to assume that corporate goals are completely value-free: they reflect both the institutional differences and prevailing ideologies of the countries in which the companies are embedded in. Indeed, as Douglas North (1990) has highlighted, once a given structure is in existence, it will set up additional structures that are not easily changed and there may also be forces within a country with powerful interests in preserving the system in place. In addition, the system will tend to reinforce itself by developing a network of complementary institutions (Hall & Soskice, 2001), but it may also lead to inefficient lock-in effects for change (Bechuck & Roe, 1999). Thus in the American ideal, a finely tuned network of institutional investors, investment analysts and stockbrokers is created which at the same time seeks to improve the efficiency of the system and lobby for its continued existence, expansion and/or even conflicts (Thelen, 1991).

Convergence scholars thus ignore politics, locality and institutions. They are seen as negligible forces and rather an idealized market is privileged. Markets, however, are dissimilar and have different logic. In their major study comparing financial markets, Allen and Gale drew our attention to the fact that financial markets in various countries are different and that in some of these 'markets', 'information is exchanged, relationships are established, bargaining and renegotiation occur, search takes place (individuals are matched), innovation and security design are undertaken and institutional forms are established' (Allen & Gale, 2000: 147). National differences persist they are '"hard wired" into core corporate structures' and 'embody distinctive and durable ideologies or, as some analysts now prefer to call them belief systems' (Doremus, et. al, 1998: 113). These structures also shape and affect the parameters in terms of engagement with and within the economy, in particular the various interest groups that determine the rules of practices including those impacting on market structures, the financial system and associated control systems (Unger, 1976; Domhoff, 1979; Sumner, 1979; Dan-Cohen, 1986; Kogut, 1991; Kelsey, 1995; Usui & Colignon, 1996; Whitley, 1999).

Corporate Governance and 'Cultural' Variations

Semenov (2000) recently compared systems of governance between 12 European countries, Australia, Canada, Ireland, New Zealand and the USA, and found that culture was an important marker of difference, and the difference is better explained than their economic variables. Indeed, corporations do not exist in a vacuum; they developed within society, its laws and its practices.

Historically, corporations were social organisations established to pursue the 'public benefit' however defined (Hurst, 1970; Monks & Minow, 1995); over time they evolved into associations of individuals and became viewed as separate legal entities, enjoying their own sovereignty (Samuels, 1987). As companies developed and adapted to the corporate form, shares were issued, traded and increasingly, the ownership and control became de-linked. This gave the management agency great power and provoked public wariness (Berle & Means, 1968; Hurst, 1970; Williams 2000). In order to ensure there were no systemic abuses by managers, legislations on fiduciary restraints, disclosure regimes and directors' duties were developed. The proportion of shares held by intermediaries/institutions were generally small, both for fiduciary reasons and to retain liquidity, so that they are not locked into the fate of particular firms and as such, exposed only to limited risks. Since the end of the Second World War, this changed and fund managers and related institutions grew in numbers and strength; they also increasingly began to realise, assert and exercise their powers (Gates, 1998; Stapleton, 1998; Lazonick & O'Sullivan, 1996; Baum & Stiles, 1965). Because of the changing nature of share ownership (including the role of institutional shareholders) and growing public interest, there has been a clear shift to see corporations as embedded within an elaborate nexus of contracts. This suggests a shift in the locus of power and accountability and that shareholders do not necessarily and uniformly have shared interests and objectives e.g. between individual and institutional shareholders. It also points to a more complicated set of arrangements which while maintaining and privileging the shareholders (owners), point to the web of existing relationships between corporations and different stakeholders (including creditors, employees, consumers and even local communities).[9] The *telos* of corporate governance has accordingly shifted and to suggest therefore that there is only one form of corporate governance practice is clearly not borne out by its historical evolution. As numerous writers have pointed out, corporate structures depend in part on the structures with which the economy evolved (Whitley, 1999; OECD, 1999; Hollingsworth & Boyer, 1997; Roe, 1997; Bebchuk & Roe, 1999).[10]

---

[9] In Australia, this is perhaps best seen in the corporate collapses of Ansett Airlines, HIH Insurance and OneTel. Of course, there were the earlier cases of Alan Bond, Laurie Connell and Christopher Skase of the 1980s. Clarke, Dean & Oliver 91997) have argued that corporate collapses in Australia results from poor professional regulations and standards, particularly in accounting and auditing procedures, practices and education (for a critique of corporate excesses and practices, see Tomasic & Bottomley, 1993). In a 1997 study, Australian directors overwhelmingly consider shareholders as their first priority (74%) in their consideration of stakeholders. Employees were not part of their deliberations and the company featured over 20% while customers rated less than 5% (Francis, 1997: 353-4). The evidence on stakeholders interests and financial performance have been mixed. Freeman (1984) and Waddock & Graves (1997), amongst others, found a positive relationship between these two measures while Agle et. al (1999) found no meaningful relationship exists.

[10] Clearly, there are numerous examples globally. See van der Berghe & Ridder (1999) but in Australia, one can also discern similar forms of evolution. For example, in the nineteenth century, 'banking capitalism', where banks finance businesses usually through debt financing, was a common practice at least until the 1930s (Ma & Morris, 1982; Sykes, 1988; Bryan & Rafferty, 1999). This then shifted to a period of public ownership with its concomitant legislations on fiduciary restraints and directors' duties. The opening up of the Australian financial markets in 1983, the rise in institutional strengths and the crash of 1987 saw a shift towards corporate reform. Corporate governance, with an emphasis on self-regulation, became widely articulated. One could cynically argued that this was a pre-emptive strike against new and possibly more restrictive legislations.

These institutional arrangements are often significant, as they set *de facto* performance standards, particularly via growth and financial indicators and also affect long-term relationships resulting in elaborate cross-holdings and interlocking directorships, which enable them to exercise considerable power and influence at board levels. Potentially, these relationships engender conflicts of interest in-group transactions. These images, commonly associated with crony capitalism in 'third world' countries, are surprisingly also common in many western countries, including Australia, France, New Zealand, Canada and the USA (van der Berghe and de Ridder, 1999; Stapleton, 1999; Farrar, 1987; Daniels & Morck, 1995). Clearly, the idea of a true form of democratic corporate governance, where all shareholders have an equal voice and vote, has some way to be realised; the volume of shares held are still determinative and in the hands of institutional voters and proxies, often decisive in effecting strategies, policies and outcomes. It becomes apparent that each country's path to good governance will be different. Indeed, as the literature has suggested, the quest for convergence does not mean that corporate governance reform will be implemented identically in each country. Moreover, analyses of the major codes have acknowledged that no single model of corporate governance can be applied that will adequately solve each and every governance issue (ADB, 1995, 1999, 2000; World Bank, 1999). Instead these studies maintain that good governance needs to be contextually defined and developed as the circumstances of each country (and firm) differ.

Corporate governance cannot be simply reduced to a generic optimal form, severed from context, nor regarded as spontaneously created out of ideal market forces and proclaimed as an exemplar of institutional efficiency (North, 1991). Political, legal, social, cultural and regulatory institutions frame and define to a substantial extent the relations, the processes and the institutions governing and impacting on the firm (Gourevitch, 1996; Zysman, 1996; Roe, 1991). Bebchuk and Roe (1999: 127) thus argue that path-dependencies 'may freeze the institutions of particular countries in a non-competitive pose'. Moreover, the concept of the corporation as separate legal person and the privileging of shareholders are clearly not universally shared. In Europe, corporate practices have tended to recognise a broader range of stakeholders interests and sought to incorporate employees' interests into its business calculus (Balling, 1993; Charkham, 1994; Moreland, 1995a; Clark & Bostock, 1997; Kester, 1997; Plender, 1997; Hopt & Wymeersch, 1997; Goodijk, 2000).[11]

---

[11] The case of UK is particularly interesting as it seeks to 'harmonise' its laws and practices as required and provided for in the Treaty of Rome. There are and have been numerous studies on these aspects of integration see Edwards, (2001); Sugarman & Teubner (1990); Buxbaum & Hopt (1988) amongst others.

In Japan and parts of Asia, duties and responsibilities of corporations towards society are also given due emphasis (Charkham, 1994: chapter 3; Gerlach, 1992; Yoshimori, 1995; Westney, 1996; Kanda, 1997; Cooke & Sawa, 1998; Bradley et. al., 1999; Araki, 2005) and business groups (*keiretsus*) play important roles in corporate governance (Sheard, 1994; Berlof & Perotti, 1994; Prowse, 1992; Hoshi, Kashyap & Scharfstein, 1991; Aoki, 1990; Nishiyama, 1984). Kenichi Ohmae (1982) for example, suggests that in Japan, the concept of a corporation is fundamentally different. According to him, 'Japanese chief executives, when asked what they consider their main responsibility, will say that they work for the well being of their people. Stockholders do not rank much higher than banks in their list of concerns' (Ohmae, 1982: 218-9). These varying practices have prompted some writers to suggest that economic and legal practices are rooted, shaped and affected by prevailing social and cultural institutions and cannot simply be wished away (North, 1990; Orru, 1997; Hollingsworth & Boyer, 1997; Whitley, 1999; Griffiths & Zammuto, 2003). Concerns have indeed been expressed that the search for ideal-type forms of corporate governance neglect many other developing, emerging and transitional economies (Tam, 1999; Weimer & Pape, 1999; Reed, 2002; Cernat, 2004), and that other possible systems exist and are emerging (Wong, 2005a; Griffiths & Zammuto, 2003; Tam, 1999; Whitley, 1999).

Searching for Good Governance

The principal driving forces for global corporate reforms have been capital market imbalances, innovations in information and computer technologies, a global push towards deregulation and a new emphasis on business management, risk management and flexible practices (including networks, joint ventures and strategic alliances) (Rosen, 2000; Castells, 2000; Volcker, 2000; Child & Faulkner, 2000; Clegg, Ibarra-Colado & Bueno-Rodriquez, 1999; Held, et. al. 1999; Thurow, 1999; Gray, 1998; Clarke & Clegg, 1998; Nalebuff & Brandergurger, 1996; Ohmae, 1995; Reich, 1992). These forces prompt financial investors, national governments and regulators to seek a new, more effective and comprehensive economic architecture to facilitate and improve greater transparency, accountability and more effective regulation of economic, business and financial markets.[12] This of course has led to a revamping of

---

[12] George Soros, a financial speculator and investor, one charged as the cause of the 1997 Asian financial crisis, has been vociferous in calling for a re-regulation of the global financial markets. According to him, the present system is inherently unstable and that more appropriate and rigorous supervisory practices and systems with enforcement powers need to be developed (Soros, 2000). The debate on international corporate governance has traditionally been dominated by concerns over transnational corporations and their practices. This has led the UN to develop and proclaim various codes of conduct but there was clearly no possible consensus. Since then, professional and non-governmental bodies (for example, the International Federation of Accountants, the International Accounting Standards Committee and the International Organisation of Securities Commission), have taken the lead and been active in pushing for new similar international standards and practices. Of course, the WTO and its various committees have now taken over this drive for global standardisation.

GATT (General Agreement on Trade and Tariffs), giving birth to the WTO and its attendant agreements and protocols, including the General Agreement on Trades and Services (GATS).

Market proponents claim that nation states are not effective in regulating their own economic activities and that corporations are already subjected to the disciplining logic of the competitive global capital market. Managerial practices, in their view, have to realise the most efficient and uniform form of practice, and in this case, the market is the best guide and marker of competent governance. This has to be rule bound and legally derived. This model, however, has a tendency to be reductionistic and confines itself to questions of method, housekeeping practices and maintaining a minimalist obligatory business ethical practice. Minimalist legislative changes clearly are not effective; the spirit and substance of good corporate practice is elusive and may not be attainable standards and practices will differ from persons to persons and organisations to organisations. Indeed, in so far as the international economy does continue to become more integrated, it can be argued that societies with different institutional arrangements will continue to develop and reproduce varied systems of economic organization with different economic and social capabilities (Orru, et. al., 1997; North, 1990).[13] Such variations, as I have shown above, reflect long-standing contrasts in the characteristics of national legal systems, political, cultural and institutional and financial systems (North, 1990; Hollingsworth, Schmitter & Streeck, 1994; Griffiths & Zammuto, 2003). Therefore, despite legislations, formal compliance of corporate governance regulations will not be effected unless these 'ethereal' and substantive issues are resolved.

The assumptions and concepts implicit in the good governance model are culturally derived. Indeed, this has been well recognised. Despite the claims of universal applicability of governance principles, many organisations including the OECD, noted the need for the 'observance of environmental and social standards' in reform (OECD, 1999: 23). National cultures, as international businesses and multinational corporations, will not go away anytime soon but instead continue to manifest and exercise their residual effects. What is required is a solution aimed at implementing and addressing the inherent issues embedded in governance practices within contextual realities. Culture influences our social preferences and consequently our interpersonal rules and institutions including legal rules and corporate structures. As such, I will further examine the impact of culture on: (1) the idea of transplant; (2) ownership structure, shareholder protection and relationship-based businesses and systems and (3) resilience of family firms, and show that culture is a significant factor in these structures and practices. Consequently, corporate governance practices are affected accordingly.

---

[13] Firms are by no means the same sorts of economic actors in different economies the ways in which private ownership is organized and connected to authority hierarchies as well as how these latter hierarchies are structured are able to delimit production and pricing levels and coordinate investment decisions of legally autonomous entities (Hamilton & Feenstra, 1997)

Transplanting Change

Corporate governance practitioners and proponents of reforms have assumed that corporate governance practices and systems can be merely replaced and transplanted from a more 'developed' system to one 'less developed'. Typically, it assumes a superior Western model, which needs to be adopted. This flies in the face of various international management and organisational change (OC) literature, particularly those that have investigated and analysed international joint ventures, mergers and acquisitions (M&As). The OC literature suggests that a forced application of corporate culture is and has been disastrous; and the literature on M&As similarly noted this trend. Corporate culture and practices, including governance principles and practices are local, specific and organic, and they evolve out from local contexts. Philip Alston (1999), an eminent international law scholar in reviewing the idea of legal transplants, has argued rather persuasively that such transplants generally do not succeed. The ADB similarly concurs: 'lessons derived directly from the experience of any one country or group of countries, regardless of how successful it or they have been, cannot be transplanted directly' (ADB, 1999: 15). Implicit here is the idea that despite our beliefs in universality, culture transcends legal practices and regimes. Contemporary social theorising have recognised this and suggest that as 'hosts' and local cultures interact, they construct new reciprocities and a host of new local networks and practices. This hybrid effect will lead to incremental adaptation and institutional transformation. This process is gradual, rather than an abrupt radical structural and strategic transformation.

Another theme in this transplant literature is the notion of sovereignty and imperialism. Many developing economies have been colonised and see such governance principles and practices as a means of (re)introducing 'soft' imperialism via legal precepts and practices. These unduly compromise their sovereignty as they are now subjected to a new set of principles, standards and regime that are imported from elsewhere and take no cognisance of their particular specificities. Indeed, some analysts have argued that the 1997 Asian financial crisis was the result of the 'neo-liberal' trend implicit in the US model (Chang, Park & Yoo, 1998; Jomo, 1998; Wade, 1998).

A critical interrogation of the idea of transplant would reveal that British rather than the American tradition of corporate law have a wider reach. With its highly regulatory content, protection of minorities and other features, British company law has adapted more readily to less-developed countries and their conditions than open-ended, enabling US-styled corporation law. Nonetheless, the central guiding pillar in this model is market fundamentalism (Reed, 2002). Recent literature suggests that other possible economic models have emerged and that market fundamentalism has not succeeded. This has meant a movement back to the recognition that states and regulation still matter, and that simply transplanting the market model wholesale to other economies and societies is extremely problematic and likely to fail.

Ownership, Shareholders and Relationships

A number of researchers have identified Asian firms as dominated by predominantly concentrated, family-based and dominated corporations (ADB, 2000; Claessens et. al, 1999; 2000; Whyte, 1996; Redding, 1990). More often than not, 'the distinction between owners and managers is eliminated' in most cases (Dyck, 20000: 29). Close knit and relatively dense relationships mean that the need for disclosure and transparency is often not crucial. However, as the OECD inveighs, 'a strong disclosure regime can help attract capital and maintain confidence in the capital markets' (OECD, 1999: 19). Current practices and systems in Asia clearly do not encourage disclosure and transparency and as such, can mitigate against investment decisions and pose a threat to good governance (La Porta et. al, 2000). Transparency has been identified as key feature of good governance and necessary for investor protection, particularly, the protection of minority shareholders from the abuse of controlling shareholders. However, Asian (and in developing countries) firms do not have a strong tradition of strong disclosure. This is in part due to insiders (often family and group members) who exercise control over the firms and they manage the information flows affect transparency and disclosure, within the firms. Often non-disclosure and opaque corporate dealings are the norm (Hirakawa, 2001).

Closely linked to this transparency and insider nexus is the relationship among participants in the governance system, and in Asia, the extent of bank-corporation relationship. Because of rather lax and/or the lack of prudential systems, Asian firms rely more on personal affiliations to raise capital. This is often achieved through bank lending (and close government-business clientele-like relationships) rather than equity market capitalisation for their growth (Blyer & Coff, 2003; Carney & Gedajlovic, 2002; Rajan & Zingales, 2001; Lasserre & Schutte, 1995; McVey, 1992). This, however, as a number of commentators have alluded to, has more to do with control than seeking growth, and can be counter-productive as it can constrain growth rather than encouraging it (ADB, 2000; Berglof & von Thadden, 1999; Weinstein & Yafeh, 1998). However, in Asia, control is linked to the use of effective power and here, ownership confers that right.

The ADB notes that 'companies are sometimes interconnected through ownership or other business relationships with their creditors, which is a further obstacle for creditors to take legal action against their borrowers' (ADB, 20000: 44). Indeed, where banks are represented on boards, it has been found that there is less discipline and less stringent monitoring. Such bank-corporation relationship is typically characterised and driven more by relationships and cronyism rather than any sound business backing. This 'derives from the conflict of interest that may arise when banks are both owner and creditor' (ADB, 2000: 7). The ADB also found that 'creditors have little or no influence over management decisions and, in cases where they do, the influence is exercised mainly through loan covenants' (ADB, 2000: 41). Clearly, the implication is that Asian firms are as susceptible to governance and management faults as their debtors. International analysts and financial institutions also charge East Asian governments for misguided policies by being derelict in monitoring economic activities and thus failed to reduce exposure to foreign exchange risks in both the financial and corporate sectors.

While there have been reforms since the 1997 crisis and lending requirements tightened, monitoring ability and/or influence on management decision-making have not increased. Relationships still matter and dominate much of management decisions, practices and strategies. Not unsurprisingly, a number of scholars have suggested that two distinct patterns of industrial capitalism can be discerned (Dore, 2000; Hall & Soskice, 2001). Moreover, there is the recognition that the state looms writ large in Asia and 'managed markets'. Clearly, Asian firms have innovated to accommodate this exigency senior executives stay in their role for long periods of time and assiduously cultivate their political relationships. Such organisational and business response, as such is highly rational, and indeed crucial for the firms to survive and grow. Changing the boards of management and directors to one of a shifting population of chosen executives would destroy and weaken this source of advantage and hence, unlikely to succeed. Indeed, recent research points out that the commonly held view of the separation between ownership and control in public listed corporations is a myth. Many of the largest corporations are family controlled and there is very little distinction made between ownership and management (La Porta, Lopez-de-Silanes & Shleifer, 1998).[14] Despite popular perception, Demsetz (1983) and La Porta and his associates also found that concentration of ownership and control exists in western developed countries, including among the largest American corporations.[15] Similar trends are discerned in Australia. These research findings are of grave concern for they suggest that contrary to the popular public view of greater public regulation, accountability and control, many large contemporary businesses are in fact governed by a small, interlocking oligarchic elite, usually via family ties and other business relationships. As such, calls for reforms which privilege voluntary compliance have been and are largely ineffectual. Rather, the need for greater participation into governance structures by stakeholders might induce more cooperative and effective forms of governance.

Family Capitalism

The dominant form of capitalism in many countries is not US-styled capitalism but rather one that is family-based (Colli, Fernandez-Perez & Rose, 2003). Viewed throughout much of the world as destructive of social cohesion and to be avoided rather than emulated (Gray, 1998: 101, 115-6), the US model is seen as bereft of social and political relevance to many developing countries. Rather, a society-centred and

---

[14] Amongst the more interesting findings, La Porta and his fellow researchers found globally were: many of the largest firms are controlled by families; In family-controlled firms, there is very little separation between ownership and control; Family control is more common in countries with poor shareholder protection; State control is common, particularly in countries with poor shareholder protection; Deviations from one share, one vote are most common in countries with poor shareholder protection; and corporations with controlling shareholders rarely have other large shareholders

[15] There is a view and the myth that this exists solely in East Asia see for example, Fukuyama (1996) and Backman (1999).

more humane and collective form of capitalism are desired.

In Asia, firms are typically 'molecular organisation heavily networked family firms' that tend toward vertical integration. This is of course, not a continental exception the economic topographies of France and Italy has been and is dominated by family firms (Faccio & Lang, 2002; Brunello, Graziano & Parigi, 2003). Here, networks and the institutions of trust and reciprocity work to foment and build up relationships and alliances of firms, banks, sub-contractors, customers, and suppliers and even extend into government agencies. The emphasis on reciprocity induces and strengthens the ideals of trust, social harmony, role compliance and obligations.

Firms, as such, are not seen merely as a matrix of enforceable, limited term contracts between principals and agents that delimit individual responsibilities but as entities which people make commitments to. They are seen almost as communities of the people working in them. There is thus a moral compact: the role of the firm is akin to a larger village providing for its population and the workers willingly contribute to the well-being of the firm through their hard work. Superiors likewise provide for the subordinates and the amount of respect and authority granted to the boss is a reflection of that obligation. Thus, this enables the boss to be decisive, fairly didactic and even paternalistic. The freedom to exercise their managerial decision and discretion intuitively and decisively is advantageous in contexts marked by organisational and product uncertainty and innovation (Khanna & Palepu, 2000). Because of this low agency costs, versatility and flexibility, many private firms, particularly family-controlled firms have been found to be more efficient than private firms (Durand & Vargas, 2003; Anderson & Reeb, 2003).

Efficiency in these firms is related of course to trust, particularly the exercise of reciprocal power relationships. Power as such, is not a mere accident of politics or an evolution of economics but rather reflective of acceptable social ideals. Where there is an infraction of acceptable norms through the exploitation of power or advantage, disgrace for the perpetrator is guaranteed. This moral force becomes a technology of power and control through which the players subject themselves to. This exercise of power as Wong (2005b) has shown in his critical analysis of Confucian capitalism, can be likened to as a 'new moral technology' of control and is applied assiduously by managers to legitimise their business management practices morally and also to press their employees into the employ of the firms through a conflation of the self with the firm.

Conclusion

The study of a converging global governance practice is a globalisation story (Gugler, Mueller & Yurtoglu, 2004; Dore, 2003). By presenting corporate governance as the market mechanism most effective in protecting investors' rights, corporate governance has become the *de facto* disciplinary tool for markets via-a-vis governments, and for a time, it appears that there was only one model. However this globalisation is weak, as events have attested to. The 1997 Asian financial crisis, developments in eastern Europe, South America, UK, Europe and the USA, all raised questions of the wisdom and/or viability of embracing only a model. No model of capitalism or business system has been or is perfect. Each country has its own unique traditions maintained in their institutions such as families, schools and forms of governments. Douglas North (1990) has classified cultural factors as 'informal constraints' on societies and has put them on par with formal constraints via institutions. Institutions arguably can be seen as the crystallisations of culture and culture creates and enables institutional arrangements. For example, the differences found in the relative importance attributed to family interests between and even parts of the world are reflected in the role of families in business ownership. Similarly, whilst growth, continuity and reputation may be universal, these goals and many other goals are and have been modulated and moderated by culture and institutions. The national origin of firms remains significant; its leaders give effect to its goals and these are again influenced by local histories and specificities. As such, the traditional shareholder wealth maximisation model[16] is not easily transportable and transferable to the rest of the world where corporations pursue diverse and even different objectives (Boatright, 1999). Unless and until the world is unified by a universalist culture, firms will continue to maintain a multi-pronged, multi-faceted approach to meet their *specific* objectives.

I do not, however, like many others, believe that good corporate governance systems and practices can be merely legislated for nor is there a singular model. There is no perfect system; it involves tradeoffs between competing goals and as such, can only involve 'second best' options. Moreover, convergence has its limits; (local) institutional systems, practices and arrangements are all pervasive and highly influential in effecting economic directions and outcomes. Therefore, despite the global economy, a singular mode of governance is unlikely. A singular mode of corporate governance would require a reorganisation of central institutional structures and relationships, as well as a restructuring of interest-group relations and perhaps, of their constitution and organisation. This is unlikely to be realised given the different social and economic histories of countries and very strong held beliefs of political arrangements e.g. sovereignty, individualism, liberalism and collectivism. As such, Rubach and Segora wrote, 'differences in corporate governance systems reflect the paths by which each came to exist'. These path-dependencies suggest that institutional structures are critical influencing variables; moreover political and legal realities mitigate against a mere transplant outcome. Resistance is likely and adaptations more likely to be the outcome.

These adaptations will of course be compounded by the diversity, interactions and changes (and integration) in the increasingly complex global economic system, ensuring varying practices and arrangements. Thus, rather than proclaiming 'the end of history' and a universal mode of corporate governance, we need to be more circumspect and seek to locate our understandings of particular economies within their specificities. Indeed, complementarity might be equally valid and useful in enabling us to understand different corporate governance systems and practices (Schmidt & Spindler, 1998; Shleifer & Vishy, 1997). Analytically, this would involve

---

[16] This view of the SWT model according to some is a total misconception. For a critique and elaboration, see Miller (1994).

a move away from abstract, idealised forms and a commitment to historical and institutional contexts and realities (North, 1990). This would require us, therefore, to undertake the task of continually and constantly developing, adapting and re-writing corporate governance practices capable of meeting our new needs and challenges.

Richard Whitley wrote that 'distinctive ways of organising economic activities become established and effective because of major differences in key social institutions such as the state, the financial system, the education and training system', including labour market organisation as well as the indirect influence 'of more general and diffuse attitudes and beliefs about work, material values and authority relations...(and) family and kinship relations, identities and authority structures' (Whitley, 1992: 13, 16). The implication is that business systems, including corporate governance systems, are historically, socially and culturally determined. If these observations are accurate, corporate governance systems and practices cannot merely be legislated for; getting the law and the model right is not enough. There is the issue of local details, of the capacity of institutions which are if not more critical in enabling the required outcomes. Without attending to one's locale, history, culture and particularities, such 'best' practice may be ineffective and like weeds, turn out to be a nightmare.

Therefore, rather than looking for one best way, it is more important to find ones that work for the circumstances. This paper has sought to highlight two key points. The first is the heterogeneity of governance patterns and the need to explore in great depth the linkages between the political and institutional environment, on the one hand and corporate trajectories on the other. This point is certainly not novel and can be seen in the 'varieties of capitalism' literature and certainly acquired a new relevance in a world of ineffectual governance and steadily increasing corporate power (and its beneficiaries). The other relates to what is global? Specifically, I have suggested that what needs to be avoided is to adopt standards of governance that originated within a specific cultural and regional context be allowed to (re)present itself as the global norm. Otherwise, comparative and critical analyses would have no real value and unable to advance our heuristic understandings.

References

ADB (Asian Development Bank) (1995) *Governance: Sound Development Management*, Asian Development Bank Online Publication, www.adb.org/documents/policies/governance/govooo.asp, August 1995) accessed 21 October 2007.

ADB (1999) *Governance in Asia: From Crisis to Opportunity*, ADB Annual report, Manila: ADB.

ADB (2000) *Corporate Governance and Finance in East Asia: A Study of Indonesia, republic of Korea, Malaysia, Philippines and Thailand) Vol 1, A Consolidated Report*, Manila: ADB.

Albert, M. (1993). Capitalism vs. Capitalism: How America's Obsession with Individual Achievement and Short Term Profit Has Led it to the Brink of Collapse, New York, Four Walls Eight Windows.

Allen, F. & D. Gale (2000) *Comparing Financial Systems*, Cambridge, MA: MIT Press.

Alston, P. (1999) 'Transplanting Foreign Norms: Human rights and Other International legal Norms in Japan', *European Journal of International Law*, 10(3): 625-32.

Anderson, R.C.& D.M. Reeb (2003) 'Founding Family Ownership and Firm Performance: Evidence from the S&P 500', *Journal of Finance*, 58(3): 1301-28.

Aoki, M. (1990) 'Toward an Economic Model of the Japanese Firm', *Journal of Economic Literature*, 28: 1-27.

Aoki, M. (2001) Towards a Comparative Institutional Analysis, Cambridge, MA, MIT Press.

Araki, T. (2005) 'Corporate Governance Reforms, Labor Law Development and the Future of Japan's Practice-Dependent Stakeholder Model', Japan Labor Review, 2(1): 26-57.

Backman, M. (1999) Asian Eclipse: Exposing the Dark Side of Business in Asia, New York, John Wiley & Sons.

Balling, M. (1993) *Financial Management in the New Europe*, Cambridge, MA: Blackwell

Bargh, C., P. Scott & D. Smith (1996) *Governing Universities: Changing the Culture?* Buckingham: The Society for Research into Higher Education.

Baum, D.J. & Stiles, N.B. (1965) *The Silent Investors*, Syracuse, New York, Syracuse University Press.

Bebchuk, A. & Roe, M.J. (1999) 'A Theory of Path-Dependence in Corporate Ownership and Governance', *Stanford Law Review*, 52: 127- 69

Berglof, E. and Perotti, E. (1994). 'The Governance Structure of the Japanese Financial Keiretsu' *Journal of Financial Economics*, 36: 259-284.

Berglof, E. & E.L. von Thadden (1999) '*The Changing Corporate Governance Paradigm: Implications for Transition and Developing Countries*', Annual Bank Conference on Development Economics, 28-30 April 1999, Washington, DC: World Bank.

Berle, A. & Means, G. (1968) *The Modern Corporation and Private Property*, Revised Edn, New York ,Harcourt Brace & World.

Best, M. (1990) *The New Competition: Institutions of Industrial Restructuring*, Oxford, Polity Press.

Blyer, M. & R.W. Coff (2003) 'Dynamic Capabilities, Social Capital and Rent Appropriation: Ties that Split Pies', *Strategic Management Journal*, 24: 677-86.

Bradley, M.H. et. al (1999) The Purposes and Accountability of the Corporation in Contemporary Society: Corporate Governance at a Crossroad', *Law and Contemporary Problems*, 6: 9

Brancato, C.K. (1997) *Institutional Investors and Corporate Governance*, Chicago, Irwin.

Branson, D. (2002) 'The Very Uncertain Prospects of Global Convergence in Corporate Governance', *Cornell International Law Journal*, 34, 321-62

Brunello, G., C. Graziano & B. Parigi (2003) 'CEO-Turnover in Insider-Dominated Boards: the Italian Case', *Journal of Banking and Finance,* 27: 1027-51.

Bryan, D. & Rafferty, M. (1999) *The Global Economy in Australia*, Sydney, Allen and Unwin.

Budros, A. (1997) 'The New Capitalism and Organisational Rationality: The Adoption of Downsizing Programs, 1979-1994', *Social Forces*, 76: 229-50.

Buxbaum, R. & Hopt, K. (1988) *Legal Harmonisation and the Business Enterprise*, Berlin, Walter de Gruyter.

Carney, M. & E. Gedajlovic (2002) 'The Co-evolution of Institutional Environments and Organizational Strategies: The Rise of Family Business Groups in the ASEAN Region', *Organization Studies*, 23(1): 1-31.

Castells, M. (2000) 'Information Technology and Global Capitalism' in W. Hutton & A. Giddens (Eds.) *Global Capitalism*, New York, New Press

Cernat, L. (2004) 'The Emerging Corporate Governance Model: Anglo-Saxon, Continental or Still the Century of Diversity?, *Journal of European Public Policy*, 11(1): 147-66.

Chandler, A. (1990) *Scale and Scope*, Cambridge, Mass, Harvard University Press.

Chang, H.J., H.J. Park & C.G. Yoo (1998) 'Interpreting the Korean Crisis: Financial Liberalisation, Industrial Policy and Corporate Governance', *Cambridge Journal of Economics*, 22: 735-46.

Charkham, J. (1994) *Keeping Good Company A Study of Corporate Governance in Five Countries*, Oxford, Clarendon Press.

Chen, M. (1995) *Asian Management Systems: Chinese, Japanese, Korean Styles of Business*, New York, Routledge.

Child, J. & Faulkner, D. (1998) *Strategies of Cooperation Managing Alliances, Networks and Joint Ventures*, Oxford, Oxford University Press.

Child, J. & McGrath, R.G. (2001) 'Organisations Unfettered Organisation Form in an Information-Intensive Economy', *Academy of Management Journal*, 34: 1135-48.

Claessens, S. S. Djankov J.P.H. Fan & L.H.P. Lang (1999) *Corporate Diversification in East Asia: The Role of Ultimate Ownership and Group Affiliation*, World Bank Working Paper 2089, Washington DC: World Bank.

Claessens, S. S. Djankov & L.H.P. Lang (2000) 'The Separation of Ownership ad Control in East Asian Corporations', *Journal of Financial Economics*, 58(1/2):

81-112.

Clarke, F. Dean, G.W. & Oliver, K.G. (1997) *Corporate Collapse: Regulatory, Accounting and Ethical Failure*, Cambridge, Cambridge University Press.

Clarke, T. & Bostock, R. (1994) 'International Corporate Governance: Convergence and Diversity' in T. Clarke & E. Monkhouse (Eds) *Rethinking the Company*, London, FT Pitman.

Clarke, T. & Clegg, S. (1998) *Changing Paradigms*, London, HarperCollins Business.

Clegg, S. Ibarra-Colado, E. & Bueno-Rodriquez, L. (1999) *Global Management: Universal Theories and Local Realities*, London, Sage.

Coase, R. (1937) 'The Nature of the Firm', *Economica*, 4: 387-405.

Colli, A., F. Fernandze-Perez & M. Rose (2003) 'National Determinants of Family Firm Development: Family Firms in Britain, Spain and Italy in the 19th and 20th Centuries', *Enterprise and Society*, 4(1): 28-65.

Collier, B. & Pitkin, S. (Eds.) (1999) *Corporations and Privatisation in Australia*, Sydney, CCH Australia.

Cooke, T.E. & Sawa, E. (1998) 'Corporate Governance Structure in Japan - Form and Reality', *Corporate Governance*, 6(4): 217-23.

Dan-Cohen, M. (1986) *Rights, Persons and Organisations A Legal Theory for Bureaucratic Society*, Stanford, Stanford University Press.

Daniels, R. & Morck, R. (Ed.) (1995) *Corporate Decision-Making In Canada*, Calgary, University of Calgary Press.

De Alacantra, C.H. (1998) 'Uses and Abuses of the Concept of Governance', *International Social Science Journal*, 155: 105-13.

Delhaise, P. F. (1998) *Asia in Crisis: The Implosion of the Banking and Finance Systems*, New York, John Wiley & Sons.

Demestz, H. & Lehn, K. (1985) 'The Structure of Corporate Ownership: Causes and Consequences', *Journal of Political Economy*, 93: 1155-77.

Demestz, H. (1983) 'Corporate Control, Insider Trading and Rates of Return', *American Eonomic Review*, 86: 313-16.

Dicken, P. (2003) *Global Shift: Reshaping the Global Economic Map in the 21st Century*, London, Sage.

Dobbin, F. (1994) *Forging Industrial Policy: The United States, Britain and France in the Railway Age*, Cambridge, Cambridge University Press.

Dodd, C.H. (1991) *Dynamics of Intercultural Communication*, Wm.C. Brown, Dubuque, IA.

Dore, R. (2000) *Stock Market Capitalism: Welfare Capitalism*, Oxford, Oxford University Press.

Dore, R. (2003) 'The Globalization of Corporate Governance: External and Internal Mechanisms of Control', *Journal of Interdisciplinary Economics*, 14: 125-37.

Drucker, P. (1992) 'The New Society of Organisations', *Harvard Business Review*, Sept-Oct: 95-104.

Dugan, R., McKenzie, P. & Patterson, D. (2000) *Closely Held Companies Legal and Tax Issues*, Auckland, CCH New Zealand Ltd.

Duncan, I. & Bollard, A. (1992) Corporatisation and Privatisation Lessons from New Zealand, Auckland, Oxford University Press.

Durand, R. & V.Vargas (2003) 'Ownership, Organization and Private Firms' Efficient Use of Resources', *Strategic Management Journal*, 24: 667-75.

Dyck, I.J.A. (2000) *Ownership Structure, Legal Protections and Corporate Governance*, Annual Bank Conference on Development Economics, 28-30 April 1999, Washington, DC: World Bank.

Edwards, V. (2001) *EC Company Law*, Oxford, Oxford University Press.

Faccio, M. & L.Lang (2002) 'The Ultimate Ownership of Western European Corporations', Journal of Financial Economics, 65(3); 365-95.

Fama, E.F. & Jensen, M.C. (1983) 'Separation of Ownership and Control', *Journal of Law and Economics*, 26: 301-

Farrar, J. (2001) *Corporate Governance in Australia and New Zealand*, Oxford, Oxford University Press.

Farrar, J. H. (1987) 'Ownership and Control of Listed Public Companies Revising or Rejecting the Concept of Control' in B. Pettet (Ed.) *Company Law in Change*, London, Stevens & Sons.

Fligstein, N. (1990) *The Transformation of Corporate Control*, Cambridge, Mass., Harvard University Press.

Fligstein, N. & R. Freeland (1995) 'Theoretical and Comparative Perspectives on Corporate Organisation', *Annual Review of Sociology*, 21: 21-43.

Francis. I (1997) *Future Directions The Power of the Competitive Board*, Melbourne, FT Pitman.

Freeman, R.E. (1984) *Strategic Management: A Stakeholder Approach*, Boston, Pitman.

Fukuyama, F. (1992) *The End of History and the Last Man*, London, Penguin.

Fukuyama, F. (1996) *Trust: The Social Virtues and the Creation of Prosperity*, New York, Free Press.

Gates, J. (1998) *The Ownership Solution Towards a Shared Capitalism for the Twenty-First Century*, London, Penguin Books.

Geertz., C. (1973) *The Interpretation of Cultures*, Basic Books, New York.

Geertz, C. (1984) 'Anti Anti-Relativism', *American Anthropologist*, 86: 263-78.

Gerlach, M. (1992) *Alliance Capitalism*, Berkeley and Los Angeles, University of California Press.

Gilson, R. J. (1994) 'Corporate Governance and Economic efficiency' in M. Isaakson & R. Skog (Eds.) *Aspects of Corporate Governance*, Juristoforlaget, Stockholm.

Gilson, R.J. & Roe, M.J. (!993) 'Understanding the Japanese Keiretsu: Overlaps between Corporate Governance and Industrial Organisation', *Yale Law Journal*, 102: 871-906.

Giradin, E. (1997) *Banking Sector Reform and Credit Control in China*, Paris, OECD.

Goodijk, R. (2000) 'Corporate Governance and Workers' Participation', *Corporate Governance*, 8(4): 303-10.

Gordon, J.N. & M.J. Roe (2004) *Convergence and Persistence in Corporate Governance*, Cambridge, Cambridge University Press.

Gourevitch, P. (1996) 'The Macropolitics of Microinstitutional Differences in the Analysis of Comparative Capitalism' in S. Berger & R. Dore (Eds.) *National Diversity and Global Capitalism*, Ithaca, Cornell University Press.

Gray, J. (1998) *False Dawn: The Delusions of Global Capitalism*, London, Granta

Books.

Gugler, K. (ed.) (2001) *Corporate Governance and Economic Performance*, Oxford, Oxford University Press.

Gugler, D.C. Mueller & B.B. Yurtoglu (2004) 'Corporate Governance & Globalization', *Oxford Review of Economic Policy*, 2(1): 129-56.

Hall, E. (1955) 'The Anthropology of Manners', *Scientific American*, 192(4): 85-90.

Hall, P. & D. Soskice (2001) *Varieties of Capitalism*, Oxford, Oxford University Press.

Hamilton, G. & Feenstra, R.C. (1997) 'Varieties of Hierarchies and Markets: An Introduction' in M. Orru et. al. (Eds.) *The Economic Organisation of East Asian Capitalism*, London, Sage.

Hampden-Turner, C. & Trompenaars, F. (1993) *The Seven Cultures of Capitalism*, London, Piatkus.

Hampden-Turner, C. & Trompenaars, F. (1997) *Mastering the Infinite Game: How East Asian Values are Transforming Business Practices*, Oxford, Capstone.

Handy, C. (1995) *The Empty Raincoat: Making Sense of the Future*, London: Arrow Books.

Hannerz, U. (1992) *Cultural Complexity*, Columbia University Press, New York.

Hansmamm, H. & R. Kraakerman (2001) 'The End of History for Corporate Law', *Georgetown Law Review*, 89: 439-68.

Harbison, F. & Myers, C.A. (1959) *Management in the Industrial World*, McGraw Hill, New York.

Hay, C. & marsh, D. (Eds.) (2000) *Demystifying Globalisation*, London: Palgrave.

Held, D. et. al. (1999) *Global Transformations*, Cambridge, Polity Press.

Herrigel, G. (1996) *Industrial Constructions: The Sources of German Industrial Power*, Cambridge, Cambridge University Press.

Hirakawa, H. (2001) 'East Asia's Financial and Economic Crisis and Its Lessons', *Journal of Tokyo Keizai University*, 223: 41-51.

Hirshhorn, R. (1995) 'The Governance of Non-Profits' in R. Daniels & R. Morck (Ed.) *Corporate Decision-Making In Canada*, Calgary, University of Calgary Press.

Hirst, P. & Thompson, G. (1999) *Globalisation in Question*, Cambridge: Polity Press.

Hofstede, G. (1991) *Cultures and Organizations: Software of the Mind*, New York, McGraw-Hill.

Hollingsworth, J.R. (1991) 'The Logic of Coordinating American Manufacturing Sectors' in J.L. Campbell et. al. (Eds.) *Governance of the American Economy*, Cambridge, Cambridge University Press.

Hollingsworth, J.R., Schmitter, P. & Streeck, W. (1994) (Eds.) *Governing Capitalist Economies*, Oxford, Oxford University Press.

Hollingsworth, J.R.& Boyer, R. (1997) *Comparing Capitalisms: The Embeddedness of Institutions*, Cambridge, Cambridge University Press.

Hopt, K.J. & Wymeersch, E. (Eds.) (1997) *Comparative Corporate Governance*, Berlin, Walter de Gruyter.

Hopt, K.J. et. al. (1999) Comparative *Corporate Governance The State of the Art and Emerging Research*, Oxford, Oxford University Press.

Hoshi, T, Kashpay, A. & Scharfstein, D. (1991) 'Corporate Structure, Liquidity and Investment: Evidence from Industrial Groups', *Quarterly Journal of Economics*,

106:33-60.

Hurst, J. W. (1970) *The Legitimacy of the Business Corporation*, Charlottesville, University Press of Virginia.

Jensen, C.M. & W. Meckling (1976) 'Theory of the Firm: Managerial Behaviour, Agency Cost and Capital Structure', *Journal of Financial Economics*, 3: 305-60.

Joint Committee of Public Accounts and Audit (1999) *Corporate Governance and Accountability for Commonwealth Government Business Enterprises*, Report 372, Canberra, AGPS.

Jomo, K.S. (Ed.) (1998) *Tigers in Trouble: Financial Governance, Liberalization and Crises in East Asia*, London, Zed Books.

Jordan, C. (1997) *International Survey of Corporate Law in Asia, Europe, North America and the Commonwealth*, Melbourne, Centre for Corporate Law and Securities Regulation.

Kanda, H. (1997) 'Corporate Governance, Country Report: Japan' in K. Hopt et. al. *Comparative Corporate Governance   The State of the Art and Emerging Research*, Oxford, Oxford University Press.

Keasey, K., Thompson, S. & Wright, M. (Eds) (1997) *Corporate Governance Economic, Management and Financial Issues*, Oxford, Oxford University Press.

Kelsey, J. (1995) *Economic Fundamentalism*, London, Pluto Press.

Kester, C. (1997) 'Governance, Contracting and Investment Horizons: A Look at Japan and Germany' in D.H. Chew (Ed.) *Studies in International Corporate Finance and Governance Systems*, New York, Oxford University Press.

Khanna, T. & K. Palepu (2000) 'Is Group Membership Profitable in Emerging Markets? An Analysis of Indian Business Groups', *Journal of Finance*, 55(2): 867-91.

Kogut, B. (1991) 'Country Capabilities and the Permeability of Borders', *Strategic Management Journal*, 12: 33-47.

Konig, K. & Siedentopf (1988) 'An International Perspective II: Privatisation and Institutional Modernisation in Asia and Europe' in I. Thynne & M. Ariff (Eds) *Privatisation: Singapore's Experience in Perspective*, Longman, Singapore.

Kristensen, P. H. (1997) 'National Systems of Governance and Managerial Strategies in the Evolution of Work Systems: Britain, Germany and Denmark Compared' in R. Whitley & P.H. Kristensen (Eds.) *Governance at Work: The Social Regulation of Economic Relations*, Oxford, Oxford University Press.

La Porta, R. et. al. (1999) 'Corporate Governance Around the World', *Journal of Finance*, 52: 1131-50.

La Porta, R. F. Lopez-De-Silanes, A. Shleifer & R.Vishy (1998) 'Law and Finance', *Journal of Political Economy*, 106: 1113-55.

La Porta, R. F. Lopez-De-Silanes, A. Shleifer & R.Vishy (2000) 'Investor Protecton and Corporate Governance', *Journal of Financial Economics*, 58(1/2): 3-27.

Lasserre, P. & H. Schutte (1995) *Strategies for Asia-Pacific*, London, Macmillan.

Lazonick, W. & O'Sullivan, M. (1996) 'Organisation, Finance and International Competition', *Industrial and Corporate Change*, 5: 1-49.

Lindberg, L.N. & Campbell, J.L. (1991) 'The State and the Organisation of Economic Activity' in J.L. Campbell et. al. (Eds.) *Governance of the American Economy*, Cambridge, Cambridge University Press

Lusting, M.W. & Koster, J. (1996) *Intercultural Competence: the Fundamentals of Intercultural Communication*, Morris, Englewood, CO.

Ma, R. & Morris, R.D. (1982) *Disclosure and Bonding Practices of British and Australian Banks in the Nineteenth Century*, Sydney, University of Sydney Accounting Research Centre.

McCahery, J.A., P. Moerland, T. Raaijmakers & L. Reeneboog (Eds.) (2002) *Corporate Governance Regimes: Convergence and Diversity*, Oxford, Oxford University Press.

McDonnell, B. (2002) Convergence in Corporate Goverance: Possible but not Desirable', *Villanova Law Review*, 341: 350-3.

McGregor-Lowdes, Fletcher, K. & Sievers, A.S. (Eds.) (1996) *Legal Issues for Non-Profit Associations,* Sydney, Law Book Co.

McVey, R. (1992) 'The Materialisation of the SouthEast Asian Enrepreneur' in R. McVey (Ed.) *Southeast Asian Capitalism*, New York, NY, Cornell University Southeast Asia Program.

Marcus, G. and Fisher, M. (1986) *Anthropology as Cultural Critique*, University of Chicago Press, Chicago.

Mead, R. (1990) *Cross Cultural Management Communication*, John Wiley & Sons, Chichester

Miller, M.H. (1994) 'Is American Corporate Governance Fatally Flawed?', *Journal of Applied Corporate Finance*, 6(4): 32-9.

Monks, R. A. G. and Minow, N. (1995) *Corporate Governance*, Cambridge, MA: Blackwell.

Moreland, P.W. (1995a) 'Alternative Disciplinary Mechanisms in Different Corporate Systems', *Journal of Economic Behaviour and Organisation*, 26: 17-34.

Moreland, P.W. (1995b) 'Corporate Ownership and Control Structures: An International Comparison', *Review of Industrial Organisation*, 10: 443-64.

Morgan, G. (1993) 'Paradigm Diversity in Organisational Research' in J. Hassard & D. Pym (Eds.) *The Theory and Philosophy of Organisations*, Sage, London.

Morrison, T. et. al. (1994) *Kiss, Bow or Shake Hands: How to Do Business in Sixty Countries*, Adams Media, Holbrook, MA.

Nalebuff, B.J. & Brandenburger, A.M. (1996) *Co-opetition*, London, HarperCollins Business.

Neubauer, F. & Lank, A.G. (1998) *The Family Business: Its Governance for Sustainability*, Basingstoke, Macmillan.

Nishiyama, T. (1984) 'The Structure of Managerial Control: Who Owns and Controls Japanese Businesses' in K. Sato & Y. Hoshino (Eds) *The Anatomy of Japanese Business*, London, Provident House.

North, D. (1990) *Institutions, Institutional Change and Economic Performance*, Cambridge, Cambridge University Press.

OECD (1998) *Corporate Governance: Improving Competitiveness and Access to Capital in Global Markets*, Paris, OECD.

OECD (1999) *Principles of Corporate Governance*, Paris, OECD.

Ohmae, K. (1982) *The Mind of the Strategist*, London, McGraw-Hill.

Ohmae, K. (1995) *The End of the Nation State*, New York, Free Press.

Orru, M. (1997) 'The Institutionalist Analysis of Capitalist Economies' in M. Orru et.

al. (Eds.) *The Economic Organisation of East Asian Capitalism*, London, Sage.

Pascale, R.T. & Athos, A.G. (1981) *The Art of Japanese Management*, Warner Books, New York.

Platteau, J.P. (1994) 'Behind the Market Stage where Real Society Exist, Part II: The Role of Moral Norms', *Journal of Development Studies*, 30(3): 753-817.

Plender, J. (1997) *A Stake in the Future: the Stakeholding Solution*, London, Nicholas Breaery.

Prowse, S. (1992) 'The Structure of Corporate Ownership in Japan', *Journal of Finance*, 47: 1121-40.

Rajan, R.G. & L. Zingales (2001) *The Great Reversals: The Politics of Financial Development in the 20th Century*, Working Paper, University of Chicago.

Redding, G. (1990) *The Spirit of Chinese Capitalism*, New York: de Gruyter.

Redding, G. (2004) 'The Conditional Relevance of Corporate Governance Advice in the Context of Asian Business Systems', *Asia-Pacific Business Review*, 10(3-4): 272-91.

Reed, D. (2002) 'Corporate Goverance Reforms in Developing Countries', *Journal of Business Ethics*, 37(3): 223-47.

Reich, R. (1992) *The Work of Nations*, New York, Simon and Schuster.

Roe, M. (1991) 'A Political Theory of Corporate Finance', *Columbia Law Review*, 1: 10-67.

Roe, M. (1997) 'Path Dependence, Political Options and Governance Systems' in K.

Hopt & D. Wymeersch (Eds) *Comparative Corporate Governance*, Berlin, Walter de Gruyter.

Roe, M.J. (1994) *Strong Managers, Weak Owners The Political Roots of American Corporate Finance*, Princeton University Press, Princeton.

Roe, M. (2002) 'Corporate Law's Limits', *Journal of Legal Studies*, 31: 233-71.

Rosen, R. (2000) *Global Literacies*, New York, Simon and Schuster.

Roy, W.G. (1997) *Socializing Capital: The Rise of the Large Industrial Corporation in America*, Princeton, NJ, Princeton University Press.

Rubach, M.J. & Sebora, T.C. (1998) 'Comparative Corporate Governance: Competitive Implications of an Emerging Convergence', *Journal of World Business*, 33(2): 167-84.

Samovar, L.A. & Porter, R.E. (1991) *Communication Between Cultures*, Wadsworth, Belmont, CA.

Samuels, W. (1987) 'The Idea of the Corporation as a Person' in W.J. Samuels & A.S. Miller (Eds) *Corporations and Society: Power and Responsibility*, New York, Greenwood Press.

Schmidt, R.H. & G. Spindler (1998) *Path Dependence, Corporate Governance and Complementarity: A Comment on Bebchuk and Roe*, Working Paper Series, Finance and Accounting, Goethe University.

Semenov, R. (2000) *Cross-Country Differences in Economic Governance: Culture as Major Explanatory Variable*, PhD Dissertation, Netherlands: University of Tilburg.

Sheard, S. (1994) 'Interlocking Shareholdings and Corporate Governance' in M. Aoki & R. Dore (Eds.) *The Japanese Firm The Sources of Competitive Strength*, Oxford, Oxford University Press.

Shleifer, A. & Vishny, R.W. (1997) 'A Survey of Corporate Governance', *Journal of Finance*, 52: 737-83.

Soros, G. (2000)'The New Global Financial Architecture' in Hutton, W. & Giddens, A. (2000) *Global Capitalism*, New York, New Press.

Stapleton, G. (1996) *Institutional Shareholders and Corporate Governance*, Oxford, Oxford University Press.

Stapleton, G. (1998) 'Australian Sharemarket Ownership' in G. Walker, B. Fisse & I. Ramsay (Eds) *Securities Regulation in Australia and New Zealand*, Sydney, LBC.

Sugarman, D. & Teubner, G. (eds.) (1990) *Regulating Corporate Groups in Europe*, Ban Baden, Nomos Verlagsgesellschaft.

Tam, O.K. (1999) *The Development of Corporate Governance in China*, Cheltenham, Edward Elgar.

Thelen, K. (1991) *Union of Parts*, Ithacea, NY, Cornell University Press.

Thurow, L. (1992) *Head to Head: The Coming Economic Battle Among Japan, Europe and America*, Sydney, Allan & Unwin.

Thurow, L. (1999) *Building Wealth*, New York, Harper Collins,

Tomasic, R. & Bottomley, S. (1993) *Directing the Top 500 Corporate Governance and Accountability in Australian Companies*, Sydney, Allen & Unwin.

Tricker, R.I. (1984) *Corporate Governance*, Aldershot, Gower.

Tricker, R.I. (1994) *International Corporate Governance*, New York, Prentice Hall.

Turnbull, S. (1997) 'Corporate Governance: Its Scope: Concerns and Theories', *Corporate Governance*, 5(4): 180-205.

Unger, R. (1976) *Law in Modern Society*, New York, Free Press.

Usui, C. & Colognon, R. (1996) 'Corporate Restructuring: Converging World Pattern or Societally Specific Embeddedness?', *Sociological Quarterly*, 4: 361-78.

Van der Berghe, L. & De Ridder, L. (1999) *International Standardisation of Good Corporate Governance*, Boston, Kluwer Academic Publishers.

Volcker, P. A. (2000) 'The Sea of Global Finance' in W. Hutton & A. Giddens (Eds.) *Global Capitalism*, New York, New Press.

Waddock, S.A. & Graves, S. (1997) 'The Corporate Social Performance-Financial Performance Link', *Strategic Management Journal*, 18: 303-17.

Wade, R. (1998) 'From 'Miracle' to 'Cronyism': Explaining the Great Asian Slump', *Cambridge Journal of Economics*, 22: 693-706.

Weimer, J. & Pape, J.C. (1999) 'A Taxonomy of Corporate Governance', *Corporate Governance*, 7(2): 152-66.

Weinstein, D.E. & Y Yafeh (1998) 'On the Costs of a Bank-Centered Financial Systems: Evidence from the Changing Main Bank Relations in Japan', *Journal of Finance*, 53: 635-72.

Weiss, L. (1998) *The Myth of the Powerless State*, Ithaca, Cornell University Press.

Westney, E. (1996) 'The Japanese Business System: Key Features and Prospects for Change', *Journal of Asian Business*, 12: 21-50.

Whitley, R. (1992) *Business Systems in East Asia: Firms, Markets and Societies*, London, Sage.

Whitley, R. (1999) *Divergent Capitalisms*, Oxford, Oxford University Press.

Whyte, M.K. (1996) 'The Chinese Family and Economic Development: Obstacle or

Engine?', *Economic Development and Cultural Change*, 45(1): 1-30.

Williams, A. (2000) *Who Will Guard the Guardians: Corporate Governance in the Millenium*, Chalford, Management Books 2000 Ltd.

Williams, R. (1981) *Culture*, Fontana, London

Williamson, O. (1996) *The Mechanisms of Governance*, NY, Oxford Universit Press.

Wong, L. (2005a) Chinese Management as Discourse: 'Chinese' as a Technology of Self and Control?, Asian Business and Management, 4: 431-53.

Wong, L. (2005b) "Corporate Governance in China: A Reflexive Critical Approach" in C.Lehmann (Ed.) *Advances in Public Interest Accounting* (special Edition on Corporate Governance) 11: 117-43.

World Bank (1997) *China's Management of Enterprise Assets: The State as Shareholder*, Washington, DC, World Bank.

World Bank (1999) *Corporate Governance: A Framework for Implementation*, Washington DC: World Bank.

Yoshimori, M. (1995) 'Whose Company is it? The Concept of the Corporation in Japan and the West', *Long Range Planning*, 28(4): 33-44.

Zysman, J. (1996) 'How Institutions Create Historically-Rooted Trajectories of Growth', *Industrial and Corporate Change*, 3(1): 243-83.

Chapter 9

Social Responsibility at the grassroots the influence of '*mahalla*' community organisations on the CSR practices of small and medium enterprises (SMEs) in Uzbekistan

Daniel Stevens and Lobar Mukhamedova

Introduction

In this chapter we examine the way in which a particular feature of culture in Uzbekistan, the *mahalla* community organization, plays a central role in the way in which corporate social responsibility (CSR) is understood and practiced amongst small and medium enterprises (SMEs) in Uzbekistan.

First we examine the institution of the '*mahalla'* community organization in Uzbekistan and how its nature reflects two aspects of 'culture' in shaping CSR. Second we analyse the critical role the promotion of SMEs has within the development ambitions of the government of Uzbekistan in promoting social welfare and addressing poverty. Third we briefly outline the potential for SMEs, by embracing CSR, to magnify their contribution to the overall well being of society.

Fourth we draw from a survey of SMEs in Uzbekistan and interviews with both SME managers and *mahalla* community leaders to examine the way in which the *mahalla* institution shapes the understanding and approach of SMEs to CSR.

Finally we conclude with some observations about how the particular case of SMEs in Uzbekistan suggests broader lessons about how corporate social responsibility evolves as it encounters new cultures and institutional frameworks.

Mahalla as culture tradition and institution

When considering the impact of culture on CSR the definition of 'culture' is of course pivotal. Normally in studies of culture and CSR the term culture is used interchangeably with political states (for example Maignan 2001 and Ardichvili & Kuchinke 2002, cited in Ahunov 2006) largely due to the way in which data is normally collected at the country level. The validity of this approach has been extensively debated around the case of Hofeste's dimensions of culture. Hofeste himself admitted that states are not the best units for studying cultures, but 'they are usually the only kind of units available for comparison and better than nothing.' (Hofstede 2002: 2)

Others have tried to use broader cultural categories such as 'Asian' (Baugn et al 2006) though normally this represents an amalgamation of different countries rather than a cross-cutting category. Another broader cultural category has been to take religion and explore the relationship, for example, between Islam and CSR (Zinkin 2006, cited in Ahunov 2006) and across different religious affiliations (Brammer et al 2007). The inconclusive nature of the findings of such research suggests that generalizing according to religious affiliation is difficult when the nature of this affiliation and how it shapes approaches to CSR may depend greatly on the individual country.

For not only is analysis at the nation-state level accessible, a la Hofstede, but maybe the most relevant given the importance of regulatory regimes that shape a company's approach to CSR. In short, broader notions of culture are very limited in explaining differing approaches to CSR, and need to be combined with analysis of more prosaic factors such as the regulatory and broader political system within a nation-state.

The analysis of CSR in Uzbekistan is a case in point. Firstly it is not clear which cultural grouping to fit Uzbekistan into how 'Asian' is a country that for about a century was ruled from Moscow, only becoming independent in 1991. Likewise, while the county's population is predominantly Muslim, again the experience of being largely isolated from the larger Muslim world when part of the Soviet Union means that the impact of religious affiliation differs from that in other parts of the Muslim world.

Thus when we look at the influence of a community organization like the 'mahalla' we need to recognise that while on the one hand this organization reflects a broader cultural tradition that transcends Uzbekistan's borders, on the other hand it's impact is shaped by the political landscape particular to Uzbekistan. In this section we discuss both this broader cultural aspect of the *mahalla* as well as the way in which it has now become part of the broader state structure in the country.

The term '*mahalla*' is an Arabic term meaning "local community" (Aminova 2006) is a tradition held in common with other parts of Central Asia and the Moslem world. The traditional focus of the *mahalla* has been organizing community events such as the 'rites of passage' rituals around birth, marriage and death, played a philanthropic role of directing charity to the needier residents, and a social work role resolving family conflicts and generally keeping '*tinch*' or peace and stability in the neighbourhood. It also organizes something known as '*hashar*', in which community members assist each other on a reciprocal basis in tasks that require extensive labour input particularly building houses. The *mahalla* is traditionally are coordinated by a council of elders, known as *oksakals* (literally white beards).

Having origins from as far back as the ninth century, the *mahalla* has demonstrated a considerable resilience over time, particularly during the Soviet period, which has lent it an aura of legitimacy as a mediator between community members and the state, particularly during the 1990s when Uzbekistan became independent from the Soviet Union and was freer to celebrate its cultural distinctives. At the same time it is important to note that this tradition is largely restricted to the older quarters of the cities of Uzbekistan, and also a feature of 'sedentary' ethnic groups of Uzbekistan (the dominant Uzbeks and also the Tadjiks) and less so of the 'nomadic' groups (such as Kazakhs, Kyrgyz or Karakalpaks) and the European ethic groups such as the Russians, which made up a significant part of the urban population. Thus upon independence in 1991 it was only in these Uzbek/Tadjik urban neighbourhoods that the tradition remained, and other more European areas of the city and rural areas there were different state led structures for organizing community relations.

This allure and legitimacy of the tradition, and the potential for the *mahalla* in ensuring social cohesion during the disruptive period of transition away from the Soviet system, meant that the *mahalla* was increasingly co-opted by the government and metamorphosed into what is officially classified as an organ of self governance but what is widely perceived as the lowest level of the state.

Firstly the *mahalla* was given a role in the delivery of social security benefits, beginning in 1994 when benefits for families with low-incomes were distributed in this way, then in 1997 for child benefits and finally in 1999 for maternity benefits (Coudouel and Marnie, no date). Such benefits had previously been universal, but the need to move towards a means tested approach meant that the government needed a mechanism for determining who were eligible, and the *mahalla* seemed an ideal fit as a body able to determine need and administer the payments.

As well as combating poverty, another challenge in post independence Uzbekistan was security, and a series of car bombings in 1999 marked the emergence of a terrorist threat, rooted in social dislocation and economic hardship, nourished by radical Islamic ideologies and reinforced by a perceived lack of alternative channels for expressing the frustrations of those who were not benefiting from the new opportunities opening up in the country. Once again the local knowledge of the *mahalla* seemed an ideal ally for the state in both identifying terrorists and also preventative work in educating young people about the dangers of getting involved in such groups. So secondly the *mahalla*s were given a role in both identifying suspects and educating young people, with a post created of '*posbon*', part community policeman part educator, who would work closely with the security services (IWPR 2004).

In addition to these two central themes, *mahalla*s have been involved in programmes to support entrepreneurship, public health and a whole other range of issues including basic administrative issues such as confirming residence and providing documentary support for other administrative processes.

In using the *mahalla* institution for these state functions, the institution needed to be rolled out across the whole country, to include the newer, more European districts of the cities, as well as the rural regions where about two-thirds of the population live. At the same time it had to be more formalized, with a committee structure created that included an official chair (*rais*) and other positions such as a secretary. Because of its administrative functions, it also worked closely with the district (*tumon*) level of government. Where it has been rolled out beyond the old urban quarters the *mahalla* institution looks and feels very similar to the *domkom,* the Soviet community administrative structure and as such is widely perceived as a state body. However, in these older quarters the *mahalla* has taken a dual identify reflecting both a traditional community organization busy with organizing weddings and resolving family conflicts, as well as an administrative body distributing social security and keeping a watchful eye on the youth, activities which had already been carried out informally.

As such the *mahalla* is a mixture of both traditional community relations and modern state governance. This suggests that when considering the impact of culture we should be attuned both to the historically rooted traditions that it reflects, as well as the way in which it is often transformed into institutions of a modern state, i.e. recognizing that culture reflects traditions that cross borders, as well as the system of governance within each individual state.

SMEs and their wider social role

Transitioning from the Soviet command economy, dominated by large scale enterprises, the concept of the SME is quite novel for Uzbekistan. However, with encouragement from International Finance Institutions such as the IMF, World Bank and Asian Development Bank, along with other international organizations, the government has identified the growth of SMEs as fundamental to the country's development prospects. They look to the example of more developed nations and see that, for example, in the UK SMEs constitute over 99% of all businesses and 'make significant contributions to employment, wealth creation, investment, innovation and overseas trade' (Worthington et al. 2006: 201) In 16 years of independence, through a policy of privatization of small state enterprises, SMEs now contribute over 45% of GDP and are described by the President as 'the main source of supplying the market with necessary goods and services, increase of incomes and well being of population, and the most important factor in tackling the problems of employment' (Karimov 2007). As such the government is looking to increase the share of SMEs in GDP to over 50% by 2010 (Government of Uzbekistan 2007: 7).

The potential contribution of SMEs to unemployment is emphasized by the government, particularly given the restructuring in the agriculture sector which has involved the shedding of many workers from inefficient collective farms, and the hope is that SMEs in both manufacturing and the services sector will create new jobs. At the same time conditions for small business have been difficult. Uzbekistan scored poorly in the World Bank 2007 Doing Business report, though another joint World Bank/EBRD Business Environment and Enterprise Performance Survey (2006) concluded that Uzbekistan had performed well recently compared to other CIS countries and was improving, particularly in terms of the improving macroeconomic conditions in the country. This report noted that there had been a fall in the number of firms reporting problems in doing business in 2005 compared to 2002, though a relatively high and increasing percentage of firms reported 'problems regarding unofficial payments when dealing with taxes, business licensing, and accessing public services.'(IMF 2007: 2).

Thus there is a realization of the potential of SMEs in having a wider positive social impact, but at the same time continued challenges in ensuring a favorable business climate to operate in.

SMEs and CSR

In addition to their contribution to economic growth, particularly employment, there is also the potential that SMEs might develop their own brand of corporate social responsibility and in doing so further increase the benefits they bring to society.

That SMEs can also engage in CSR is well established (Sarbutts 2003, Jenkins, 2004: 52, Castka et al 2004, Luken & Stares, 2005). By being rooted in communities, rather than separated in campus style company headquarters, the social pressure on mangers to ensure that their business is perceived as benefiting the community is potentially stronger. By virtue of being small, and privately managed, it also gives them greater room for maneuver to address these expectations. Georges Enderle (2004: 62) argues that SMEs 'are supposed to have some spaces of freedom and corresponding responsibilities, at least under the conditions of most business environments around the globe.' In the rest of this article we investigate the amount of freedom and sense of responsibility that exists in the particular business environment that is Uzbekistan. Given the centrality of the *mahalla* in the local governance of the country, our hypothesis was that it would significantly shape this operating environment, and consequently the approach to CSR, found amongst these locally rooted SMEs.

How does the *mahalla* influence SME's approach to CSR

In answering this question we draw from research carried out by Westminster International University in Tashkent in partnership with the Chamber of Commerce and Industry in Uzbekistan[1]. This research, undertaken at the end of 2006, involved a survey of over 200 SMEs in Uzbekistan, in depth interviews with 28 managers, and also 15 *mahalla* leaders, representing seven regions of the country[2].

The interviews with the managers of SMEs were designed to identify their business objectives, along with their understanding of the notion of social responsibility, and the activities that they had taken with respect to the environment and also work conditions for their employees. The interview also explored the role of the *mahalla* in the entrepreneurs' life. These managers were also invited to express their opinion on how the social activity of entrepreneurs could be increased.

While there is no formal definition of what counts as an SME in Uzbekistan, this is normally calculated in terms of employees and for the 28 SMEs that we interviewed

---

[1] Funding for the project was provided by the British Embassy, Tashkent, Uzbekistan
[2] The following cities were visited by the participants of the project Andijan, Samarkand, Bukhara, Termez, Navoi and Tashkent.

the number of employees ranged from 1-100. In terms of the background of these SME managers, the majority of them are in the services, production and agricultural sectors and their activities include provision of medical services, consulting services and educational centers. Most of the enterprises are quite new, having been founded between 1993 and 2005. All of these managers have a higher education.

The majority of the interviewed entrepreneurs were involved in some form of charity activities. This includes assistance to orphanages, provision of free training education in handicrafts to young people, donations to the poor, and providing food for the celebration of national holidays. Most of the SMEs were sponsoring orphanages or old peoples homes. In terms of the motives cited, the majority made reference to religious factors. Only one respondent explained these activities in terms of social responsibility. A number of managers emphasized that CSR was primarily about treating one's workers well, with one expressing the ambition ;to make something pleasant for the people who work with me. Friendly atmosphere is the key to success and it is crucial that besides the money side there should be a real satisfaction with work. Only in this case we can talk about social responsibility at the workplace.'

One key finding was that only 14 % of the SME manager respondents do not work closely with the mahalla committees. It seems clear that while the concept of CSR may not be developed, cooperation with the *mahalla* community organization is pivotal to their activity.

The interviews with the representatives of the *mahalla* were focused on the on social activities of *mahalla* and the role of *mahalla* in promoting entrepreneurship. Within the framework of project, 15 representatives of different *mahalla*s in 7 regions were interviewed. As the result of the interviews it was identified that *mahalla* assists in conducting such social activities as the *subbotnik* (the Soviet term for voluntary public works, normally involving cleaning the streets or buildings in preparation for a public holiday), holiday celebrations, provision of rooms and places for work, recommending young people for learning handy craft and work.

It is particularly in the area of handicrafts that the *mahallas* seem to play an important intermediary role between entrepreneur and those in the community in need of employment opportunities. These crafts include gold-embroidery, stamping, the manufacture of leather products, weaving, jewelry   all of which require basic workshops. The *mahalla*, which often has some building space, can provide a location for such workshops as well as recommending apprentices. Since the *mahalla* itself has detailed information on the residents, it plays a role of connecting the needy and the entrepreneurs who can help address their needs not just with short term handouts but with a long term investment in developing a skill. This seems to complement the *mahalla*s role of administering social security payments.

The *mahalla* leaders also actively seek out the help of SMEs - writing letters and directly asking entrepreneurs to take part in the activities of the *mahalla*. In the opinion of *mahalla* committees, in order to involve SMEs more in the life of the community, some prior explanatory work is necessary. It is likely that greater awareness of each other and the concept of CSR might help entrepreneurs and representatives of the *mahalla* to work in closer cooperation. Mahallas are keen for the SMEs to understand that the further strengthening of the role and status of the *mahalla* within the governance system as well as more broadly the social and economic life of society, will strengthen the level of social protection within society. The *mahalla* sees that it has a role in mobilizing action to preserve and promote national values and traditional customs related to a healthy way of life, social justice and the spiritual and moral education of the people. They see SMEs as needing to make a contribution to this. The weight of this argument translates into considerable pressure on some SMEs to accede to the requests of the *mahalla*, whether or not they see it as linked to their business model. It becomes a defensive ploy, to ensure that the *mahalla*, or the broader system of state governance that it is linked to, keeps off their backs.

What was interesting about the interviews with the SME managers is that none of the respondents knew about the positive privileges given by the state for carrying out social action. However, when invited to suggest what would help them to engage more in social activity it was state support that was often mentioned including greater tax privileges, and preferential loans, to go along with more broader suggestions such as greater mutual trust and increasing knowledge about the issue of corporate social responsibility.

This suggests that, as cited above, a primary concern for SMEs is the regulatory environment and what they seem to be looking for is more of a two-way process of mediation played by the *mahalla*. At present it appears rather one way with the *mahalla*, itself subject to government priorities, relaying these demands onto the SMEs which feel obliged to accede to requests for funding various events, often with little relation to their business processes or long-term strategic plans. This is largely defensive CSR, used to maintain positive relations with the government. What SMEs seem to be looking for is that *mahalla*s would also lobby for them and support them in their representations to higher levels of government. SME managers suggested that maybe the *mahalla* could help them as a guarantor for loans, or in securing licenses.

Conclusions

This analysis of the relationship between SMEs and the community '*mahalla*' organization, in the context of the SME's approach to CSR, is an illustration of how, while broader notions of culture may have some explanatory power, this is always going to take second place to the influence of the particular business environment within each country, in particular the regulatory regime and the attitude of the government to small business. For the rich tradition of mutual assistance represented by the *mahalla* seems to have had a weakening impact on SME managers when it comes to the notion of social responsibility, with most of the managers identifying religious factors as more directly contributing to their social activities. The impact of the *mahalla* seems to be more in its new role as representative of the state at the local level, mediating the government expectations that SMEs in the country should make a significant contribution to the broader development of the country. The form this contribution is to make is partly determined by the *mahalla*, in the form of the requests it makes for SMEs to contribute to its own activities.

However, SME managers were not overly negative about the role of the *mahalla*, and came up with constructive suggestions as to how it might play a role in not only representing state interests to business, but also their interests to the state, in other words for the *mahalla* to play a mediatory role in which there is give and take on both sides. This suggests that rather than seeing the *mahalla* as obstacle they see the potential for it to play a role of enhancing cooperation between business and government. This reflects the role the traditional *mahalla* seems to have played during Soviet times, where its greater perceived independence from the state enabled it to play a more neutral role in ensuring cooperation between individual communities and the government what is referred to as its 'institutional dualism'- "being both a genuine community and an administrative unit" (Makarova 1999: 128).

This points the way forward in fostering CSR amongst SMEs. It is clear the *mahalla* plays a pivotal role in advancing social welfare at the community level, and that for any SME interested in engaging with the local community it makes sense to work with the *mahalla*. The *mahalla* also seems positive, and eager to interface with SMEs. Indeed one mahalla leader explained that 'We are to address the financial interests of SMEs by giving preferential loans and tax breaks, and by reducing the bureaucratic procedures.' This suggests that some are aware of the needs of SMEs, what is missing seems to be a greater balance in the give and take required for the mutual trust between entrepreneur and state to flourish.

This analysis is also instructive about how CSR evolves when it moves into emerging markets. We have seen that much of the CSR of SMEs in Uzbekistan is defensive as a result of the particular regulatory regime they face which denies them the space to develop more strategic CSR approaches in the context of a competitive market in which reputation needs to be proactively built. The regulatory regime is thus vital when considering how CSR might travel to new emerging markets. The transition to a market economy in Uzbekistan has been relatively gradual, and state involvement in the economy still quite extensive, such that the CSR activities of SMEs are primarily focused on ensuring good relations with the authorities, and less focused on seeking competitive advantage and meeting consumer expectations. How culture shapes these consumer expectations is an issue not covered by this current research, though is clearly an area worthy of investigation. For as firms are freed up to compete more, the focus will gradually shift away from the demands of the bureaucrat and more towards the preferences of the buyer.

References

Ahunov, Muzaffarjon (2006) Literature Survey: Culture, and CRS among SMEs, unpublished paper, Westminster International University in Tashkent

Aminova, Munira (2006) Aspects of CSR, SMEs and other businesses practice in the *mahalla*s of Uzbekistan, unpublished paper, Westminster International University in Tashkent

Ardichvili, Alexander & Kuchinke, Peter (2002) Leadership styles and cultural values among Managers and subordinates: a comparative Study of four countries of the former soviet union, Germany, and the US, *HRDI* 5:1 (2002), pp. 99-117

Baughn, C. Christopher & Bodie, Nancy L & McIntosh, John C. (2006) Abstract Submitted to Conference on Corporate Social Responsibility: Agendas for Asia,

http://www.nottingham.ac.uk/nubs/ICCSR/AsiaConf06/AbstractPdfs/Baughn.
    pdf
Brammer, S., Williams, Geoffrey and Zinkin, John (2007) Religion and Attitudes to
    Corporate Social Responsibility in a Large Cross-Country Sample, *Journal of
    Business Ethics*, Volume 71, Number 3, March, 2007
Castka, Pavel., Balzarova, Michaela A., Bamber, Christopher J. & Sharp, John M.
    (2004) How can SMEs Effectively Implement the CSR Agenda? A UK Case
    Study Perspective, *Corporate Social Responsibility and Environmental
    Management*, 11, pp. 140-149
Coudouel, Aline & Marnie, Sheila (no date) From Universal to Targeted Social
    Assistance: an Assessment of the Uzbek Experience, draft paper
Enderle, Georges (2004) Global competition and corporate responsibilities of small
    and medium-sized enterprises, *Business Ethics: A European Review* Volume 13
    Number 1 January 2004, pp 51-63
Government of Uzbekistan (2007) Welfare Improvement Strategy of Uzbekistan: Full
    Strategy Paper for 2008-2010, Tashkent
Luken, Ralph & Stares, Rodney (2005) Small Business Responsibility in Developing
    Countries: A Threat or an Opportunity? *Business Strategy and the Environment*
    14, pp. 38-53
Maignan, Isabelle (2001) Consumers' Perceptions of Corporate Social
    Responsibilities: A Cross-Cultural Comparison, *Journal of Business Ethics*, 30:
    5772, 2001.
Makarova, Ekaterina (1999) Paradoxes of Development in Soviet and Post-Soviet
    Central Asia: With Special Reference to the Role of the Mahalla in Uzbek Cities,
    Ph.D. Thesis: University of Manchester
Hofstede (2002) Dimensions do not exist: A reply to Brendan McSweeney, Geert
    Hofstede, *Human Relations* Volume 55(11):
International Monetary Fund (IMF) (2006) Republic of Uzbekistan: 2006 Article
    IV ConsultationStaff Report; Public Information Notice on the Executive Board
    Discussion; and Statement by the Executive Director for the Republic of
    Uzbekistan, IMF Country Report No. 07/133, 2007
IWPR (2004), 'Uzbekistan: Neighbourhood Watch', IWPR's *Reporting Central Asia*,
    No. 303, July 27, 2004
Karimov, Islam (2007) Speech of President Islam Karimov at the joint meeting of the
    Oliy Majlis (parliament), Cabinet of Ministers, and Staff of the President of the
    Republic of Uzbekistan dedicated to the 16th anniversary of the Independence of
    Uzbekistan
Sarbutts, Nigel (2003) Can SMEs 'do' CSR? A practitioner's view of the ways
    small- and medium- size businesses are able to manage reputation
    through corporate social responsibility, *Journal of Communication
    Management*; 2003; 7, 4; pp. 340 - 347
Worthington, Ian, Ram, M. & Jones T. (2006) Exploring Corporate Social
    Responsibility in the U.K. Asian small Business community, *Journal of Business
    Ethics*, 67: pp. 201-217

Chapter 10

Cultural Diversity at Work and the Need for Wholeness

Ana Maria Davila Gomez

Abstract

Increasingly, with globalization, organizations become a space where multiculturalism is a source of conflicts or agreements that needs to be addressed. Inside a competitive paradigm of exclusion, the concept of Corporate Culture establishes that the values of shareholders and the managerial board are those that represent the identity of the organization. However, inside a multicultural reality, an encounter of sets of values becomes a source of conflicts at work, not only for attaining organizational goals, but also for representing mental health issues and human development interest of the individuals at work. Therefore, the corporate culture discourse does not fit reality, as new identities are formed in an on-going transformation of organization and cultures, hence, transculturality needs to be addressed as a social phenomena at work. Traditional deterministic approaches of culture in organizations, that separates nations in individualistic or collectivistic, may serve as a tool for identifying some of the values of a specific culture, but not as managerial criteria for stereotyping people nor for practicing negotiation. We consider that an approach that integrates the concept of wholeness in management is imperative, which includes willingness, understanding, listening and openness. With this, managers need to develop awareness of the different points of view coming from differences and complexities of stakeholders: community, groups of employees, nations and States. New qualities need to be developed such as openness and sensitivity to otherness, and all this in the aim to respect the impact of any decision and action in the wholeness. In this article, we discuss the previous reality in an aim to understand some of the causes and implications for human well-being derived as an imposition from the concept of corporate culture. Equally, we examine how organizational theory has addressed these issues, trying to unveil some limits and possibilities, in an aim to reflect at the end about some alternatives, that considering transculturality, may help managers in the imperative to be open and active towards wholeness. We need to pass from a 'corporate culture' of competition to a transcultural experience of collaboration.

Multiculturalism at work and willingness of managers

In 2001, Unesco adopted the Universal Declaration on Cultural Diversity (Unesco, 2001). One apart of this diversity declaration states:
"Cultural diversity and international Solidarity [...] Article 11 - Building partnerships between the public sector, the private sector and civil society - market forces alone cannot guarantee the preservation and promotion of cultural diversity, which is the key to sustainable human development. From this perspective, the pre-eminence of public policy, in partnership with the private sector and civil society, must be reaffirmed."

While talking about organizations, and their responsibility towards human beings, we may assume that the previous paragraph indicates us that in the workplace there is a need for a human righteousness. A sense of goodness is required. Tolerance, acceptance and non-discrimination necessitate that people making part of organizations, reflect on their ways of doing things. With globalization, cross-cultural experiences are widely accentuated, not only in developed countries as a result of migrations, but also in developing countries given the nowadays modes of off-shoring and outsourcing that follow a positivistic approach of utilitarianism.

When questioning about the righteousness and goodness of acts, it is not difficult to identify that even following international rules for working (such as the conventions emanated from the International Labour Organization concerning equality, non discrimination and opportunities - see International Labour Organization, 2007), or even inside what is stipulated inside some countries' legislations, there is a space to act with liberty for shareholders. We know that legislation worldwide is not the same. Therefore, it is possible to act legally in a country whose legislation allows things that are prohibited in another one. With such disparities in countries' legislation, it comes the possibility to be unethical, even though following the law.

By the same token, a certain kind of value in an organization does not assure that people working inside adhere to the institutional set of beliefs. It is socially understood that public institutions work for the well-being of citizens. However, nothing assures that the service that is delivered to a citizen will be at the same time delivered with a certain degree of human righteousness, as it is the hope of the universal human rights declaration. We talk here about the treatment experienced in the relationship: discrimination, ethics, respect, acknowledgment or listening, to only mention some aspects of the interaction established between two human beings: one, the citizen, and the other, the employee of the public institution. Even though we can establish that in this interaction there will always be a person representing the values of the public institution, reality shows that it is not always the case.

Furthermore, with globalization, information technology has gain the attention of highly instructed professionals that will fit the modernized demands of productivity in order to achieve the competitive level asked in almost all kinds of organizations. On the one hand, information allow us to take more conscious decisions, but on the other hand, as it may be manipulated or ignored depending on the finalities of those who posses it, it may also become a mask of the real image of the organization (see for example how Crowther and Davila (2007), Crowther and Green (2004) discuss about the righteousness and validity of information content in Corporate Reports that will arrive to citizens and community). Inside this information, we also may consider what is valued by an organization, and inside this, the term of 'corporate values' is extremely important, given that what culture and values mean may represent the norms, the beliefs, or the ways of conducting the individuals. However, as reality shows, for instance, the fact of working in a public organization, does not assure that organizational actions within will certainly show a coherence in the sense that people are treated equally.

While considering the point to which human groups have arrived to elaborate noble ideas like the one presented before (I.e. righteousness in the human treatment), we ask, as human beings that we are, how is it possible that, simultaneously, in the same world, such distant thoughts may coexist: one of peace and understanding, and another of hatred and mistrust. On the one hand, we have people who fight beautiful intellectual battles in an aim to contribute at least a little in order to obtain a better world. We see many of these in academies, religious congregations, non profit international organizations, or even public institutions in some States, among others. On the other hand, we have people who disregard a common view of a better world for all of us. And paradoxically, we find many of these in the same kind of citizen-oriented institutions aforementioned, and also, anywhere in the world. Is there a concentration of good people somewhere? Or, more than a question of geographical matter, is it more a question of individual and intrinsic characteristics of the being? Why are some people more acknowledging of the need for improvement and solidarity, while others disregard their connection with their fellow men like them, or even worse, with the wholeness?

In the next points we reflect about some of the possible causes of the previous, trying to elaborate about some alternative ways of managing within multiculturalism. We explore the appropriateness of the concern for the wholeness, and therefore, the need for otherness (as claimed by Tsoukas, H. and Chia, 2002) as a key element needed in organizations nowadays.

Being competitive as a 'Corporate Culture' of exclusion

With globalization, the managerial paradigm of rationality and increasing of share value asks of organizations to become more competitive. This reality puts management education and practices to privilege the strategic orientation of concurrent forces presented by Porter (1980), in which, the external organizational context is seen as a set of forces (clients, competitors, substitution products and suppliers). There is a need to understand the influence of these forces in order to identify how to face them. In this sense, an additional set of managerial tools helps managers to formulate their strategies depending on the internal strengths and weaknesses of the organization, in order to answer to the opportunities and dangers established while doing the aforementioned analysis of the forces in the external context. In this perspective, one organization at a time is considered as the most important and the solely objective for a manager. As we see, in this dominant tendency, no major consideration for other stakeholders is taken into account. As customers are not considered as citizens, their meaning is only identified as a transactional target. In the same way, communities are rarely recognized. Furthermore, employees, who are also stakeholders, are considered only as work force, not necessarily as integral beings who also have a familiar and social role in the community.[1]

We may consider this as a culture of the management practice, in which the values of the 'corporate culture' that will allow the organization to be competitive are: productivity, exigency, force for negotiations. This refers, for instance, to the actions taken when organizations deal with other organizations that are their competitors, or even with their clients or suppliers, or furthermore, when negotiating with governments of foreign countries once the firm wants to install factories or offices overseas. With these values, managers are asked to continuously improve and demonstrate competency in the following skills: influence towards others, convincing leadership, stress acceptance, communication assertiveness, among others. Inside this need to convince others about the declared corporate values, there are two objectives: one, to obtain from the employees acceptance and assertiveness to the corporate culture, in order to gain fidelity and loyalty, therefore implication and efficiency at work, and second, to influence actual or possible counterparts while doing negotiations like fusions and acquisitions, mergers, or simply while working at places where the workforce has a high degree of multiculturalism (e.g. Adler, 2002; Trompenaars and Hampden-Turner, 1998).

As such, we could see a tendency to impose a culture of the minority (the powerful shareholders or managers) towards the majority: employees, members of communities, or even more, members of governments of different countries. In this sense, culture is understood not as something natural but as something intentionally constructed. It is not rare to hear how, inside the positivistic approach, various organizational development (OD) projects on organizations, leaded by the high directors, seek to establish the values and the culture of directors which will be, subsequently, implemented in the whole of the organizations throughout various workshops, in which almost every member of the firm's personnel participates, under the supervision of the human resources department. Even though these techniques seek the employees allegiance, the results are not always as expected. On the contrary, while the employees values are openly disregarded, the directors values are widely acknowledged and are considered as the values worth retained; the result is an increasing lack of motivation and trust from the personnel. Employees start recognizing that they are only viewed as instruments of increasing share value and not as individuals that have values which may help the organization in its mission and also may help to their self realization as human beings. It is as if the results are worse than the aims of the project. A neither consultative nor conciliatory exercise of acknowledging the diversity of values among the different groups of the organizations may lead to distrust, lack of honesty, and closes the door for innovation and creativity.

---

[1] See the need for a broader consideration of the human being at work in Davila-Gomez and Crowther (2007) and in Crowther and Green (2004).

Without recognizing it, our modern managerial techniques of 'top-down' strategies and culture dissemination, are reviving what Taylor (1856-1915) and Fayol (1841-1925) structured as one of the core principles of scientific administration. We talk here about the principle that establishes that directors are placed in the higher levels of the hierarchy because they are those who posses the knowledge to decide and it is up to them to identify how to conduct the business. At the same time, this principle orders that employees with no hierarchy have the only duty to accept what has been well planed by directors, therefore, employees do not need to be distracted of their work routines and do not need to be worried by strategic issues.

As we see, even though this could be seen as very dramatic, and also a little archaic, given that this principle has been formulated long time ago, the reality is that the dominant positivistic approach of our management still endures its finality by means of productivity techniques, and as discussed previously, by some OD tools such as 'culture change' or 'culture dissemination'.

Contrary to the dominant practice, history and anthropology teach us that culture is something that occurs mostly in a spontaneous way when various individuals of any given group agree to accept some values as a common understanding that will rule their interactions, many times, their social and political life, and all that with the acknowledgement of the members (e.g. Morin, 2001). Hereby, the values answer mostly to inner conviction of the individuals. It is like saying, when someone belongs to a culture, he or she, inherits the community values that are cherished as the way in which actions need to be conducted. In some cases, when the collective to which these values belong is considerably strong and large, there is an external recognition by other cultures, therefore delimitations (by means of comparison) are established between the individuals of different groups, and the concept of culture of nations takes place (Juteau, 2000). Consequently, these identifications of associativeness lead to the concepts of ethnicity, or in some cases, gender.

With this approach, we may understand that inside organizational culture we find not only the values of the community (employees at any hierarchical level), but also the famous 'corporate culture' interacting with the first one. As explained by Zghal (2003) and Mercier (2001), more than one imposed organizational culture, we experience a multiplicity of values and preferences given the fact that people come from different contexts and groups of associations (nations, professions, gender). A good understanding of the reality will imply the need for recognition of this diversity and the need for interaction between the different groups. As demanded by Chevrier (2004), in management, there is a need to pass from multiculturalism, which addresses mostly the recognition of diversity, to interculturalism, which implies as well the interaction and recognition of diversity, making it possible to obtain agreements that are more beneficial for all the parties involved.

In interculturalism, Chevrier proposes to the manager to be more open towards other individuals, to encourage conviviality within the social life of the organization, and to develop a transcultural environment at work. Taking the previous to a practical level, Vulpe et al. (2000) establish some competences that will help managers, mostly but not exclusively to public managers, such as: adaptation, modesty, respect, comprehension, information and formation in the foreign culture and traditions, respects of accords, among others. Moreover, Henriette (2005), propose to managers the importance of developing intercultural competences based on human qualities by means of gaining experience within living events of diversity as a tool to improve their know-to-be and their know-to-act. This reminds us of what Kierkegaard (1813-1855) claims as necessary in the continuous development of the being through self-examination and self-reflection.

A critical regard of the 'cultural dimension' in organization theory

Continuously, new generations of people try to learn how to live, within the frame of the founding rules. Yet, modifications are made depending on the continuous questioning of the actual validity of the old rules or simply by the appearance of new values. For instance, Turiel (2002) shows how society influences the way in which individuals, inside a social regime, internalize and accept (or deny) the rules by means of coherent or disobedient behaviours towards the rule.

Throughout a series of journalistic examples, Turiel shows that even inside culture agreements characterized by strong hierarchy and highly organized rules of conduct (some of which are sometimes very restrictive or unfair), there is a possibility for the individual to seek a sense of righteousness through actions, that aim to attain a change, that may provide more justice and equality. In this sense, Nucci and Turiel (2000), explain that in some cases, a disobedience to the social rules is conducted by some individuals in a quiet environment where they cannot be caught by the surveillance of the regime; therefore, in some cases, it is inside home that some disobedience to, what some would call 'archaic rules', take place (i.e. gender equity, authoritarian disagreement, among other behaviours).

For the latter to represent a truly social change, a social movement is needed. A collective reflection may take not only a generation, but sometimes even centuries. Sometimes, this is done quietly, but others, as history tells us, it entails intellectual or military revolutions, which are now still occurring. Nonetheless, it is not necessary to change an entire whole national culture to see that also little modifications are continuously made in a collective when, for instance, new legislation, or its amendments, is made, or when, as a result of the aforementioned globalization, different cultural groups work together in neutral soil or as result of expatriation (see Philippe, 2004) by the organization. Whatever the case, the validity of the concept of 'corporate culture' is in continuous questioning.

In the case of legislation amendments, we may cite the example of the Canadian legislation preoccupation for a national value of equity and non-discrimination as it is stated in the Canadian Multicultural Act 1988 amendment 1993 (see Canadian Heritage, 2004), which while encouraging immigration, establishes, for example, some orientations for including and respecting cultural diversity at work. However, reality shows immigrants facing problems and not necessarily fitting well in their workplace. For instance, in the Employment Equity in the Federal Public Service 2004-2005 Annual Report to Parliament (see Canada Public Service Agency, 2005) we may see how the Canada Public Service Agency intend to open the willingness of managers and private firms owners by means of starting setting the example by applying the inclusive cultural diversity politics on governmental organizations.

Some initiatives of the same kind have been done already for various years upon the concept of Equality Equity Option, and/or Affirmative Action, in various countries such as United States and Australia, among others, and in which enrolment policies in companies include positively the openness to cultural diversity, moreover women at work. In the Canadian case, the aforementioned report shows how public institutions have started to integrate multicultural and affirmative action at work in terms of recruitment, meetings for conflict resolutions, among other activities. Regardless of the fact that these legislations intend to gain more acceptance in the whole community, there is still the need for individuals who own power, to acknowledge this need. Therefore, even in governmental institutions, the aim is not an easy task to complete.

Additionally, in the case of organizations containing a high concentration of multiculturalism, or for those that go overseas, various attempts to address the difficulties of the situation have been conducted. For instance, in the domain of management and culture, the works of Hofstede (2001, 1980) have been widely cited and acknowledged in the praxis because they allow managers to identify various sets of behaviour from different national cultures. Some other authors criticize the determinism and stereotyping of this approach given that, by means of four dimensions (hierarchy distance, feminine / masculine, control incertitude and universalism / collectivism), it is not always possible to identify qualitative particularities of societies or communities (i.e. what d'Iribarne, 1998, 1989, explains as the need to connect society traits with organizational realities). Even though this approach may give us a first glimpse of reality while encountering others different to us, it is certain that the person as a whole has attachments to various groups, therefore, the person has different values and a uniqueness that is worth to acknowledge. In fact, each one of Hofstede's dimensions can be measured. For instance, as an example, we can see how a culture has more respect for hierarchies than another. Being aware of this difference may provide insight when, for instance, we are going to address the managers of another country, or when we are going to conclude some negotiations (see Adler, 2002).

In this case, some other authors have already recognized the need to identify other cultural characteristics that do not need to be so deterministic, but more symbolic and interpretative. For instance, Hall (1983) identify the importance of other dimensions like 'time' or 'space' and how differently they are perceived in the understanding of reality, depending on the national culture (see how Sabelis (2004) examines the importance of acknowledging these differences while working in transcultural environments). Equally, when Hampden-Turner and Trompenaars (2004) accept the individualistic/collectivistic dissociation, they ask multicultural groups at work to conciliate in praxis these two orientations in order to obtain positive outcomes for organization's learning and success (even though inside a competitive approach) as well as the individuals' professional development. They acknowledge the fact, that inside collectivist cultures, an individual may be affected by suffering, even depression, if he or she wishes to excel and perform by him or herself outside the already pre-arranged social set of possible success. At the same time, they recognize that inside individualistic cultures, socially oriented persons who wish to work for a social cause, have to do it harder and in some cases, they even work incognito, in order to exercise actions that are more just or ethical than what the actual regime would allow them to do.

As such, we see how some managers that have the intrinsic value, principle or belief, that their organizations should contribute with the improvement of the collective, will entail, in various cases, some sort of crusades as they wish to be listened and followed by a quiet society in which individuals take for granted the social benefits that the State, as an entity, pursue.

However, by itself alone, the Hofstede scales are not necessarily very complete and useful when a manager has already lived a process of merge and he or she is the representative of the holding firm in another country. Calori, Lubatkin and Very (1996) explain that in addition to the physical and procedural integration within two companies working together (or in merge process), there is another process going on that contains the socio-cultural and managerial diversity, which at the end, is the most difficult and complex to execute. Here, the manager, as an expatriate, needs to manage people who may act differently than him or her in some ways, and equally in another, depending on the uniqueness of the collective history to which the personnel belongs. In this sense, upon a critical and interpretative perspective, d'Iribarne (1998, 1989) explains that culture in organizations answers mostly to social behaviours and historical experiences. For him, organizational culture is a reflect of social behaviour, moreover, community values, that are shaped by power, tensions, groups of domination, and furthermore, meaning of honourableness.

In his texts, d'Iribarne explains, for instance, that what is honourable for a culture has a different connotation in another. D'Iribarne explores the impact of culture in managerial practice on various nations in Europe, North America and Africa, but we limit our references here to three: United States, France and some African countries. He identified that, for instance, in France, it is very important to discuss any decision or action in order to unveil purposes for the society, therefore, the role of hierarchy is imperative in the sense that those in the higher end of the hierarchy may foresee how things might turn out in that particular society. In contrast, this concern means, for some African cultures, that power in a community entails the responsibility to take care for each one of the members, and in this community, the leader must know every member and the deepness and complexity of their needs. And finally, for American corporations and their directors, it is imperative to respect signed contracts and formalized agreements.

With these examples it is not difficult, therefore, to identify how the collectivism/individualism of Hofstede is perceived. In Hofstede's examples, France and some African cultures are collectivists. Nevertheless, aided by d'Iribarne's analysis, we may see that the French case is more socially oriented, and the African case is more communitarian oriented. Taking here the scales of Hofstede, we identify also that there are other cultures in which collectivism overcomes the sense of a nation. Those are some of the Asian cultures, where the concept of 'wholeness' entails not only their nation, but also the Earth as a component of the Universe, inclusively, the Universe as the Whole. Therefore, the idea of collective may have different dimensions depending on the reality of the established boundaries of responsibility. In a different spectrum, we see then how the United Stated is classified by Hofstede as an individualistic oriented country, as the importance of the contract is what leads managerial concern, therefore, society and the collective is left to the worries of the

State, which have to govern the people by means of public institutions.

In this sense, various organizations ruled by individualistic oriented individuals, may encounter more difficulties to start thinking in terms of stakeholders concerns, because, historically, values have been placed into individualistic development. Coming from that, we understand why the Western Corporate Culture encourages competition instead of collaboration between firms, therefore, the concept of strategic alliance will succeed where economical interests are shared by both parts of the alliance. Otherwise, we encounter difficulties to make alliances work easily. For instance, Miller et al. (2005) show how cultural diversity is lived in an alliance between a US firm and an Indian firm. They establish that even after having conducting workshops for mutual understanding and mutual co-construction or enrichment of procedures, the results after some years of operation indicate that cultural diversity and integration are still issues that need to be continuously addressed, for both, organizational success and the individual's satisfaction at work.

In our reflection, we identify that alliances might work in terms of performance (productivity wise and from a competitive point of view), but at high costs like repetition of tasks, lack of human motivation, an impoverishment of the corporation's image in the community, a high rate of rotation of the staff; everything due to the fact that the corporate values coming from the top directors may not be those of the employees that belong to other cultures that cherish, for instance, collective development, or even universal integration with the wholeness.

In this sense, all sorts of critics fall upon Hofstede's scales given that it has been already demonstrated that even inside very individualistic oriented nations (such as the Anglo-Saxon countries) various good actions of environmental responsibility and social responsibility take place[2]. Additionally, in this sense, it has been already demonstrated, either by history or scientific work, that the fact of belonging to an individualistic culture does not imply that all individuals of the culture are individualistic oriented. Strauss (2000) discusses and presents evidence concerning that matter in the United States, while exploring individuals' interpretations and actions of their own being, their own self. Moreover, there has also been done some critical analysis of this phenomena in the aim to reform business education to include more reflective activities (e.g. Davila-Gomez and Santos, 2007; Reynolds, 1998; Rosile and Boje, 1996). At the same time, the fact that the capital of an organization belongs to an Asian owner, a-priori understood as collective oriented, does not imply that the actions taken will be socially responsible. For instance, Chikudate (2002) denounces the case of some Japanese director's corruption, and the complete disregard of this fact in business education, which ignores the problem and continues to reinforce management theories and practices of human and social abuse. Additionally, we now see how in China and other South Asian countries,

---

[2] See for instance, naming only a few, the works and achievement of some groups and organizations such as the Social Responsible Research Network directed by Professor David Crowther, in the United Kingdom (see http://www.socialresponsibility.biz/); the Research Center *Chaire de Responsabilité sociale et de développement durable* at the Univerisity of Québec - Montréal (see http://www.crsdd.uqam.ca/).

industrialization takes place accompanied with foreign investments that implies the adoption, in many cases, of a Corporate Management individualistic culture.

The latter implies that as globalization expands worldwide, the dominant positivistic approach of management that seeks competition instead of collaboration, will be held to the edge of adoption even in foreign cultures and countries. Even though d'Iribarne explains how in France the concern for society development is a honourable value, we see however how the American way of doing business is taken to the *Écoles de Gestion* without questioning the values of the unified 'Corporate Culture' that comes from the times of Taylor and Fayol as we already discussed. This phenomena happens also in Latin-American nations (see Davila-Gomez, 2003).

This individualistic oriented 'corporate culture' poses a dilemma in the responsibility of managers. For those managers working in corporations, in private firms, the boundaries of responsibility are those of increasing the share value, and when mandatory, answering to governmental prerogatives by law. And, for those managers working at public institutions, the responsibility will extend to the frontiers of their institutional mission: welfare, education, taxes, among others. Even in public institutions, dissociation with the collective, and the wholeness, is done, given that managers learn how to manage in business schools that promote the corporate individualistic values, and in some cases, in programs adapted for public administration, but, taught and experienced by people who are increasingly more immersed in the culture of individualization.

However, when we ask some of the employees that work at public institutions, even in what Hofstede consider as very individualistic nations, we find repetitively, in the words of individuals, that they prefer to work in those kind of public establishments, because they allow them to experience a sense, a meaning of fulfilment. Many people decide to work for less salary when they encounter a reciprocity in their own values rather than those of the organization. For instance, in the educational system, there is a concern for the development of the young citizens that will rule society in a short time. This value is shared by both the director board and the professors. The fact of sharing one of the most important values of the *raison d'être* of the institution, gives employees a sense of comfort, a continual inspiration for ongoing inner motivation. Nevertheless, it does not imply that management practice inside the educational system will be totally stakeholder concerned. It is well know that in public institutions there are also conflicts of interest, dissatisfaction in the workplace climate, psychological abuses, tyranny or even disregard for other members of the community. This separation of values, in a same community, leads to some individuals asking continuously about their own identity.

Transculturality and the need for Wholeness

We may explain some of the phenomena in which individualism/collectivism is collapsing, and in which the individual's identity is on a constant questioning, while looking at the concept of transculturality. Transculturality answers the reality in which at any given moment, in any place of the planet, there is a complexity of various and diverse cultural values coming, not only from ethnic or national diversity, but also from different stages of industrialization (see Chan and Ma, 2002). Pütz (2003) explains how in this reality, the intersubjective perspective of individuals and his/her social relations influence the individual's actions in their context of practice, which are hybrid and heterogeneous. Chan and Ma explain that every nation experiences industrialization differently depending on the time in which their doors were open to globalization. When a government opens those doors, some nations are better prepared in terms of protection for national industries, legislation concerning the respect of cultural diversity and gender opportunities, and even preparation and development of programs of business schools.

Additionally, and at the same time, we identify that regardless of the time in which the doors are open, a huge difference is made by the political regime of the nation. As such, a different process of globalization and modernization is experienced in China than in Russia or in any Latin-American country. Political regimes entail also cultural values and agreements of the population, which, as discussed previously, may change quietly in time (decades, centuries) or suddenly by revolution. Whatever the case, the history of each nation is different, therefore, more than an adoption of a culture, or a 'corporate culture' of doing business, there is an adaptation. A process in which the persons who live the transformation will have a different and new culture than that of their ancestors or their children. Consequently, a phenomena arrive such as 'acculturation' takes place. For some authors, this is something negative as it will rip out the original values of the person and will transform him or her in a different being. Other authors see this as an experience in which the person will learn something from others and vice versa (see Berry et al., 1992), and in this exchange, each individual decides what to believe and what to transform in him or herself; some events of this transformation may occur, however, unconsciously as we live without necessarily rationalizing each one of our actions. For instance, Palazzo (2005) recognizes the richness in terms of innovation and creativity that a transcultural working environment offers to organizations and individuals within.

From an ethical point of view, what might be considered is mostly the way in which this transformation is being made. Is it by imposition, by means of threats (e.g. going to prison, being fired of a job, etc.) or by constraint? Or, is it a natural and spontaneous process that takes place, for instance, when an immigrant comes to a country that is transforming itself and that is aiming to be more inclusive of the nowadays multicultural diversity? Or, is it a mandatory way of practicing management, when a foreign investor from an industrialized country comes to a developing country in which the workforce is cheaper and the process of imposition of new rules is imposed regardless of the existence of different cultural values?

With this, we come to the point in which the phenomena of globalization, therefore, transculturality, is already occurring at almost a non-stoppable rate (see Adler, 1994), and some of the critical issues to address, after having understood the complexity of their cultural diversity, are mostly the way in which actions are conducted and what are the consequences of those actions. Therefore, it is imperative to acknowledge the importance of including in transculturality these ways of management corporations and public institutions. Hence, managers who live in this ongoing, constantly transforming transculturality, as well as those managers whose personnel are from multicultural origin (gender, nations, professions), need to develop other skills than those demanded by the competitive prerogative. There is a need to pass from competition to collaboration. To pass from taking decisions only at the director's level, to consult them (and their possible impacts - scenarios) with different stakeholders. In other words, we need to pass from multicultural theories of understanding, to intercultural possibilities of action. With this consultation and interaction of different points of views, we will be practicing what Crowther and Rayman-Bacchus (2004) propose as stakeholders' participation in corporate decisions.

Therefore, a new approach to address different points of view in organizations, to recognize cultural diversity and real values of various stakeholders is needed. An answer to the dominant way of exercising management worldwide, the stakeholders paradigm expands our frontiers of analysis. On the one side, it allows to consider citizens, groups, governmental organizations, international accords or prerogatives, among others. And, on the other side, while acknowledging the role of other counterparts, there is an openness to listen to different interpretations of an organizational action or decision. In this sense, here we talk about the need to recognize what will be the consequences and implications of our actions. But how has this been already implemented in some organizations? How could this be applied in a broader extent, perhaps worldwide?

Our experience and researches indicate us that various factors influence in this openness. First of all, it demands collective and social actions, as well as individual's willingness. For instance, while talking about collective action, we identify what already some governments are willing to do in terms of legislation while demanding not only financial reports to corporations, but also social reports is something that needs to be more broadly spread. Nevertheless, as pointed out by Crowther and Davila-Gomez (2007), while doing corporate reporting, it is important to show the real image of the organizational acts and not only a mere cover for entertaining the members of the community. We talk here about the need for honesty and transparency. Otherwise, legitimacy in the eyes of the collective cannot be achieved.

As a result, social responsibility concerns helps us to increasingly exercise integration of different points of views within the transcultural realities of our ongoing transforming multi-cultural work environments. In this sense, we see how, for instance, Garcia et al. (2003) propose that for acting ethically during this integration of different points of view, it is imperative to count with collaboration, inclusion and cooperative values, and for all that, managers need to develop sensitivity towards the members' diversity, involve members in ethical decisions, and gain awareness.

The previous indicates us that managers who deal constantly with this transcultural reality need to gain expertise and confidence during their professional career, which means in other words, openness to the challenges of integration and collaboration, awareness of others' needs and preoccupations (as an authentic sentiment), of stakeholders' needs. Managers need to invest in their continual personal development and not only in their intellect in order to obtain the best competitive deal in negotiations (either by mergers, or by multicultural points of view in a work environment). When collaboration becomes the strategy, competition is seen not as the individualistic goal of an organization, but as the result of various organizations (or groups inside various, or one organization) that seeks attaining the realization of the aims of all the parties of the group.

Thus, even though we may identify with the aid of Hofstede and d'Iribarne, that there are more collective or individualistic oriented nations than others, we need to disseminate, in a broader spectra of management practice and education, the sense of 'wholeness', especially in the western hemisphere. With wholeness it comes the concern for consequences of our acts. As expressed by some western philosophers such as Marcel (1965) and Kierkegaard (1813-1855), in a more profound level of transcendence, the reality of the aim of each human being, the significance of any act coming from any entity of the whole, will impact the reality of all other components of the whole. Thus, in our corporate world, it means that behind cultural values there are not only axiological norms or agreements, but also the individual's sense of life. That is what we identify as ontological meanings, which may or may not be aligned with the already established social agreement. As we discussed it previously, a culture is in constant redefinition when individuals inside the group question the validity of those norms. Quiet, simple, complex or huge revolutions lead to transformation and, as a consequence, some values are added while others remain or are excluded of the social agreement.

Therefore, when there is disagreement in organizations, there is the possibility for change, moreover, for improvement of the situation. In this sense, the stakeholders approach furnishes multicultural work spaces with possibilities of acknowledgement of others' understandings, others' points of views and also, the possibility for the individuals who are experiencing the disagreements, to become aware and sensible to the implication that those individual actions also have an impact in others. This means acknowledgement, development of otherness. While acting with a sense of wholeness, we develop also the otherness and vice-versa.

Conclusion

Management practice as a set of ways of doing things represents a culture. Norms, tools and expectations of what management practice should produce, become values. In this, management culture answers to the traditional notion of 'corporate culture'. As such, the mix of two modern events portraits what we identify nowadays as organization's reality: the industrialization historical phenomena produced in the western hemisphere by the 1800's and 1900's (still ongoing), and the conformation of the neo-liberal economy theory since the 1700's to our days. This entails corporate culture with competitive values, as well as imposed by shareholders and managers, regardless of the fact that globalization nowadays opens to nations and other groups of people where values of cooperation and collaboration might be more cherished than those of competition. However, inside any cultural group, there are individuals who entail some values that are contrary to those imposed, and as such, social responsibility as an example, may be practiced and defended even in western cultures. Hence, transculturality as a result of a blend of cultures and values, allows the beginning of new transformed cultures that will be in constant redefinition. Learning as a result contains some roots for the individual's human development; learning of oneself as well as of others. In the path, learning while becoming a better collective.

Individual willingness and managerial ethical conduct, help managers to confront the values of corporate culture that entails separation and dissociation in the organizational live. Openness to diversity, efforts to mutual understanding, and practice of acknowledgement of different sentiments or portraits of reality, help managers to develop the sense of otherness and wholeness needed in stakeholders interactions. We need more organizations which image is perceived by the collective as based upon the values of collaboration, inclusion, conciliation and respect. As individuals, we need to conduct our organizations righteousness.

References

Adler, N. (2002), *International dimensions of organizational behavior*, Cincinnati, Ohio, South-Western.

Adler, N. (1994), "Globalization, Gouverment and Competitiveness", *The 1994 John L. Manion Lecture*, Canadian Centre for Management Development, Ottawa, 20 pages.

Berry, J. W. et al. (1992), *Cross-cultural psychology: research and applications*, Cambridge: Cambridge University Press.

Calori, R., Lubatkin, M. and Very, P. (1996) , "Une étude emporium des formes et déterminants de l'intégration post-acquisition", *Management international*, Vol. 1, No. 1, pp. 41-53.

Canadian Heritage (2004), *Canadian Multiculturalism Act 1988 - amendment, 1993* -, http://www.pch.gc.ca/progs/multi/policy/act_e.cfm, consulted in November 2007.

Canada Public Service Agency (2005), *Employment Equity in the Federal Public Service 2004-2005 Annual Report to Parliament*, http://www.psagency-agencefp.gc.ca/ee/ar-ra/ar-ra_e.asp, consulted in November 2007.

Chan, J. M. and Ma, E. (2002), "Transculturating Modernity: A Reinterpretation of Cultural Globalization", in Chan and McIntyre (eds.), *In Search of Boundaries - Communication, nation-States, and Cultural Identities*, Conneticut, Ablex publishing, pp. 3-18.

Chevrier, S. (2004), "Le management des équipes intercultural", *Management international*, Vol. 8, No. 3, pp. 31-40.

Chikudate, N. (2002), "Collective Myopia and Defective Higher Educations Behind the Scenes of Ethically Bankrupted Economic Systems: A Reflexive Note from a Japanese University and Taking a Step Toward Transcultural Dialogues", *Journal of Business Ethics*, Vol. 38, pp. 205-225.

Crowther, D. (2007), *Social Responsible Research Network*, http://www.socialresponsibility.biz/, UK, consulted in November 2007.

Crowther, D. and Davila-Gomez, A.M. (2007), "Psychoanalysis and the Myths of Corporate Communication", in A.M. Davila Gomez & D. Crowther (eds.) *Ethics, Psyche and Social Responsibility*, Aldershot, UK; Burlington, USA: Ashgate, pp. 107-127

Crowther, D. and Green, M. (2004), "Re-placing People in Organizational Activity", in A. Das Gupta (ed.), *Human Values in management*, Aldershot, Ashgate, pp.

264-282.

Crowther, D. and Rayman-Bacchus, L. (2004) "The Future of Corporate Social Responsibility," in Crowther, D. and Rayman-Bacchus, L. (eds.) *Perspectives on Corporate Social Responsibility* Ashgate, Aldershot, Great Britain, pp.229-249.

Davila Gomez, A.M. 2003, *Hacia un Management Humanista desde la educación a distancia: intersubjetividad y desarrollo de cualidades humanas* Doctoral thesis, École des HEC de Montréal, Canada.

Davila-Gomez, A. M. and Crowther, D. (2007), "Psychological Violence at Work: Where does the Human Dignity Lie?"in A.M. Davila Gomez & D. Crowther (eds.) *Ethics, Psyche and Social Responsibility,* Aldershot, UK; Burlington, USA: Ashgate, pp. 15-33.

Davila-Gomez, A.M. and Santos, J. N. (2007), "Critical Pedagogy as a Strategy for Management Development: Introducing Intersubjectivity as a Practical Application Tool", in A.M. Davila Gomez & D. Crowther (eds.) *Ethics, Psyche and Social Responsibility*, Aldershot, UK; Burlington, USA : Ashgate, pp.143-155.

d'Iribarne, P. (1998), *Culture et modularisation*, Paris, du Seuil.

d'Iribarne, P. (1989), *La logique de l'honneur: gestion des enterprises et traditions nationales*; Paris, du Seuil.

Fayol, H. (1841-1925), *Administration industrielle et générale*, Paris, Dunod, 1979.

Garcia, J. et al. (2003), "A Transcultural Integrative Model for Ethical Decision Making in Counseling", *Journal of Counselling ε Development*, Summer 2003, Vol. 81, pp. 268-277.

Hall, E.T. (1983), *The dance of life: the other dimension of time*, Garden City, N.Y.: Anchor Press/Doubleday.

Hampden-Turner, C. and Trompenaars, F. (2004), *Au-délà du choc des cultures : dépasser les opositions pour mieux travailler ensemble*; trad. By Larry Cohen Paris Ed. d'Organisation.

Henriette, M. R. (2005), "Les resources individuelles pour la compétence intercultural individuelle", *Revue internationale sur le travail et la société*, Vol. 3, No. 2, pp. 668-691.

Hofstede, G. (2001), *Culture's Consequences: Comparing Values, Behaviors, Institutions, and Organizations Across Nations,* London: Sage Publications.

Hofstede, G. (1980), *Culture's consequences: international differences in work-related values*; Sage, Berverly Hills Calif.

International Labour Organization (2007), *International Labour Standards*, http://www.ilo.org/public/english/standards/norm/subject/equality.htm, consulted in November 2007.

Juteau, D. (2000), "Ethnicité, nation et sexe-genre", *Les Cahiers du groupe de recherché etchnicité et société (GRES)*, Vol. 1, No. 1, pp. 53-57.

Kierkegaard, S. (1813-1855) *For Self-examination and Judge for Yourselves! -1851,* 1974, Oxford University Press, London, Princeton University Press, USA.

Marcel, G. (1965), *Homo Viator,* Harper Torchbooks, United States of America.

Mercier, S. (2001), "L'instrumentalisation des valeurs : une ressource stratégique pour l'entreprise? La démarche du groupe Fournier", *Gestion*, Vol. 26, No.2.

Miller, M. et al. (2005), "Appreciative Inquiry in Building a Transcultural Strategic

Alliance - The Case of biotech between a U.S. Multinational and an Indian Family Business", *The Journal of Applied Behavioral Science*, Vol. 41, No.1, pp. 91-110.

Morin, E. (2001), *La Méthode. -Vol. 5 L'Humanité de l'humanité : l'identité humaine*, Paris, Editions du Seuil.

Nucci, L. P. and Turiel, E. (2000), "The Moral and the Personal: Sources of Social Conflicts, in L. P. Nucci, G. B. Saxe and E. Turiel (eds.), *Culture, thought and development*, Mahwah, new Jersey, Lawrence Eribaum Associates, Inc. pp. 115-139.

Palazzo, G. (2005), "Postnational Constellations of Innovativeness: A Cosmopolitan Approach", *Technology Analysis & Strategic management*, Vol. 17, No. 1, pp. 55-72.

Philippe, P. (2004), "Mondialisation et construction identities de cadres de l'industrie pétrolière", *Revue française de gestion*, 30, 148, pp. 87-118.

Porter, M. (1980), *Competitive Strategy: techniques for analyzing industries and competitors*, New York, Free Press.

Pütz, R. (2003) "Culture and Entrepreneurship - Remarks on Transculturality as Practice", *Tijdschrift voor Economische en Sociale Geografie*, Vol. 94, No. 5, pp. 554-563.

Reynolds, M. (1998) "Reflection and Critical Reflection in Management Learning," *Management Learning*, vol. 29, no. 2, pp.183-200.

Rosile, G.A. and Boje, D.M. (1996), "Pedagogy for the Postmodern Management Classroom: Greenback Company", in D.M. Boje, R.P. Gephart and T.J. Thatchenkery (eds.) *Postmodern Management and Organization Theory*, Thousand Oaks: Sage, pp. 225-250.

Sabelis, I. H. J. (2004), "Global Spedd: A Time View on Transnationality", *Culture and Organization*, Vol. 10, no. 4, pp. 291-301.

Strauss, C. (2000), "The Culture Concept and the Individualism-Collectivism Debate: Dominant and Alternative Attributions for Class in the United States", in L. P. Nucci, G. B. Saxe and E. Turiel (eds.), *Culture, thought and development*, Mahwah, new Jersey, Lawrence Eribaum Associates, Inc. pp. 85-113.

Taylor, F. (1856-1915), *The principles of scientific management*, (c 1911), Harper, New York, 1934.

Trompenaars, F. and Hampden-Turner, C. (1998), *Riding the waves of culture: understanding cultural diversity in global business*, New York, McGraw Hill.

Tsoukas, H. and Chia, R. (2002) "On Organizational becoming: Rethinking organizational change" *Organization Science* vol. 13, no.5 pp. 567-582.

Turiel, E. (2002), *The Culture of Morality - Social Development, Context and Conflict*, Edinburgh, New York, port Melbourne, Madrid, Cape Town, Cambridge University Press.

Unesco (2001), *Unesco - Universal Declaration on Cultural Diversity*, http://unesdoc.unesco.org/images/0012/001271/127160m.pdf, consulted in November 2007.

Univerisity of Québec Montréal (2007), *Chaire de Responsabilité sociale et de développement durable* http://www.crsdd.uqam.ca/ , consulted in November 2007.

Vulpe, T. et al. (2000), *A profile of the interculturally effective person*, Ottawa, Department of Foreign Affairs and National Trade - Canadian Foreign Service Institute.

Zghal, (2003), "Culture et gestion: gestion de l'harmonie ou gestion des paradoxes?", *Gestion* Vol. 28, No. 2, pp 26-32.

Chapter 11

Islam and Corporate Governance

Riham Ragab Rizk

Introduction

Culture, which governs how individuals perceive their responsibilities and carry out their duties, has long been recognised as a likely determinant of business practices and ethical values (Hofstede, 1980; Gray, 1988; Perera, 1989). The influence of religion upon accounting and finance is an issue which is only starting to gain more attention in the conventional academic literature (see Lewis, 2001; Cone, 2003). Traditionally, religion has had a role in shaping and enforcing ethical behaviour such as truthfulness, honesty and social justice. A community in which such values are held in high regard may be marked by an elevated degree of trust in business dealings and financial affairs (Rizk, 2005).

It has been argued (Cone, 2003), that the Islamic understanding of corporate responsibility shares some fundamental similarities with the Rawlsian concept of social justice, as mutual agreement among equals motivated by self-interest. All parties must be fully aware of the risks attendant on a particular course of action and be accepting of equal liability for the outcomes, good or bad.

Although it is difficult to find a Muslim majority country in which the true teachings of Islam are implemented in every aspect, in the Qur'an, Islam's primary authority in all matters of individual and communal life, as well as theology and worship, and in the teachings and example of the Prophet Muhammad (pbuh), preserved in a literary form known as *hadith*, there is much with which to construct an authentic Islamic doctrine for corporate governance, responsibility and citizenship. It is these aspects of Islamic law, *Shari'ah*, that are the focus of this chapter.

The Origins of the Shari'ah

Muslims refer to the last phase of pre-Islamic Arabia as the time of ignorance (*jahiliyah*). The Meccan tribe of Quraysh had become the era's nouveau riche because it controlled access to Arabia's most important shrine, the Ka'aba. The populace had become spiritually desolate and enjoyed little in the way of physical or social security. Their longing for a divine revelation was fulfilled in 610 A.D. when Muhammad, a respected merchant already so renowned for his personal integrity that he was known to all as *al amin* (the trustworthy), felt himself enveloped by a divine presence.

The *Shari'ah*, wherein Muslim ethics are anchored, has four sources:

a) the **Qur'an**, which expresses the work and will of God;

b) the **Sunnah**, which is the body of customs and practices based on the words and deeds of Muhammad and elaborated on by scholars;

c) **Islamic law**, which draws on the first two sources and is solidified by consensus;

d) an individual's own **conscience** when the path has not been clarified by the first three sources. As a result, the *Shari'ah* addresses all questions facing society and individuals with interpretive jurisprudence (*ijtihad*) and deduction by analogy (*qiyas*) providing mechanisms for meeting the challenges of different periods.

Ethical teachings of most religions are largely compatible with each other and with secular views. Religious imperatives on ethics reflect a steady evolution: God revealed the truth of monotheism through Abraham, the Ten Commandments were revealed to Moses, Jesus taught us that we are to love our neighbours as ourselves, and Muhammad explained how we were to love that neighbour.

The Qur'an, like the divine scriptures that preceded it, forbade lying, stealing, adultery, and murder. It also went one step further by providing a new perspective in the form of rules for such fundamental societal institutions as marriage, kinship, inheritance, warfare, and economic activity. It also focused on commerce and politics, interest and debts, contracts and wills, and industry and finance. Every act that would estrange righteousness and bring evil, whether it benefits the perpetrator or not, is forbidden. The Qur'an is quite explicit in this regard: *"it is immoral to acquire possession of income or wealth by stealing, cheating, dishonesty, or fraud."*

The laws developed by the Islamic legists drew on the concrete obligations declared in the Qur'an and supplemented by the recorded recollections of the sayings (*hadith*) and deeds of the Prophet. The *Shari'ah*, as such, has remained unsurpassed as a statement of social justice and ethical principle (Pomeranz, 2002). Although its importance is primarily spiritual and moral, some of its aspects have been written into the civil law in numerous countries. Moreover, there is a current tendency to move towards an Islamic economic system in some Islamic nations and to restore the *Shari'ah* as the basic source of legislation. There are currently 38 Muslim states, 4 of which (Afghanistan, Iran, Saudi Arabia, and Sudan) have the *Shari'ah* as their primary law. In another 23 countries, such as Egypt and Jordan, the *Shari'ah* influences civil law, and in the remaining 11 it has no influence al all.

Islamic Business Ethics

Islam supports private property and competition but remains firm on the goal of achieving an equitable distribution of wealth. It seeks to promote such a distribution by urging the rich to help the needy. Wealth is believed to belong to God, who has entrusted the individual only with spreading its positive effects. Islam stresses the sharing of wealth among fellow Muslims and fairness in such matters as management-labour relations. The accumulation of idle wealth is penalized through the obligatory giving of a predetermined part of one's wealth (*zakat*) and by encouraging rapid reinvestment, especially in projects designed to increase employment. Wasteful consumption (*israf*) is discouraged, while avoiding waste and saving wealth for the purpose of direct investment (*istithmar*) are encouraged. Islamic doctrine includes an elaborate mechanism for securing minority rights, for Muhammad is reported to have recognized the need for pluralism and tolerance. Islam even calls on its followers to rationalize the use of natural resources and to protect the environment. In fact, of more than 6,000 verses in the Holy Qur'an, some 750, one eighth of the Book, exhort believers to reflect on nature, to study the relationship between living organisms and their environment, to make the best use of reason and to maintain the balance and proportion God has built into His creation.

Islam holds that man's life is given significance by the promise of eternal bliss for those who have qualified for such a reward by having followed God's commands (Endress, 1998). Muslims express their faith in life after death-a prior appointment on Judgment Day, but an eternal life in Paradise (Fisk, 1996). In other words, each soul will be judged for the moral and ethical choices made on earth by that individual; his happiness or misery in the hereafter depend on how well he has observed God's laws (Smith, 1986) and exercised responsibility.

The Holy Qur'an designates the Muslim community as witness before God, as well as mankind, in regard to the espousal of justice:

Ye who believe! Stand out firmly for justice, as witnesses to God. Even as against yourselves, or your parents or your kin, and whether it be (against) rich or poor: For God can best protect both (4:135)

Just as the religion of Islam requires individuals to adore God, so too do the social system and the ethics of Islam regulate the corporate or organisational life of individuals. It is made clear that each person is responsible for his actions (Endress, 1988).

The record of economic crimes of the past decade alone is vast. Meaningful discussion of individual crimes is beyond the scope of this paper. However, a survey by Joseph Wells, a prominent US fraud auditor, estimates the value of the annual U.S. gross national product attributable to fraud at a staggering 400 billion dollars (Pomeranz, 1997); well before the days of Enron and Parmalat.

Certain types of fraud seem to be by-products of our late era of the industrial age. For example, consider such types of fraud, as collusive bidding, paying for substandard work, or unneeded "change orders". As might be expected, the Qur'an deals with crime and potential crime in rather broad terms, and not in specifics. Nonetheless, the condemnations are clear with Qur'anic injunctions refering to fraud and other violations of prescribed conduct vis-à-vis contracts and trusts. Below, are a few samples of Qur'anic prescriptions, which can be applied to different categories of transgressions.

- **On Contracts**
  Ye who believe! When ye deal with each other, in transactions involving future obligations in a fixed period of time, reduce them to writing. Let a scribe write down faithfully as between the parties (2:282)

- **On Trusts**
  Allah doth command you to render back your trusts to those to whom they are due; And when ye judge between people that ye judge with justice: (4:58)
  Ye that believe! Betray not that trust of Allah and the Messenger, nor misappropriate knowingly things entrusted to you. (8:27)
- **On Fraud**
  Woe to those that deal in fraud. Those who, when they have to receive by measure from men, exact full measure, but when they have to give by measure or weight to men, give less than due. (83:1-3)

While Qur'anic prescriptions may be vague, the legacy of Prophet Muhammad is very specific. Throughout his life, Muhammad is said to have allowed his actions to speak for themselves. For example, al Tin ilidhi, whose writings are an important source of Islamic law, relates the following story:

The Prophet passed a pile of grain. He put his hand into its midst and felt moisture. He exclaimed: "Oh merchant, what is this?' The owner of the grain responded: "It has been damaged by the rain, oh Prophet Muhammad." The Prophet asked: 'If this is the case, why did you not put the damaged grain on top of the pile so that people can see it?' The Prophet concluded by making clear that "whoever practices fraud is not one of us".

Islam, Accounting and Accountability

In an Islamic society, the development of economic theory and practice should be based on the provisions of Islamic law along with other necessary principles and postulates that are not in conflict with Islamic law. Two approaches have been suggested:
- Establish objectives based on the spirit of Islam and its teachings and then consider these established objectives in relation to contemporary economic thought.
- Start with objectives established in contemporary economic thought, test them against Islamic *Shari'ah,* accept those that are consistent with *Shari'ah* and reject those that are not.

Practitioners and professional bodies, such as the Accounting and Auditing Organization for Islamic Financial Institutions (AAOIFI, 2000) have followed the second approach when formulating accounting, auditing and governance standards for Islamic financial institutions. Academics, on the other hand, such as Gambling and Karim (1986), Adnan and Gaffikin (1997), Askary and Clarke (1997), Alam (1997), Baydoun and Willett (1997) and Lewis (2001), have tended to favour the first approach.

The global scene is characterised by a lack of universal rules or standards in the area of corporate governance. Instead, a variety of national codes and regulatory frameworks have emerged, reflecting the many different legal, economic and cultural environments . The European Corporate Governance Institute (www.ecgi.org) offers a comprehensive list of links to the major corporate governance offers a comprehensive list of links to the major corporate governance codes around the world. Nevertheless, a set of emerging global guidelines and principles of good practice are emerging. The OECD corporate governance guidelines, updated in 2004, are often taken as a reference point as they are broad enough to allow comparisons across governance environments and more importantly, to overcome potentially contentious, prescriptive approaches. It is for this reason that the current study breaks with academic tradition and follows the practitioner approach. Table 1 below depicts the OECD Principles as revised in 2004.

Table 1 : OECD Principles, 2004

Elements of an Effective Governance Framework The corporate governance fr amework should promote transparent and efficient markets, be consistent with the rule of law and clearly articulate the division of responsibilities among different supervisory, regulatory and enforcement authorities.
Rights of Shareholders and Key Ownership Functions The corporate governance framework should protect and facilitate the exercise of shareholders' rights.
Equitable Treatment of Shareholders The corporate governance framework should ensure the equitable treatment of all shareholders, includi ng minority and foreign shareholders. All shareholders should have the opportunity to obtain effective redress for violation of their rights.
Role of Stakeholders in Corporate Governance The corporate governance framework should recognise the rights of stakeholders established by law or through mutual agreements and encourage active co -operation between corporations and stakeholders in creating wealth, jobs, and the sustainability of financially sound enterprises.
Disclosure and Transparency The corporate governance framework should ensure that timely and accurate disclosure is made on all material matters regarding the corporation, including the financial situation, performance, ownership, and governance of the company.
Responsibilities of the Board The corporate governance framework should ensure the strategic guidance of the company, the effective monitoring of management by the board, and the board's accountability to the company and the shareholders.

From the preceding discussion on Islamic values and ethics, it is clear that there is nothing inherently un-Islamic or *haraam* in the notion of corporate governance in general or the OECD Principles in particular. On the contrary, there is a high degree of compatibility. Islamic guidelines are arguably, even more detailed, prescriptive and regulatory with particular reference to OECD principle 4 regarding disclosure and transparency. Certain Islamic ethical principles have a direct impact on accounting policy and principles. These principles include not only the interest-free economic system, but also the institution of *zakat* (religious levy) and specific business methods of full disclosure and bookkeeping discussed in detail in the following section.

Social Responsibility and Accountability

In Islamic thought, individuals and organisations are expected to feel socially responsible for others in the community. In general, the aim of the Islamic economic system is to allow people to earn their living in a fair and profitable way without exploitation of others, so that the whole of society may benefit. Islam also emphasizes the welfare of the community over individual rights. Where Muslims live under a non-Islamic government, *zakat* must still be collected from Muslims and spent for the good of society.

Islam also preaches moderation and a balanced pattern of consumption. Luxury and over-consumption is condemned, as is poverty. Every being has a minimum requirement to be able to live in dignity. The system is balanced out through the act of *zakat*, which is an essential part of the economic system, as well as an individual's faith. If this source were not enough, an Islamic government would apply a temporary tax on the rich and affluent as a religious duty (*fard kefaya*), in order to balance the budget.

In the Holy Qur'an, the word *hesab* is repeated more than eight times in different versus (Askary and Clarke, 1997). *Hesab* or account is the root of accounting, and the references in the Holy Qur'an are to 'account' in its generic sense, relating to one's obligation to 'account' to God on all matters pertaining to human endeavour for which every Muslim is 'accountable'. All resources made available to individuals are made so in the form of a trust. Individuals are trustees for what they have been given by God in the form of goods, property and less tangible 'assets', such as good health and even time. The extent to which individuals must use what is being entrusted to them is specified in the *Shari'ah*, and the success of individuals in the hereafter depends upon their performance in this world. In this sense, every Muslim has an 'account' with God, in which is recorded all good and bad actions, an account which will continue until death, for God shows all people their accounts on judgment day (4:62). This adds an extra dimension to valuation of things and deeds compared to those already embodied in conventional financial statements (Lewis, 2001).

Thus, the basic similarity between *hesab* in Islam and 'accounting' lies in the responsibility of every Muslim to carry out duties as described in the Qur'an. Similarly, in a business enterprise, both management and the providers of capital (institutional as well as individual) are accountable for their actions both within and outside their firm. Accountability, in this context, means accountability to the community (*umma*) or society at large. Many of the conventional accounting practices, which are most applicable to the concept of private accountability, do not seem to be relevant to the type of accountability required under *Shari'ah*. One of the main objectives of Islamic accounting is to provide information which discharges those involved in firms from their accountability to the *umma* (Lewis, 2001).

Full Disclosure

Related to the concept of social accountability in Islam is the principle of full disclosure. Six verses in the Qur'an refer to '*relevance*'. One meaning of the '*relevance*' referred to is disclosure of all facts (Qur'an, 2:71) '...*now you have brought the truth...*' also '*be maintainers of justice*' (Qur'an, 4:135). Financial information is relevant from an Islamic point of view only when it includes the attribute of '*truth*' fair and accurate disclosure of the matters at hand (Lewis, 2001).

   Therefore, if the purpose of accounting information is to serve the public interest, it follows that, in an Islamic context, the *umma* has the right to know about the effects of the operations of the organisation on its well being and to be advised within the requirements of *Shari'ah* as to how this has been achieved. Accountability is, thus, interpreted as being, first and foremost, accountability to God through making information freely available. Truthful and relevant disclosure of information is important, in different aspects of Islamic life. There are responsibilities such as paying *zakat*, the calculation of which requires disclosure of the value of assets and liabilities in terms of the religious obligation to aid the poor, for it indicates a Muslim's capacity to do so. Full disclosure is necessary for predicting future obligations and assessing investment risk in Islamic partnership arrangements. Considerable doubt must arise as to whether compliance with conventional accounting practice of being 'conservative' regarding asset valuation and income measurement can conform with *Shari'ah*, any more than would deliberate optimism and overstatement.

Materiality

Adequate disclosure requires that a financial statement should contain all material information necessary to make it useful to its users, whether it is included in the statement itself, the notes that accompany it, or in additional presentations. Since the Holy Qur'an '*discloses the truth and best way for living in the world*' (Qur'an 5:16), so the disclosure of all necessary information for the accomplishment of faithful obligations and the making of economic and business decisions consistent with that ethos, is the most important tenet of an Islamic accounting system (Lewis, 2001). Verses 282 and 283, in the second chapter of the Qur'an, put particular emphasis on commercial morality with regards to the evidence to be provided and doubt to be avoided. Understandability is a precondition of financial information in an Islamic accounting framework. Information is not to deceive the user, nor decrease understanding in such a way as to mislead decision-making.

Verifiability

Muslims are required to keep records of their indebtedness. In this regard, the Qur'an reads:

> *'Believers, when you contract a debt for a fixed period, put it in writing. Let a scribe write it down fairly ... and let the debtor dictate, not diminishing the sum he owes ...' (Qur'an, 2:282)*

Islam, thus, provides general approval and guidelines for the recording and reporting of financial transactions. Underpinning Islamic belief is the requirement that doubt and uncertainty be removed from interpersonal relationships. In business affairs, it is clear that all parties' rights and obligations are to be documented for verification and exploration. Other Qur'anic verses advise credit transactions to be recorded as well as signed by debtors to acknowledge their indebtedness and the amount thereof, the ultimate in verification processes (Lewis, 2001).

Reliability

Askary and Clarke (1997) identified nineteen versus, in eleven different chapters of the Qur'an, which place emphasis on the reliability of matter. If published financial information is unreliable, Muslims will be unable to fulfil their religious responsibilities, such as assessing their ability to assist the disadvantaged and pay *zakat*. In addition to other verses that emphasise the need to fulfil obligations, verse 58 in chapter four deals explicitly with the need for managers of business entities to produce true, accurate, complete and reliable financial disclosure to the owners of capital. Reliable information must also be presented correctly and completely, including all the details of transactions undertaken. True disclosure of financial facts, and their provision without any deceit or fraud, in order to satisfy users' requirements, is therefore, essential in fulfilling obligations and facilitating investment decision-making. Qur'anic verses 84 and 85 in chapter 11 emphasise this by stating *"....give full measure..."*.

Conclusion: A Model of Islamic Corporate Citizenship

Muslims see Islam as the religion of trade and business, making no distinction between men and women and seeing no contradiction between profit and moral acts. Evidence for this can be found in the fact that only a small portion of the Qur'an is devoted to matters of theology. The bulk of the Holy Book has to do with rules of conduct, both social and economic. All actions are judged according to their congruence with the guide to living found in the Qur'an. The Qur'an contains numerous references to economic practice, including the right to private property, as one of the principles on which the Islamic economic system is built. This right is protected as long as the means of acquisition is lawful. There are references to unlawful means of acquiring wealth, including usury (2: 278-79), cheating (9: 3), gambling and chance (5: 91-92) and theft (5: 38). However, the right of possession, given its lawful nature, is not absolute, since Allah is seen as the ultimate owner of all wealth (6: 165; 57: 7). Given these antecedents it is no surprise that Ernest Gellner, a long-time researcher and scholar of Islam, suggests that Islam is the ideal social model for commercial activity. He writes (1992: 14):

> *Weberian sociology leads us to expect certain congruence between a modern economy and its associated beliefs and culture. The modern mode of production is claimed above all to be rational. It is orderly, sensitive to cost effectiveness, thrifty rather than addicted to display, much given to a division of labor and the use of the free market. It requires those who operate it to be sensitive to the notion of obligation and contract, to be work oriented, disciplined and not addicted to economically irrelevant political and religious patronage networks. If this is indeed what a modern economy demands and above all if it is required by the construction of a modern economy, Islam would seem to be custom made.*

Muslims ought to conduct their business activities in accordance with the requirements of their religion to be fair, honest and just toward others. Rahman (1994) notes that there are a large number of Islamic concepts and values that define the extent and nature of business activity. There are many positive values, such as *iqtisad* (moderation), *adl* (justice), *ihsan* (kindness), *amana* (honesty), *infaq* (spending to meet social obligations), *sabr* (patience) and *istislah* (public interest). Similarly, there are a number of values that are negative, and thus to be avoided: *zulm* (tyranny), *bukhl* (miserliness), *tam'* and *gash'* (greed), *iktinaz* (hoarding of wealth) and *israf* (extravagance). Economic activity within the positive parameters is *halal* (allowed and praiseworthy) and within the negative realm *haram* (prohibited and blameworthy). Production and distribution, which are regulated by the *halal-haram* code, must adhere to the concept of *adl* (justice). Collectively, these values and concepts, along with the main injunctions of the Holy Qur'an, provide a framework for an equitable business and commercial system (Lewis, 2001).

Islam, in its purest form, is much more than a faith: it is an indivisible unit, a political system, a legal system, an economic system and a way of life. The economy, like other activities, is governed by moral rules and mechanisms designed to achieve progress through the ideal use of resources and the protection of human values. Although it is not easy to locate societies where Islamic values, morals and ethical principles are truly implemented in every sphere of life, as dictated by the Qur'an and Sunna, this does not nullify the validity of the model itself. The desire for such a model has always been, and will always exist in both Islamic and non-Islamic societies as evidenced by the emergence of a variety of national codes and regulatory frameworks on corporate governance and responsibility. Empirical studies investigating how far the affairs of businesses in Muslim majority societies actually fit with the prescribed model could be quite revealing and hence, worthy of pursuing.

References

Abdul-Rahman, Abdul Rahim and Andrew Goddard (1998); "An Interpretive Inquiry of Accounting Practices in Religious Organizations"; *Financial Accountability and Management*; Vol. 14, No. 3; pp 183-201.

Afshari, R., (1994); "An Essay on Islamic Cultural Relativism in the Discourse of Human Rights"; *Human Rights Quarterly*; Vol. 16, No.2 (1994): pp 235-276.

Alhabshi, Syed Othman (2001); *Social Responsibility of the Corporate Sector*; Institute of Islamic Understanding Malaysia; pp 1-5.

Ali, A. J (1995); "Cultural Discontinuity and Arab Management Thought"; *International Studies of Management & Organization*; Vol 35, No.3; pp 3-70.

Ali, A. Yusuf (1983); *The Holy Qur'an: Text, Translation, and Commentary*; Amana Publications; USA; 1862 pp.

Badawi, Jamal (2001); "Toward a Spirituality for the Contemporary Organization" in Conference Paper *Bridging the Gap Between Spirituality and Business*; Santa Clara University; USA; pp 66-79.

Bashir, A (1993); "Ethics, Individual Rationality and Economic Gains: An Islamic Perspective"; *Humanomics* ; Vol 9, No.3 ; 66-73.

Baydoun, Nabil and Roger Willet (2000); "Islamic Corporate Reports"; *Abacus*; Vol. 36, No. 1; pp. 71- 90.

Beekun, Rafik Issa and Jamal Badawi (1999); *Leadership: An Islamic Perspective*; Amana Publications; Maryland, USA

Beekun, Rafik Issa (1997); *Islamic Business Ethics*; International Institute of Islamic Thought, Virginia; USA.

Cone, M (2003); *"Corporate Citizenship: The Role of Commercial Organizations in an Islamic Society"*; Journal of Corporate Citizenship; Vol. 9; pp 49-66.

Cook, Michael (2001); *Forbidding Wrong in Islam*; Cambridge University Press; United Kingdom

Denny, F. M., J Corrigan, C Eire & M Jaffee (1998a); *Jews, Christians, Muslims: A Comparative Introduction to Monotheistic Religions*; Upper Saddle River, N.J.; Prentice Hall.

Denny, F. M., J Corrigan, C Eire & M Jaffee (1998b); *Readings in Judaism, Christianity and Islam*; Upper Saddle River, N.J.; Prentice Hall.

Endress, G (1998); *An Introduction to Islam*; Columbia University Press, USA; pp. 294.

European Corporate Governance Institute (www.ecgi.org); accessed on 12/18/2007.

Fisk, R (1996); "Between Faith and Fanaticism"; *The Independent*, p. 20.

Gibb, H.A.R (1962); *Studies on the Civilization of Islam*; Princeton University Press; pp 369

Harahap, Sofyan Syafri (2003); "The Disclosure of Islamic Values- Annual Report"; *Managerial Finance*; Vol. 29, No. 7; pp 70-89.

Husted, Bryan (2003); "Governance Choices for Corporate Social Responsibility: to Contribute, Collaborate or Internalize?"; *Long Range Planning*; Vol. 36; pp. 481-498.

Jaggi, Bikki and Pek Yee Low (2000); "Impact of Culture, Market Forces and Legal

System on Financial Disclosures"; *The International Journal of Accounting*; Vol. 35, No. 4; pp 495-519.

Lewis, Mervyn (2001); "Islam and Accounting"; *Accounting Forum*; Vol. 25, No. 2; pp 103-127.

Mutahhari, M; (1985); *Fundamentals of Islamic Thought*; Mizan Press; USA; pp. 235.

Organisation for Economic Development (OECD), 2004; *Principles of Corporate Governance*.

Pomeranz, Felix (1997); "The Accounting and Auditing Organization for Islamic Financial Institutions: An Important Regulatory Debut"; *Journal of International Accounting, Auditing and Taxation*; Vol. 6 No. 1; pp 123-130.

Pramanaik, A.H (1994); "The Role of Family as an Institution in Materializing the Ethico-Economic Aspects of Human Fulfilment "; *Humanomics* 10, No.3 ; 85-110.

Rahman, A.R.; (1996); "Administrative Responsibility: An Islamic Perspective"; *American Journal of Islamic Social Sciences* ; Vol 3, No.4; pp. 497-517

Roxas, Maria and Jane Stoneback (1997); "An Investigation of the Ethical Decision-Making Process Across Varying Cultures"; *The International Journal of Accounting*; Vol 32, No 4; pp 503-535.

Smith, H; (1986); *The Religions of Man*; Perennial Library; USA pp.295-334.

Conclusion

Chapter 12

The Future of Corporate Governance: A Prognosis

Güler Aras & David Crowther

Introduction

Corporate governance is fundamental to the continuing operating of any corporation; hence much attention has been paid to the procedures of such governance. A significant part of the reason for this is due to the developments brought about through globalisation. The phenomenon known as globalisation is a multidimensional process involving economic, politic, social and cultural change. However the most important discussion about globalisation is related to the economic effect it has upon countries and the corporations operating within and across these countries. There has been much written about globalisation either positive or negative and the effects which it is having. One consequence of globalisation though is manifesting itself in the structure and organization of corporations. This is concerned with the harmonisation procedures and structures which will manifest itself through the emergence of global norms for corporate governance. We have seen through the preceding chapters a variety of issues concerned with corporate governance. Equally we have seen examples of the central message of this book concerning the overwhelming importance of cultural issues in the operation of whatever systems of governance are introduced. Nevertheless some form of commonality and harmonization continues to be a subject of debate. This chapter takes this debate and the arguments from the chapters in this book in order to consider what the future might hold for corporate governance procedures and mechanisms.

Globalisation and corporate governance

Two features describe the modern world globalisation and the free market. It is widely accepted almost unquestioningly that free markets will lead to greater economic growth and that we will all benefit from this economic growth. Around the world people especially politicians and business leaders are arguing that restrictions upon world economic activity caused by the regulation of markets is bad for our well-being. And in one country after another, for one market after another, governments are capitulating and relaxing their regulations to allow complete freedom of economic activity. So the world is rapidly becoming a global market place for global corporations, increasingly unfettered by regulation. We have seen the effects of the actions of some of these corporations within the United States itself the champion of the free market. We have seen the collapse of the global accounting firm Andersen; we have seen the bankruptcy of major corporations such as Enron and World.com with thousands of people being thrown out of work and many people losing the savings for their old age which they have worked so long and hard to gain.

And why has this happened? Basically there are problems with accounting, with auditing, and with peoples' expectations. We must remember that the myth of the free market is grounded in classical liberal economic theory, as propounded by people such as John Stuart Mill in the nineteenth century, which, briefly summarised, states that anything is ok as long as the consequences are acceptable. The regulatory regime of accounting which has been increasingly changed over time to serve the interests of businesses rather than their owners or society. Thus no longer is it expected that the accounting of a business should be undertaken conservatively by recognising potential future liabilities while at the same time not recognising future profit. Instead profit can be brought forward into the accounts before it has been earned while liabilities (such as the replacement of an aging electricity distribution network) can be ignored if they reduce current profitability. A study of the changes made in accounting standards over the years shows a gradual relaxation of this requirement for conservatism in accounting as these standards have been changed to allow firms to show increased profits in the present. This of course makes the need for strong governance procedures even more paramount.

Scandals, failures, problems

Every time society faces a new problem or threat then a new legislative process of some sort is introduced which tries to protect that society from a future reoccurrence (Romano 2004). Recently we have seen a wide range of problems with corporate behaviour, which has arguably led to prominence being given to corporate social responsibility (see for example Boele, Fabig & Wheeler 2001, Aras & Crowther 2007a). Part of this effect is to recognise the concerns of all stakeholders to an organisation, and this has been researched by many people (for example Johnson & Greening 1999; Knox & Maklan 2004) with inconclusive findings. Accordingly therefore corporations, with their increased level of responsibility and accountability to their stakeholders, have felt that there is a need to develop a code for corporate governance so as to guide them towards appropriate stakeholder relations.

A great deal of concern has been expressed all over the world about shortcomings in the systems of corporate governance in operation: Britain, Australia, most other Anglo-Saxon and English speaking countries, and many other countries, have a similar system of governance. Conversely Germany is a good example of where the distance between ownership and control is much less than in the United States, while Japan's system of corporate governance is in some ways in between Germany and the United States, and in other ways different from both (Shleifer & Vishny 1997). By contrast, in India the corporate governance system in the public sector may be characterized as a transient system, with the key players (viz. politicians, bureaucrats, and managers) taking a myopic view of the system of governance. Such international comparisons illustrate different approaches to the problem of corporate governance and the problem of ensuring that managers act in their shareholders' interest. Recently of course much attention to this issue has been paid by institutional investors (Cox, Brammer & Millington 2004).

Good governance is of course important in every sphere of the society whether it be the corporate environment or general society or the political environment. Good governance levels can, for example, improve public faith and confidence in the political environment. When the resources are too limited to meet the minimum expectations of the people, it is a good governance level that can help to promote the welfare of society. And of course a concern with governance is at least as prevalent in the corporate world (Durnev & Kim 2005).

Corporate governance can be considered as an environment of trust, ethics, moral values and confidence as a synergic effort of all the constituents of society that is the stakeholders, including government; the general public etc; professional / service providers and the corporate sector. One of the consequences of a concern with the actions of an organisation, and the consequences of those actions, has been an increasing concern with corporate governance (Hermalin 2005). Corporate governance is therefore a current buzzword the world over. It has gained tremendous importance in recent years. Two of the main reasons for this upsurge in interest are the economic liberalisation and deregulation of industry and business and the demand for new corporate ethos and stricter compliance with the law of the land. One more factor that has been responsible for the sudden exposure of the corporate sector to a new paradigm for corporate governance that is in tune with the changing times in the demand for greater accountability of companies to their shareholders and customers (Bushman & Smith 2001).

Developing a framework for corporate governance

In the UK there have been a succession of codes on corporate governance dating back to the Cadbury Report in 1992. Currently all companies reporting on the London Stock Exchange are required to comply with the Combined Code on Corporate Governance, which came into effect in 2003. it might be thought therefore that a framework for corporate governance has already been developed but the code in the UK has been continually revised while problems associated with bad governance have not disappeared. So clearly a framework has not been established in the UK and an international framework looks even more remote.

One of the problems with developing such a framework is the continual rules versus principles debate. The American approach tends to be rules based while the European approach is more based on the development of principles a slower process. in general rules are considered to be simpler to follow than principles, demarcating a clear line between acceptable and unacceptable behaviour. Rules also reduce discretion on the part of individual managers or auditors. In practice however rules can be more complex than principles. They may be ill-equipped to deal with new types of transactions not covered by the code. Moreover, even if clear rules are followed, one can still find a way to circumvent their underlying purpose - this is harder to achieve if one is bound by a broader principle.

There are of course many different models of corporate governance around the world. These differ according to the nature of the system of capitalism in which they are embedded. The liberal model that is common in Anglo-American countries tends to give priority to the interests of shareholders. The coordinated model, which is normally found in Continental Europe and in Japan, recognises in addition the interests of workers, managers, suppliers, customers, and the community. Both models have distinct competitive advantages, but in different ways. The liberal model of corporate governance encourages radical innovation and cost competition, whereas the coordinated model of corporate governance facilitates incremental innovation and quality competition. However there are important differences between the recent approach to governance issues taken in the USA and what has happened in the UK.

In the USA a corporation is governed by a board of directors, which has the power to choose an executive officer, usually known as the chief executive officer (CEO). The CEO has broad power to manage the corporation on a daily basis, but needs to get board approval for certain major actions, such as hiring his / her immediate subordinates, raising money, acquiring another company, major capital expansions, or other expensive projects. Other duties of the board may include policy setting, decision making, monitoring management's performance, or corporate control. The board of directors is nominally selected by and responsible to the shareholders, but the articels of many companies make it difficult for all but the largest shareholders to have any influence over the makeup of the board. Normally individual shareholders are not offered a choice of board nominees among which to choose, but are merely asked to rubberstamp the nominees of the sitting board. Perverse incentives have pervaded many corporate boards in the developed world, with board members beholden to the chief executive whose actions they are intended to oversee. Frequently, members of the boards of directors are CEOs of other corporations in interlocking relationships, which many people see as posing a potential conflict of interest.

The UK on the other hand has developed a flexible model of regulation of corporate governance, known as the "comply or explain" code of governance. This is a principle based code that lists a nmber of recommended practices, such as:
• the separation of CEO and Chairman of the Board,
• the introduction of a time limit for CEOs' contracts,
• the introduction of a minimum number of non-executives Directors, and of independent directors,
• the designation of a senior non executive director,
• the formation and composition of remuneration, audit and nomination committees.

Publicly listed companies in the UK have to either apply those principles or, if they choose not to, to explain in a designated part of their annual reports why they decided not to do so. The monitoring of those explanations is left to shareholders themselves. The basic idea of the Code is that one size does not fit all in matters of corporate governance and that instead of a statury regime like the Sarbanes-Oxley Act in the U.S., it is best to leave some flexibility to companies so that they can make choices most adapted to their circumstances. If they have good reasons to deviate from the sound rule, they should be able to convincingly explain those to their shareholders. A form of the code has been in existence since 1992 and has had drastic effects on the way firms are governed in the UK. A recent study shows that in 1993, about 10% of the FTSE 350 companies were fully compliant with all dimensions of the code while by 2003 more than 60% were fully compliant. The same success was not achieved when looking at the explanation part for non compliant companies. Many deviations are simply not explained and a large majority of explanations fail to identify specific circumstances justifying those deviations. Still, the overall view is that the U.K.'s system works fairly well and in fact is often considered to be a benchmark, and therefore followed by a number of other countries. Nevertheless it still shows that there is more to be done to develop a global framework of corporate governance.

In East Asian countries, the family-owned company tends to dominate. In countries such as Pakistan, Indonesia and the Philippines for example, the top 15 families control over 50% of publicly owned corporations through a system of family cross-holdings, thus dominating the capital markets. Family-owned companies also dominate the Latin model of corporate governance, that is companies in Mexico, Italy, Spain, France (to a certain extent), Brazil, Argentina, and other countries in South America.

Corporate governance principles and codes have been developed in different countries and have been issued by stock exchanges, corporations, institutional investors, or associations (institutes) of directors and managers with the support of governments and international organizations. As a rule, compliance with these governance recommendations is not mandated by law, although the codes which are linked to stock exchange listing requirements[1] will tend to have a coercive effect. Thus, for example, companies quoted on the London and Toronto Stock Exchanges formally need not follow the recommendations of their respective national codes, but they must disclose whether they follow the recommendations in those documents and, where not, they should provide explanations concerning divergent practices. Such disclosure requirements exert a significant pressure on listed companies for compliance.

In its 'Global Investor Opinion Survey' of over 200 institutional investors first undertaken in 2000 (and updated in 2002), McKinsey found that 80% of the research into the relationship between specific corporate governance controls and the financial performance of companies has had very mixed results. respondents would pay a premium for well-governed companies. They defined a well-governed company as one that had mostly outside directors, who had no management ties, undertook formal evaluation of its directors, and was responsive to investors' requests for

---

[1] Such as, for example, the UK Combined Code referred to earlier.

information on governance issues. The size of the premium varied by market, from 11% for Canadian companies to around 40% for companies where the regulatory backdrop was least certain (eg those in Morocco, Egypt or Russia). Other studies have similarly linked broad perceptions of the quality of companies to superior share price performance. On the other hand,

International standards

Governance is of concerned with both the rights of shareholders and, increasingly, the rights of other stakeholders. This extended concern has been paralleled in the developments of regulations concerning financial reporting. At the start of the 20th century it was generally accepted that accounting served the purpose of facilitating the agency relationship between managers and owners of a business, through its reporting function, but that the general public had no right to such information (Murphy 1979). Thus as far as the UK is concerned, but paralleled in many other countries throughout the world (Crowther 2000), the Companies Act 1906 stated that there was no requirement for companies to produce financial statements, although the Companies (Consolidations) Act 1908 amended this to require the production of a profit & loss account and balance sheet. This was further amended by the Companies Act 1929 which required the production of these, together with a directors report and an auditors report for the AGM. Subsequent legislation has extended the reporting requirements of companies to the format seen today.

Such corporate reporting has however been extended in addition to satisfying legislative requirements. Thus the period up to the Second World War[2] saw an increasing use of accounting information for analysis purposes but with an emphasis upon the income statement. This period also saw the extension of the directors report to contain information about the company which was not to be found in the financial statements. This information was however primarily concerning the past actions of the company as corporate reporting as the emphasis in this period remained firmly upon the reporting of past actions as part of the relationship between the ownership and management of the firm. It is only in the post-war period that this emphasis changed from backward looking to forward looking and from inward looking to outward looking. Gilmore & Willmott (1992) have argued that this was a reflection of the changing nature of such reporting to a focus upon investment decision making and the need to attract investment into the company in this period of expansion.

The emphasis remained firmly upon the needs of the company however and only the emphasis had changed from informing existing investors to attracting new investors and so Jordan (1970: 39) was able to claim that:

'The purpose of accounting is to communicate economic messages on the results of business decisions and events, insofar as they can be expressed in terms of quantifiable financial data, in such a way as to achieve maximum understanding by the user and correspondence of the message with economic reality'

---

[2] From 1939 1945.

At this time the users of such corporate reports have increased so that they are no longer only the shareholders of the company and its managers, but all were however still considered to be a restricted set of the population, having specialist knowledge of and interest in such reporting. The identification of such specialists had however been extended to include both the accounting profession and investment professionals. Thus Cyert & Ijira (1974: 29) were able to claim that:

'Financial statements are not just statements reporting on the financial activities and status of a corporation. They are a product of mutual interactions of three parties: corporations, users of financial statements, and the accounting profession.'

while Leach (1975) stated that:

'In recent years there have been enormous changes in public interest in and understanding of financial statements. The informed user of accounts today is no longer solely the individual shareholder but equally the trained professional acting for institutional investors and the financial news media.'

Thus there was at this time a general acceptance that corporate reporting should be provided for the knowledgeable professional rather than the individual investor or potential investor, who was assumed to be financially naive (Mauntz & Sharif 1961), and in order to satisfy the needs of these professionals corporate reports became more extensive in content with greater disclosure of financial and other information. This pressure for greater disclosure was not however new, and Mitchell (1906) argued that the accounts produced did not give an adequate basis for shareholder judgement. All that has changed is the perception of who the reporting should be aimed at with a widening of the perceived intended audience from managers and shareholders to include other professionals. There was at this time little questioning of the assumed knowledge that the financial information is the most important part of the corporate report. The importance of the financial information contained in the reports has changed however and Lee & Tweedie (1977) claimed that the most important financial information contained in the report was details concerning profits, earnings and dividends. They equally claimed that the economic prospects of the firm are the most important information contained in the report (Lee & Tweedie 1975) but were dismissive of the private shareholder in recording (Lee & Tweedie 1977) that the majority read the chairman's report but nothing else.

This focus upon the development of the financial reporting aspects of corporate reporting of course ignores the development of the semiotic of such reporting and the changing nature of this semiotic. This lack of recognition is despite the acceptance that such reporting had changed over time to become more forward looking, to include more non-financial information including the chairman's report, and to become used by a wider range of people. It has been argued (Crowther 2002; Crowther, Carter & Cooper 2006) that this semiotic of corporate reporting is the most important use of such reporting and the prime vehicle for developing an understanding of such reporting and the changed nature of the reporting itself. Indeed the function of the semiotic is to aid social construction of corporate activity in a way which is mediated through the semiotic (Vygotsky & Luria 1994) in such a way that the interpretation of the reader is controlled from without by the creators of the semiotic. It is further argued that the lack of recognition of the semiotic of corporate reporting has also led to a lack of exploration of the dialectics inherent in such reporting.

The most recent stage in the development of reporting is epitomised by the most dramatic changes in corporate reporting. No longer is the firm seeking to communicate internally to members or potential members but rather the focus is upon the external environment. Indeed no longer do results matter, although still contained in the report but relegated to semi-obscurity, and it is only prospects that matter. Thus the report now becomes predominantly forward looking and, perhaps more significantly, the forward orientation is not upon the economic prospects of the firm but upon the prospects for the shareholder community in terms of rewards both dividends and share price increases. Additionally the report now acknowledges the rest of the stakeholder community and seeks to demonstrate corporate citizenship by commenting upon relationship with, and benefits accruing to, employees, society, customers and the local community. Indeed the report has tended to become not a communication medium but rather a mechanism for self promotion. Thus the actual results of the firms past performance no longer matter but rather the image of the firm is what matters and the production of the report is the event itself, rather then merely a communication mechanism. And of course the availability of this reporting has increased dramatically as all companies[3] now show their reports via the Internet as well as via paper, thereby making them potentially accessible to everyone.

The relationship between governance, social responsibility and business success

Often the more significant the power that multinational corporations and some groups of stakeholders in a firm have, the more is spoken about corporate social responsibility (CSR). Thus a concept that was some kind of luxury some years ago, nowadays has reached the top of the public opinion discussion. Some steps taken in the corporation's development, in the environment and in the human values can be the guilty causes of this CSR fashion. If in the beginning firms were small and there was no distinction between ownership and management, the economic development made that there was a necessity to join more capital to set up bigger enterprises. Thus, there were owners, who gave the funds, and experts in management, who managed the company and were paid by the owners. Agency Theory establishes this relationship between the principal, the shareholder, and the agent, the manager, bearing in mind that the goals of the shareholders must be got through the management of the agents. But, which are the shareholders' objectives? Obviously to increase the enterprise value through the maximization of profits.

---

[3] It is accepted that not all companies throughout the world yet do this but the number of companies which do not report via the Internet is shrinking rapidly. Moreover it is a requirement in an increasing number of countries.

But a company's structure is nowadays more complex than before and there have appeared other people, not owners, directly or indirectly implied in the company's operations known as stakeholders. This complexity has of course increased the need for governance procedures. Multinational corporations have sometimes even more power than governments in their influence, and stakeholders have gained more power through the media and public opinion in order to require some kind of specific behaviour from companies. Within this new environment, although explained in a very simply way, the primary objective of the company has become wider. Although generally speaking, the assumption may be that the first goal is to get financial performance in the company, after it the next step will be to comply with other socially responsible policies. That is because to pay attention to social objectives, or to show an orientation to multiple stakeholders group, could be considered a luxury, because it must have meant that the other basic company's goal had been met. This argument is the basis of the first hypothesis about the relationship between CSR, linked to pay attention to stakeholders, and business success: "Better performance results in greater attention to multiple stakeholders" (Greenley and Foxall, 1997, p. 264). While the other hypothesis about this relationship will run in the opposite direction: "that orientation to multiple stakeholder groups influences performance" (Greenley and Foxall, 1997, p. 264), which means to "attend" to social policies in a better way.

This double-side relationship increases the difficulty to try to empirically prove it. Intuitively it seems as if there is a clear relationship between CSR and business success, but although the measurement of business success may be easy, through different economic and financial tools, such as ratios; the measurement of the degree of compliance of a company with social policies is really difficult. We can have in mind some kind of indicators such as funds donated to charitable objectives, but a company can spend immeasurable quantities of money on charitable questions and have problems in the relationship with labour unions because of bad working conditions, or low wages, for example. In this sense there are, since a long time ago, some companies whose objectives include philanthropic aims. It may be understood as the initial values are ones, and then the market and the capitalism forces the firm to change them in order to survive in this maelstrom. Although at the same time the double sided relationship operates, because people socially concerned bear in mind these basic aims and the image of the saving banks is improved, which has got a direct relationship with the economic performance.

This example may be only one speaking about the market inefficiencies[4] and the trend to acquire human values and ethics that must be forgotten when we are surrounded by this society and the market.

The relationship between good governance and business performance is however clearer. As we stated in chapter 1, investors are increasingly willing to pay a premium for good governance in a business because of the expected improvements in sustainable performance which will, over time, be reflected in future dividend streams. And the relationship between social responsibility and governance is similarly clear and described by us previously (see Aras & Crowther 2007b, 2008). In

---

[4] See Baumol & Batey (1993).

an attempt to satisfy the necessities of the stakeholders there can appear other conflicts between the interests of the different groups included in the wider concept of stakeholders. Sometimes due to this conflict of interests and to the specific features of the company it tries to establish different levels between the stakeholders, paying more attention to those ones that are most powerful, but are there some goals more socially responsible than others? In the end the hierarchy will depend on the other goals of the company, it will give an answer to those stakeholders that can threaten the performance of the economic goals.

The difficulties in measuring the social performance of a company are also due to the ownership concept. This is because the concept of corporate social responsibility is really comprehensive. There are companies whose activities are really different but all of them have to bear in mind their social responsibility, and not only companies, but also people in whatever activity they do. From a politician to a teacher: ethics, code of conducts, human values, friendship with the environment, respect to the minorities (what not should be understood as a dictatorship of the minorities) and so on are values that have to be borne in mind and included in the social responsibility concept. A good example of this diversity can be seen in this directory where are included opinions of different experts in such different topics as "building and construction" or "auditing", although everyone has got a deep relationship with the other. The same can be said about the regions, besides the classification according to topics in the directory has been included another classification of CSR in accordance with regions. The point of view of the concept can vary depending on the country or the region, because some important problems linked to basic human values are more evident in some countries than in other ones. These social problems cannot be isolated because they have got an important relationship with the degree of development of the country, so in the end it is the economy that pushes the world. Capitalism allows the differences between people, but what is not so fair is that these differences are not only due to your effort or work but are also due to have taken advantage of someone else's effort. And this can be the case with multinational corporations, which sometimes abuse of their power, closing factories in developed countries and moving them to developing countries because the wages are lower, or for example, because the security and health conditions are not so strict and so cheaper to maintain for the company. And then the same companies obtain big amounts of profits to expense them in philanthropic ways.

Development conditions of regions can determine the relationship between governance and business success, as we have highlighted, if it is allowed in some developing countries to damage the environment or there are no appropriate labour unions and so on. Because lack of requirements or government's attention, the global players use these facilities to obtain a better economic performance although they can be aware of their damaging policies. But not only the development degree has to do with governance and with social responsibility, countries or regions are also deeply associated with human values through education and culture. The values are so deep inside us that even it is said that people from different regions of the world who have shared the same education, for example, ethics courses at the university, do not share the same human values, because they are marked by their origins. Perhaps it should be understood as the inclusion of ethics courses at the university degrees is useless because finally people will go on thinking what they thought at the beginning, depending on the values of their origin culture. But everything is not so simple, because there have been proofs of situations where different values have been imported from one culture to another and accepted as their own values without any problem (only point out the success of McDonalds food all over the world and even in the former communist countries, can be understood a McDonalds restaurant in the Red Square of Moscow?). So, it shows that the questions related to CSR are complicated and not so simple as they can seem at a first glance.

This complexity can be argued as a disadvantage to take into account when speaking about the creation of global standards about companies socially responsible behaviour: there are so many different cases that to establish a general regulation may be really difficult. But at the same time this diversity can be argued to require this regulation, because there have been different initiatives, most of them private, and they have added diversity to the previous one and the subject requires a common effort to try to tackle the problem of its standards and principles. The latest financial scandals have proved that it is not enough with own codes or human values, that it is necessary to reach an agreement to establish a homogeneous regulation at least at the level of global players, multinational corporations that play globally.

Governance systems and CSR

Most people would say that corporate social responsibility is an Anglo-Saxon concept which has been developed primarily in the UK and the USA. Critics however would say that it is only under the Anglo-Saxon model of governance that there could ever be a need for CSR. They would argument that the Cartesian dichotomy is a peculiarly Anglo-Saxon development which led directly to the notion of a free market as a mediating mechanism and the acceptance of the use of power for one's own end, in true utilitarian style. This has led to the loss of a sense of community responsibility which removed any sense of social responsibility from business. This therefore necessitated its reinvention in the form of corporate social responsibility, just as it necessitated the development of codes of corporate governance.

The Latin model of governance however is founded in the context of the family and the local community and is therefore the opposite of the Ango Saxon model, being based on a bottom up philsophy rather than a hierarchical top down approach. Thus this model is based on the fact that extended families are associated with all other family members and therefore feel obigated. In such a model of governance the sense of socil responsibility remains strong and is applied to firms just as much as individuals. This sense of social responsibility has never therefore been really lost and consequently there has been no need for its reinvention. As we have seen[5] the Ottoman model is an Islamic model and built into the principles of the Ottoman religion are a sense of the conservation of the environment and the concept of helping rather than exploiting one's fellow human beings (Rizk 2005; Zurcher & van der Linden 2004). Thus in this model also there is no need for the concept of corporate social

---

[5] See chapter 1.

responsibility as it was never lost; indeed such behaviour is so entwined in societal norms that the very idea is alien. The African model is one built upon networks of relationships and rules are to a large extent irrelevant.

The Anglo Saxon system of governance is of course the dominant model throughout the world and as a consequence the concern with corporate social responsibility has spread to other systems of governance. It would be reasonable therefore to argue that the concept now permeates all business models and all systems of governance, no matter what the antecedents or the necessity might be. Consequently we are able to address global perspectives on the issues of corporate governance and corporate social responsibility in this volume without fear of being regarded as Anglo-centric.

A Prognosis

This book has constituted a contribution towards the debate concerning corporate governance and the need to develop appropriate procedures. We have sought to show that cultural issues are an important element which is often omitted from any analysis and that such cultural issues are of such significance that they will negate any attempt to introduce a global system or code of governance. Nevertheless the debate about such procedures continues and we consider that we need to complete the analysis undertaken in this book by offering some form of prognosis, albeit subject to criticism and challenge for many reasons. So we start by stating that many companies regard corporate governance as simply a part of investor relationships and do nothing more regarding such governance except to identify that it is important investors / potential investors and to flag up that they have such governance policies. The more enlightened recognise that there is a clear link between governance and corporate social responsibility and make efforts to link the two. Often this is no more than making a claim that good governance is a part of their CSR policy as well as a part of their relationship with shareholders.

It is recognised and amply demonstrated throughout contributions from the various authors in this book that these are issues which are significant in all parts of the world and a lot of attention is devoted to this global understanding. Most analysis however is too simplistic to be helpful as it normally resolves itself into simple dualities: rules based v principles based or Anglo-Saxon v Continental. Our argument is that this is not helpful as the reality is far more complex. It cannot be understood without taking geographical, cultural and historical factors into account in order to understand the similarities, differences and concerns relating to people of different parts of the world. The aim of this book is to redress this by asking subject experts from different parts of the world to explain the issues from their particular perspective. Nevertheless the debate about global codes will not end and it can be foreseen that one will be introduced, and revised, and revised...

Such a code will only survive once it is designed to be sufficiently flexible to allow for the full extent of cultural variation throughout the world.

References

Aras G & Crowther D (2007a); Is the global economy sustainable?; in S Barber (ed), *The Geopolitics of the City*; London; Forum Press pp 165-194

Aras G & Crowther D (2007b); What level of trust is needed for sustainability? *Social Responsibility Journal* 3 (3), 60-68

Aras G & Crowther D (2008); Corporate sustainability reporting: a study in disingenuity?; *Journal of Business Ethics* (forthcoming)

Baumol, W. J. and Batey Blackman, S. A. (1993): *Mercados perfectos y virtud natural. La ética en los negocios y la mano invisible.* Colegio de Economistas de Madrid. Celeste Ediciones.

Boele R, Fabig H & Wheeler D (2001); Shell, Nigeria and the Ogoni. A study in unsustainable development: II. Corporate social responsibility and 'stakeholder management' versus a rights-based approach to sustainable development; *Sustainable Development*, 9, 121-135

Cox P, Brammer S & Millington A (2004); An empirical examination of institutional investor preferences for corporate social performance; *Journal of Business Ethics*, 52, 27-43

Crowther D (2000); Corporate reporting, stakeholders and the Internet: mapping the new corporate landscape; *Urban Studies,* 37 (10), 1837-1848

Crowther D (2002); *A semiology of corporate reporting*; Escola Superior de Tecnologia e Gestao da Guarda Working Paper no 04/02; Guarda, Portugal

Crowther D, Carter C & Cooper S (2006); The poetics of corporate reporting; *Critical Perspectives on Accounting* Vol 17 No 2 pp 175-201

Cyert R M & Ijira Y (1974); Problems of implementing the Trueblood Report; *Journal of Accounting Research* supplement 1974

Durnev A & Kim E H (2005); To steal or not to steal: firm attributes, legal environment, and valuation; *Journal of Finance*, LX (3), 1461-1493

Gilmore C G & Willmott H (1992); Company law and financial reporting: a sociological history of the UK experience; in M Bromwich & A Hopwood (eds), *Accounting and the Law* pp 159-191; Hemel Hempstead; Prentice Hall

Greenley, G. E. and Foxall, G. R. (1997): "Multiple stakeholders orientation in UK companies and the implications for company performance", *Journal of Management Studies*, Vol. 34, n°2, March, pp. 259-284.

Hermalin B E (2005); Trends in corporate governance; *Journal of Finance*, LX (5), 2351-2384

Johnson R A & Greening D W (1999); The effects of corporate governance and institutional ownership types on corporate social performance; *Academy of Management Journal* 42 (5), 564-576

Jordan J R (1970); Financial accounting and communication; in G G Mueller & C H Smith (eds), *Accounting: a Book of Readings*; New York; Holt, Rinehart & Winston

Knox S & Maklan S (2004); Corporate Social Responsibility: moving beyond investment towards measuring outcomes; *European Management Journal*, 22 (5), 508-516

Leach R G (1975); presentation at the launch of The Corporate Report, July 1975

Lee T A & Tweedie D P (1975); Accounting information: an investigation of private shareholder understanding; *Accounting & Business Research*, Autumn 1975, 280-291

Lee T A & Tweedie D P (1977); *The Private Shareholder and the Corporate Report*; London; ICAEW

Mauntz R H & Sharif H A (1961); *The philosophy of auditing*; American Accounting Association

Mitchell T W (1906); Review of corporate reports: the report of the Americam Locomotive Company; *Journal of Accountancy*

Rizk R R (2005); The Islamic Perspective to Corporate Social Responsibility; in D Crowther & R Jatan (eds), *International Dimensions of Corporate Social Responsibility* Volume 1; Hyderabad; ICFAI University Press

Romano R (2004); The Sarbanes-Oxley Act and the making of quack corporate governance; *European Corporate Governance Institute Finance Working Paper* No 52/2004

Shleifer A & Vishny R W (1997); A survey of corporate governance; *Journal of Finance*, 52 (2), 737-783

Vygotsky L & Luria A (1994); Tool and symbol in child development; in R Van Der Veer & J Valsimer (eds), *The Vygotsky Reader* pp 99-173; Oxford; Blackwell

Zurcher E J & van der Linden H (2004); Searching for the fault line in Netherlands Scientific Council for Government Policy, *The European Union, Turkey and Islam*; Amsterdam; Amsterdam University Press; pp 83-174

Index